ADVICE AND
DISSENT

ADVICE AND
DISSENT

Why America Suffers When
Economics and Politics Collide

ALAN S. BLINDER

BASIC BOOKS
New York

Basic Books
Hachette Book Group
1290 Avenue of the Americas, New York, NY 10104
basicbooks.com

Printed in the United States of America

First Edition: March 2018

Published by Basic Books, an imprint of Perseus Books, LLC, a subsidiary of Hachette Book Group, Inc. The Basic Books name and logo is a trademark of the Hachette Book Group.

The publisher is not responsible for websites (or their content) that are not owned by the publisher.

Library of Congress Cataloging-in-Publication Data

Names: Blinder, Alan S., author.
Title: Advice and dissent : why America suffers when economics and politics collide / Alan S. Blinder.
Description: First edition. | New York, NY : Basic Books, [2018] | Includes bibliographical references and index.
Identifiers: LCCN 2017052706 (print) | LCCN 2017054661 (ebook) | ISBN 9780465094189 (ebook) | ISBN 9780465094172 (hardcover)
Subjects: LCSH: Economics—Political aspects—United States. | United States—Economic policy. | United States—Economic conditions. | United States—Politics and government.
Classification: LCC HC106.84 (ebook) | LCC HC106.84 .B55 2018 (print) | DDC 330.973—dc23

LC record available at https://lccn.loc.gov/2017052706

ISBNs: 978-0-465-09417-2 (hardcover), 978-0-465-09418-9 (ebook)

LSC-H

10 9 8 7 6 5 4 3 2 1

To Madeline,
for all the years of good advice—and love.

CONTENTS

CHAPTER 12:

CHAPTER 13:

PREFACE

Economists offer lots of policy advice, most of which politicians routinely reject even though it would improve the quality of economic policy—and in consequence, the economy suffers. What may be a surprise is that many of these rejections of good policy advice are done for good reasons.

The solution, to the extent there is one, requires changes from both economists and politicos. Economists must change how they conceptualize issues, frame policy prescriptions, and deliver advice. Politicians need to improve their understanding of basic economics, and use it more as a guide to good policy and less as a tool for political spin. Neither is easy, however, because of the radically different civilizations from which economists and politicians hail. Plainly put, neither group understands the other. This book is an attempt to bridge the gap.

Chapter 1 distills the problem into what I call the *Lamppost Theory*: that politicians use economics the way a drunk uses a lamppost—for *support*, not for *illumination*. Chapters 2–5 elaborate on the origins of the Lamppost Theory, examining the factors that underpin the frequent (and sometimes harsh) collisions between good economics and good politics. Chapters 6 and 7 then consider how most economists, at least progressive ones, decide what constitutes good economics—an approach I call hard-headed but soft-hearted. These few pages are the proselytizing part of the book.

Precious few politicians, whether of the left or the right, think like economists, however. And of course, it is the politicians, not the economists, who make the policy decisions—as they should. Chapters 8–10 examine how the dominance of politics over economics plays out in three critical policy domains: international trade, income inequality, and tax reform. In each case, I explain how the clash of civilizations has produced either paralysis or movement in the wrong direction. This dysfunction, I argue, is not random. It follows logically from the factors underpinning the Lamppost Theory.

The good news, such as it is, comes in the final three chapters. There I search for remedies—or rather, for palliatives that might narrow the gap and make the collisions less severe. A brief summary is that we need to put more economics into politics, and put more political savvy into economics. But I'll be much more specific than that.

The ideas offered in this book have been germinating in my mind for over forty years. During a long career of teaching economics to beginning students, writing hundreds of op-ed columns (lately for the *Wall Street Journal*), advising many politicians and several presidential campaigns, serving on President Bill Clinton's original Council of Economic Advisers, and then as vice chairman of the Federal Reserve Board, I've watched Washington closely, both from the outside and the inside. And I've drawn a number of conclusions, which I share here.

Part of the book's message, especially Chapters 6 and 7, is a lineal descendant of a book I published about thirty years ago: *Hard Heads, Soft Hearts: Tough-Minded Economics for a Just Society* (Addison-Wesley, 1987). In planning for this book, I reread that one, and there was little I wanted to retract. But there was much to add because *Hard Heads* was written before I was ever immersed in official Washington. While my *economic* attitudes have barely changed over the last thirty years, my *political* attitudes have undergone several transformations—the latest thanks to Donald Trump.

After mentioning our forty-fifth president, I should perhaps make my personal politics clear. I have always considered myself center-left in the American political spectrum. If there was still such a thing as a Rockefeller Republican, I might be one. But there isn't, so I'm a longtime Democrat. I want to emphasize, however, that my intent here is not to draw a line between center-left Democrats and center-right Republicans. Fine distinctions like that hardly matter. Instead, I want to explain why most economists reject the far right as mean-spirited and the far left as naive.

Yes, Donald Trump receives much criticism in these pages. But that's mainly because I try to illustrate enduring principles with fresh examples. The truth is that this book was planned and partly drafted before I ever imagined that Trump would be elected president. The central ideas long predate Mr. Trump and will outlast him by many years.

Yogi Berra was right: you can observe a lot just by watching. When you've been thinking about something for over forty years, your intellectual debts pile up—many of them unrecognized. (*Where did I first get that thought?*) My accidental teachers include famous public figures like Bill Clinton (for whom I worked) and Alan Greenspan (with whom I worked), a long list of politicians and journalists, a few political scientists and commentators, and even some economists.

In preparing this book, I benefited specifically from literally hundreds of helpful comments from (in alphabetical order) Henry Aaron, Ben Bernanke, Joseph Blasi, Barry Bosworth, Gary Burtless, Philip Friedman, Michael Froman, Carol Graham, Bradley Hardy, John Hudak, Joseph Kennedy, Aaron Klein, Don Kohn, Robert Lerman, Avi Lerner, Ephraim Liebtag, Ofer Malamud, Norman Ornstein, Eswar Prasad, Jamie Raskin, Jonathan Rauch, Richard Reeves, Alice Rivlin, Howard Rosen, Leslie Samuels, Isabel Sawhill, Alan Schwartz, Philip Wallach, Vin Weber, David Wessel, and Cliff Winston. I thank them all and hold them blameless for any errors.

Many of these people were colleagues of mine at the Brookings Institution, where I did most of the writing during a sabbatical year in 2016–2017. I thank Princeton University for the sabbatical and its Griswold Center for Economic Policy Studies for continued support of my research. And I'm grateful to Brookings and its director of Economic Studies, Ted Gayer, for their hospitality and for providing me with a fine research assistant, Eric Koepcke. It is no exaggeration to say that, without that year at Brookings, this book never would have been written. The two nonsecret ingredients were peace and quiet and interested colleagues to bounce ideas off. Brookings provided both in abundance.

Turning a long document into the book you have in your hands is a laborious process made easier by my astute literary agents, John and Max Brockman, and by the talented folks at Basic Books, especially editorial director T. J. Kelleher and editorial assistant Carrie Napolitano, and project editor Collin Tracy, and copyeditor Beth Wright of Trio Bookworks. Here I must single out Brian Distelberg, whose thorough and perceptive reading of the penultimate draft led me to make several major changes. When the task turned to marketing and publicity, I acquired further debts to Isadora Johnson, Kait Howard, and Connie Capone.

Never mind that we were two hundred miles apart when most of the drafting was done; email makes geography almost irrelevant. My longtime and exceptional assistant at Princeton University, Kathleen Hurley, was always there when I needed her, performing many essential tasks with her usual efficiency, care, and good cheer.

But my biggest thank-you goes where it's most deserved: to my wonderful wife, Madeline Blinder. For over fifty years now, she has offered me a constant stream of good advice, some of which was met by dissent, but most of which was taken—to my good fortune. It is to her that this book is lovingly dedicated.

ALAN S. BLINDER
Princeton, New Jersey
January 2018

Chapter 1

The Lamppost Theory
of Economic Policy

Politicians use economics in the same way that a drunk
uses lamp-posts—for support rather than illumination.

—variation on a theme of Andrew Lang (1910)

May I start by dispelling a myth? Many people seem to believe that
economists have enormous influence over public policy. After all, we
pop up frequently on television, have our own Council of Economic
Advisers within the White House, serve in many advisory posts,
sometimes occupy cabinet positions, and dominate one of the US
government's most powerful agencies, the Federal Reserve System.*
All this provides superficial credence for the popular misconception
that economists play pivotal, if not indeed decisive, roles in public
policy decisions.

But it's a myth. The truth is better summarized by the epigram
above: like a drunk, politicians use economics for support, not illumination. Consider Donald J. Trump. He was elected president of the
United States on November 8, 2016, and assumed office on January
20, 2017. That was plenty of time to acquire some economic advisers,
not to mention some economic *advice*. If he wanted any. Instead, the

---

*Prior to Jerome Powell, five of the last six chairs of the Federal Reserve Board, dating
back to 1970, were economists. The other lasted just seventeen months on the job.

new president killed the Trans-Pacific Partnership, presented a budget to Congress, embraced a radical House plan to replace Obamacare (which later failed in the Senate), backed America out of the Paris Agreement on climate change, and made menacing noises about bank deregulation—all before he had a single member on his Council of Economic Advisers (CEA).

That "momentous" event finally arrived on September 12, 2017, when Kevin Hassett was confirmed as chairman of the CEA. Until that day, a campaign aide named Peter Navarro was the only PhD economist in Trumpworld. What's that? You've never heard of Navarro? That's my point. If Mr. Trump thought *either* illumination *or* support from economists was important, he certainly didn't show it.

As a longtime member of the tribe, I'd like to believe that economists are essential pieces in the economic policy puzzle. But it's a myth, and one purpose of this book is to explode it. The truth is that the Lamppost Theory, which predates President Trump by decades, has it about right. To be sure, there are instances in which economic reasoning has provided *illumination* that influenced policy profoundly, maybe even decisively. Deregulation of trucking and airlines in the 1970s and 1980s comes to mind, as does tax reform in 1986. But it's hard to think of a recent example. There are far more cases in which politicians knew what they wanted to do, and then just leaned on economics—sometimes very bad economics—for *support*.

The Lamppost Theory may be good for politicians. Many of them like to trot out economists to support their favored policies in public. It's good for political messaging—or so they believe. It certainly adds a patina of intellectual respectability. And, especially in a world where hardly anyone believes politicians, economists can add putatively disinterested—maybe even "scientific"—voices to the debate.

There is even a name for this support activity. It's called "validating." I have served as a validator for Democratic politicians numerous times, typically being asked to speak or write approvingly about policy positions I had no role in formulating. (After all, if you've helped formulate a policy, how can you validate it?) If I agree with the policy,

I often accept this role willingly. If I disagree, I don't. Many other economists, both Democrats and Republicans, do the same. Notice that validating is only about lending *support*. It comes way too late in the game to provide any *illumination*. And after the way the 2016 election and its aftermath denigrated expertise, even the political usefulness of support is now open to question.

Is the Lamppost Theory good for economists? Not likely. Being used as a stage prop is usually harmless, and some economists enjoy seeing their names in the papers and their faces on TV. But in truth, most of us are naturally what Harry Truman once disparagingly called "two-handed" ("On the one hand, . . . but on the other hand, . . . "). Complex policy proposals are rarely all good or all bad. The world is a messy place in which purist solutions hardly ever make sense and, even when they do, are politically infeasible. So real-world policy proposals run the gamut from mostly attractive with a few warts to mostly ugly with some pleasant features. And choosing policies that are mostly good, albeit with some blemishes, is a huge step up from choosing policies that are mostly bad, though with some bright spots.

Genuine illumination would present the full picture, including all the pros and cons and the weak points in each side's arguments. But when you're serving as a validator, the politicos are seeking support, not illumination. Giving voice to "the other hand" might provide fodder for your opponents—which is not helpful to your side. This political reality creates a tension for many academics, for whom exceptions, fine points, and shades of gray are their stock-in-trade. So many won't venture anywhere near the political arena, and even those who do may fill the role of validator clumsily. In politico-speak, they pose a constant risk to stray "off message," a place where political handlers never want you to be.

My favorite all-time example of this hazard happened way back in 1982. The Reagan administration trotted out George Stigler, an illustrious conservative University of Chicago economist who had just been awarded the Nobel Prize, to (they hoped) sing the praises of supply-side economics—the "theory" that underpinned the Reagan tax cuts by claiming miraculous effects of tax cuts on growth. What a fantastic validator, they must have thought: a Reagan supporter who had just been anointed an oracle. But when Stigler was put in front of the TV cameras, lights blazing, and asked about supply-side economics, the iconoclastic economist opined that "it's a gimmick, or, if you wish, a slogan." Ouch. That didn't help Ronald Reagan. I presume it didn't help George Stigler either, who was quickly hustled off stage. (But it did *not* hurt Stigler's lofty reputation in academia.)

Is the Lamppost Theory good for public understanding of economic policies? Definitely not. When presented with dueling teams of economic experts making opposing claims, ordinary people are likely to be confused, to conclude that economists don't know what they're talking about, and to tune out. The best spinners, not the ones with the best arguments, are likely to prevail in the public debate. And in a democracy, a confused electorate opens the door to poorly conceived policies.

Once again, supply-side economics, a doctrine that was born in the 1970s but lives on today, offers a marvelous example. Early in the Reagan presidency, supply-side economics was flying high politically, even though it had never left the ground economically. At the time, perhaps eighteen thousand members of the American Economic Association would have told you that the Reagan tax cuts would *not* stimulate enough new economic activity to pay for themselves; maybe about eighteen would have told you they would (though I can't name eighteen). But that "division" of opinion meant that every TV show that wanted to demonstrate how fair it was could produce an economist on each side of the phony debate. Most did. There never was a real *intellectual* debate, just a few quacks advocating a nutty position with no evidence behind it. Nonetheless, the media dutifully reported that economists were divided on the issue. So the public was first befuddled and then buffaloed.

Finally, the most important question by far: Is the Lamppost Theory good for public policy? Certainly not, and here the stakes are high. Public opinion matters in our rough-and-tumble, media-driven, hyper-democratic system—more than most people realize. In a sense, election campaigns never end. Since votes in Congress are swayed by popular attitudes, politicians often engage in intense message war-fare—a process that resembles commercial advertising more than it does the Lincoln-Douglas debates (*and may the best spinner win*). Unfortunately, only by sheer coincidence are the best crafters of policy also the best crafters of message.

Thus the Lamppost Theory appears to be good for many politicians but bad for almost everyone else. Please don't jump to the wrong conclusion, however. The chapters that follow are not a paean to the remarkable wisdom and insight of economists. I will *not* suggest that the body politic should hand over critical policy decisions to a bunch of wonks with PhDs in economics. With some rare exceptions, such as the Federal Reserve's monetary policy, the division of labor that has economists *advising* and elected politicians *deciding* is approximately right. We call that democracy.

The real questions are: Can the status quo be improved in ways that use economics for illumination somewhat more and for support somewhat less? And if so, how?

The search for answers must begin at the beginning—with an understanding of what can, without exaggeration, be viewed as a clash of civilizations between politicos and economists. That is the subject of Chapter 2, which analyzes in detail how and why politicians seek support while economists offer what they see as illumination. That same clash is the tacit subject of Chapter 3, which concentrates on the contrast between the super-short time horizons of politicians and the excessively long time horizons of economists, and of Chapter 4, which discusses the starkly different ways in which politicians and economists practice the art of messaging. (Preview: Economists are pretty bad at it.)

In Chapter 5, on the role of the media as information intermediaries, the focus shifts from the use of economics for support to the possible—and, I argue, socially more useful—uses of economics for illumination. The media, we shall see, can help or hinder each.

Following that, Chapters 6 and 7 discuss in more detail what I really mean by *illumination*. How could the quality of economic policy improve if politicians made better use of economics?

The next three chapters get down to cases. Here I apply the basic ideas and lessons from the first seven chapters to three major issues of contemporary policy: why international trade is so controversial politically even though it is not controversial among economists (Chapter 8), what might be done economically to mitigate income inequality—if politics didn't prevent it (Chapter 9), and how politics makes a hash out of economics when it comes to reforming the tax code (Chapter 10).

There are problems you *solve* and others you just *manage*. The Lamppost Theory falls squarely in the second category. The clash between political and economic civilizations runs so deep, and is so multifaceted, that no one should pretend to be able to solve it. I won't. Instead, I devote Chapters 11 and 12 to the search for palliatives, not solutions. What are some feasible changes that could make economic advice more useful to politicians, and thereby improve the quality of economic policy?

But first we must understand why economic lampposts are used so much more for support than for illumination.

Chapter 2

Clashing Civilizations

On a number of issues, a bipartisan majority of the [economics] profession would unite on the opposite side from a bipartisan majority of Congress.
—Arthur Okun (1970)

Politicos and economists speak different languages. And that's not all. Their differences go deeper and further. It is barely an exaggeration to say that politicians and economists live in two different, often clashing, civilizations.

One day long ago, I crossed the border from one strange land to the other as a fledgling member of President-elect Bill Clinton's new economic team. At our first meeting at the governor's mansion in Little Rock in January 1993, I felt like a duck out of water. The cast of characters gathered around the big mahogany table that winter day included titans of Wall Street like Robert Rubin and Roger Altman; experienced politicians like Lloyd Bentsen, Leon Panetta, and Ron Brown; and campaign figures like George Stephanopoulos, Gene Sperling, and Robert Reich. Apart from Bentsen and Brown, who have since passed away, those are all my friends now, but they were mostly strangers then. And I didn't know the rules of engagement, which made me uneasy. Only later did I learn that nobody else did, either.

Two other fugitives from academia were present at that first meeting: Laura Tyson and Larry Summers. I had agreed to join Laura as a member of the Council of Economic Advisers (CEA)—a team of three economists, typically professors on leave from their universities, who advise the president on all matters economic. Larry was headed to Treasury.

I arrived early, via connecting commercial flights from Newark through Memphis, while most of the others came directly from Washington on a charter plane. As the number two person in the smallest and least powerful agency at the briefing, I knew enough not to take a seat until the bigger shots arrived to claim theirs. When Vice President–elect Al Gore walked in, he said a round of hellos. Then Gore and Bentsen, the Treasury secretary designate, sat at the end of the table closest to the door. Interpreting that action to mark the presidential end of the table, I modestly positioned myself at the opposite end.

Whoops. Moments later the photographers swooped in and hustled Gore down to my end of the table, practically sitting him in my lap. I slid down two chairs to make room for Bentsen and a honcho to be named later. But alas, when President-elect Clinton entered the room, he chose to sit at the opposite end—near Gore's original seat—and it was musical chairs all over again. Thus did I receive my first lesson in hierarchy: where you sit depends on where you stand.

Exactly a week later, the team returned to Little Rock. This time I traveled with the others from Washington, thereby helping to overcrowd the little charter plane. Those with the highest ranks (Bentsen and Rubin) got comfortable seats in the front; we peons squeezed onto the sofas that lined the back of the bus, er, plane. Ironically, that morning's *Wall Street Journal* had carried an article on some new OSHA rules on overcrowded workplaces. I joked to Reich, the incoming secretary of labor, that this was just the sort of thing that OSHA should prevent.

After a long delay—imagine, Bill Clinton was late!—we were ushered into the dining room and took our seats around the polished mahogany table. The decor had been transformed from early American to early transient—featuring cardboard moving boxes, crated mirrors, and the like—for the First Family would be moving to Washington in a few days. This time, Clinton's end of the long table was clearly demarcated, so I headed dutifully for the opposite end.

As dictated by our respective ranks, Laura sat to my left, one seat closer to the president-elect. While we waited, I whispered to her to observe a pattern that, I predicted, would characterize all future meetings of the economic team: the Treasury would bring the most people, the Office of Management and Budget (OMB) would bring the most paper, and we (the CEA) would bring the best ideas. Snarky, but basically true.

Then Clinton arrived, followed by an orderly with a bowl of soup. I thought at the time that the poor man must not have eaten anything all day. I later learned that he ate all day long. Laura began the briefing with a quick review of the state of the economy and the basic rationale for reducing the federal budget deficit. Then it was my turn to hold forth with the details.

Armed with slides, tables, and numbers to bolster my deficit-reduction pedantry, I started. But barely three words had passed my lips when a young aide rushed in to announce that the press would be allowed in for a photo op—no reporters, just photographers. *How exciting*, I thought, *my very first photo op! I've heard so much about them.*

Realizing that I was an alien in his civilization, the president-elect looked up from his soup and instructed me graciously on proper photo op behavior: "Alan, now you're supposed to say nothing and look profound." The raucous laughter around the table gave me a much-needed moment to gather my wits, and I responded: "That's funny, Mr. President-elect. In my previous job, I was supposed to look like nothing and say profound things." (More laughter.)

Two seconds later, we were surrounded by a swarm of photographers, flashbulbs popping and cameras whirring. I thought to myself, *It's a new world, Tevye.*

The Unholy Trinity

It was. To the untrained eye and ear, the political world looks and sounds chaotic. At first, I thought there was no logic to it at all. But if you pay attention, there is an underlying logic, as I learned during my time in the Clinton White House, after that (albeit from a distance) at the Federal Reserve, and subsequently working on several presidential campaigns. It's just not the Aristotelian logic you learn in school and use in economics. Call it *political logic*.

Before going further, let me be clear: this book is not a screed complaining that those foolish politicians refuse to behave like us logical economists—and wishing that they would. Well, in all honesty, there will be a little of that—but not much, because the truth is that politicians cannot and should not follow Aristotelian logic. People who succeed at high levels of politics and government must and do have different personalities, talents, and weaknesses than people who succeed in business or in the academy. Their job applications are completely different from those in other occupations. They are chosen and succeed or fail on totally different Darwinian principles. They face dramatically different incentives. And, most important, the rules and objectives of the game are starkly different. Top government officials, especially elected ones, do not think or act like business executives or professors because they shouldn't. The early presidency of Donald Trump helped prove that point.

In the university, policy discussions always start with the merits of the case—and often end there. General principles, especially high-minded ones, figure prominently in the debate, generally crowding out dreary details of implementation. What is this policy trying to accomplish? Are the goals appropriate? What are the pros, cons, and likely side effects of the various options under consideration? Which are most likely to succeed? Which seem most consistent with other policies and other principles? Such questions are all perfectly legitimate; indeed, they are indispensable. Policymakers who ignore them court disaster—and often get it.

The best policy debates inside the government start out in more or less that same place—on the substantive merits of the case. But, unlike debates in the academy, they do not and cannot end there. Instead, the unholy trinity of *politics, message,* and *process* all demand close and protracted attention—sometimes to seemingly ludicrous degrees, sometimes overwhelming any attention to substance. But there is a method to this apparent madness. Let me take up the unholy trinity in turn.

By *politics* I mean mostly obvious but vexing matters such as: Is this policy initiative consistent with what the president promised in the campaign? (That question, I learned, is amazingly important to most politicians, who—contrary to popular opinion—want to keep their words even when they wish they could eat them.) Who in Congress will line up with us, and who will be arrayed against us? What about the interest groups—especially those blessed with legions of foot soldiers and/or piles of cash to purchase advertising? Will we wind up expending too much of our precious political capital to win this battle? Worse yet, might we lose it? What will be the political costs and benefits to the president? A class of so-called political experts—a phrase I soon added to my lexicon of oxymorons—specialize in dealing with these less-than-lofty, sometimes downright earthy, but absolutely essential issues.

That political considerations are central to politicians is hardly a striking insight, although such matters are more frequently discussed by journalists and political scientists than by economists. But in my native habitat, academia, where we never have to answer to the voters, the politics is rarely if ever considered the heart of the matter. The substance always dominates.

Things look stunningly different if you work at the White House or on Capitol Hill. There, political exigencies are never far from center stage. Should we lament that fact of life or sneer at it? Economists and other technocrats often do both. But where else should a great democracy hash out its political differences and mediate among competing claims? Decisions in Washington *are* political and *should be* political. The trick is to make sure that they are not *solely* political, to the exclusion of everything else.

By *message* I mean the sales pitch, the sizzle. Like it or not, public policies must be marketed aggressively in our heavily checked and agonizingly balanced system of government. Policies will get nowhere if they're not merchandised like smart phones or beer. Knowingly or not, James Madison and his friends saw to that in 1787, when they created a constitutional system that makes it hard to get anything done. I call it *Madison's Curse.*

To push a policy initiative through the ever-resistant maze that is the US government, you must first convince the politicians that you can win the inside game, and then convince the voters, so you win the outside game. (Actually, it may work better the other way around.) Thus American policymakers are constantly preoccupied with such cosmic philosophical questions as: What is our message? How will it play in Peoria? Where are we vulnerable to sound bites? How do we counter the objections that will be raised against our plan, for there are always objections? Brilliant as Madison was, I wonder if he factored all that in. King George, in England, was not worried about message. Neither are modern despots. Even in parliamentary democracies, salesmanship is less important if the prime minister has a healthy majority.

Message gets short shrift, or even derision, in the academy. Professors frequently discuss whether a policy suggestion is good for America, but rarely consider whether it *sounds good* to Americans. When economists do opine on message, it is often with an astonishing admixture of disdain, naiveté, and ineptitude. Mostly, they know enough to practice abstinence. But message is vital in a vibrant democracy. It's a big part of how politicians communicate with the electorate. So an entire chapter is devoted to salesmanship later in this book.

By *process* I mean such seemingly mundane questions as: How do we get organized to make this decision? Who should be at the table—both literally and figuratively? Who should be in charge? Which agencies of government, and which people within agencies, should be responsible for specific tasks? What is the appropriate timetable? How do we find the right legislative language—and the right legislative vehicle? This list is not exhaustive, but executing it skillfully can be exhausting. The litany of budgetary, political, legislative, and personnel constraints—to name just a few—often appears endless. But make no mistake about it, process matters because different processes can lead to quite different results. This is another topic that academic economists—and, I would say, the public at large—think too little about. If you really want to bore people, just start talking about the organizational structure of government or the details of legislative language. (Don't worry—you won't find much of either in this book!)

These three elements of the unholy trinity—politics, message, and process—are inextricably bound together. And each in turn is, or rather should be, closely tied to the substance of the policy. Process discussions inevitably deal with message and politics as well as substance. Political considerations involve proper processes (*We can't offend Senator Jones*), consistency with message (*Tell Ed he's way off message*), and, one hopes, even the substance of the issue (*Is that claim actually true?*). Messages are crafted with both substance and political strategy in mind. For example, politicians often sell international trade agreements as job creators, which is at best a half truth that came back to haunt supporters of open trade both after the North American Free Trade Agreement (NAFTA) passed and in the 2016 election. The full truth is that trade does create some (hopefully better-paying) jobs, but it also destroys other (lower-paying) jobs. But that's a complex, even equivocal, message. Who would storm the ramparts under such a banner? How much easier to claim—falsely—that trade either creates or destroys millions of jobs.

Since all four elements of policymaking—politics, message, process, and substance—are apt to be in motion at the same time, the overall effect is something like a Marx Brothers movie shown in fast forward. The trick is to keep Harpo under sufficient control so the substance (Zeppo?) doesn't get entirely lost in the antics.

After only a few weeks in the new Clinton administration in 1993, the appropriate metaphor for my new life dawned on me. Everyone knows the aphorism that you should never see a sausage being made—at least not if you ever plan to eat one. While the final product may be tasty, its preparation is a sight not to behold. I soon realized that we neophyte Clintonites were all learning what it feels like to be *inside* a sausage as it is being made. It's tumultuous and exhausting.

The Roots of Bad Economic Policy: The Three *I*s

As I first worked in and then watched political Washington in action, I realized that many factors conspire to produce the mess that economic policy too often becomes. Most of them fall under one of the Three *I*s: ignorance, ideology, and interest groups.

Economics is traditionally divided into two branches: macroeconomics, which deals with the national economy, booms and busts, inflation and deflation; and microeconomics, which deals with resource allocation decisions (how much does society devote to producing video games rather than growing tomatoes) and the distribution of income (who gets how much?). The Three *I*s play out differently in each domain.

The affinity for economic nostrums that seems to plague macroeconomic policy derives mainly from an unholy alliance joining scant understanding of basic economics to a distressing tendency to fly off on ideological tangents. This alliance is aided and abetted by rank disagreements among economists, who often don't know the right answer anyway. Interest-group politics matters some in macroeconomics. (Doesn't it always?) But when macro policies go astray, ignorance and ideology are normally the main culprits.

In stark contrast, interest groups are typically decisive when the best economic advice on a microeconomic issue—say, a "detail" of a trade agreement or a tax bill—is rejected. To be sure, ignorance and ideology help by obfuscating issues and ensuring that voters are confused. But they are normally bit players in these tragicomedies. After all, interest-group politics is often about fleecing the public, a fundamentally nonideological business. Politicians are unlikely to buck the vested interests if they perceive that pursuing sound economics will cost them votes. So principles routinely take a backseat to principal.

Let's take up the Three *I*s in order, starting with the one that you might think is easiest to overcome—but isn't: ignorance of basic economics.

Like merchandising, politics thrives on gimmicks that can be distilled into short, snappy slogans—often short enough to be emblazoned across a T-shirt or a baseball cap. (Example: "Make America Great Again.") After all, politicians are competing with smart phones and five-hundred-channel cable TV services for the attention of people with short attention spans.

The problem is that such superficially appealing slogans are generally based on faulty reasoning, ignorance of basic facts, rigid ideology, or folklore—maybe all of them. The more accurate versions are apt to be soporific, prolix, or both. But you gotta have a gimmick to sell the product when voters have the attention spans you'd expect from people raised on a steady diet of tweets and twenty-second TV spots. Decades ago, Newt Gingrich, as astute a politician as you're likely to find, advised his House colleagues to "practice whatever the big truth is so you can say it in 40 seconds on camera." That was in 1986. Today, the corresponding advice would be "10 seconds or 140 characters." And accuracy doesn't matter. In a political marketplace like that, complexity sells poorly—if at all.

Examples abound. Protectionists insist that restrictive trade practices "save American jobs." And who doesn't want to save American jobs from "unfair" foreign competition? But more sober and accurate analysis—which will be presented later in this book—points to a more complex reality in which import restrictions save *some* American jobs only by sacrificing others. The arguments leading to that conclusion, however, are subtle and somewhat involved. They even involve the exchange rate, a subject guaranteed to induce slumber in most listeners. And besides, there are numerous qualifications. Freer trade is not *always* the best policy, just *usually*. Every honest economist, I am afraid, is fundamentally two-handed. (*Sorry, Mr. Truman.*) But subtlety is a huge disadvantage in politics.

Another example: While economists have made important inroads, some environmentalists still recoil in horror at the idea of granting "licenses to pollute" via carbon taxes or cap-and-trade systems. On closer examination, however, those sinister-sounding licenses to pollute turn out to be an excellent way for society to acquire cleaner air and water at lower costs while imposing fewer regulations on industry. Sounds good, doesn't it? But you need to do some quiet reasoning and sweep away some ideological cobwebs before reaching that conclusion. And even then, the superiority of market-oriented policies over direct controls does not emerge as an inviolable rule. There are important exceptions. For example, you don't want to rely on pollution taxes in an acute smog emergency or when a chemical spill threatens lives.

And so it goes with other gimmicks. The supply-side boast that Ronald Reagan's or Donald Trump's tax *cuts* would actually *raise* tax revenue was a real knee-slapper. (Sorry, folks, but you don't add by subtracting.) Yet supply-siders were right to point to the disincentive effects of high tax rates. Monetary policy hawks' concern that the Federal Reserve's huge creation of money in 2009–2014 posed inflationary dangers *right away* was a wild caricature of the truth. (We are still waiting for the feared inflation.) Yet no serious economist doubts the existence of a *long-run* link between money and prices. The need to shrink the projected long-run growth of the national debt is real. But can you imagine your favorite TV anchor coherently explaining any of the nuances in twenty seconds?

When economists disagree, the public, getting little or no help from either the mass media or social media, finds it difficult to tell sound economic advice from snake oil. Politicians add to the confusion by passing off the latter as the former—often to legitimize something they seek to do for entirely different reasons. And against this we have . . . what? A few economists who deign to enter the public arena speaking English? It's a pitiful mismatch that goes a long way toward explaining why crackpot solutions with scant support among economists sometimes sweep to political victory.

What's the answer? Knowledge, we professors fancy, is the unrelenting enemy of ignorance. In the long run, deeper, more reliable, and more quantitative economic knowledge—produced through painstaking research—will contribute to greater consensus among economists and thereby to better economic policy. Or so we hope. That process is painfully slow and inherently uncertain, however. Besides, the lack of knowledge that fosters bad policy is of a totally different nature. The critical problem is not that economists know too little, true as that may be. Rather, it is that society makes such poor use of what economists do know—in large measure because politicians routinely ignore it. Advice is met by dissent.

To influence public policy debates, economic knowledge must be made accessible, intelligible, and believable to the body politic—even if it's just a matter of getting the basic facts straight. That is why people like me occasionally write books like this. There aren't many of us, however, and the writings of economists reach only a tiny fraction of the electorate. Compare our meager audience to the recipients of the daily avalanche of cable news, blogs, tweets, and posts. The real need lies in rooting out the misconceptions that permeate mass public opinion like unsightly weeds in a garden. With economic illiteracy as widespread as it is today, a popular democracy is painfully vulnerable to the self-serving machinations and hucksterism of economic snake-oil salesmen.

What can be done to ameliorate the problem? A higher caliber of economic journalism, particularly on television, would help. So would more and better economic education in the schools—and I don't mean mainly universities here, but high schools and middle schools. But those are tall orders that will not be filled soon, for journalists and schoolteachers proficient in economics are in perilously short supply. And individual citizens have little incentive to educate themselves on economics.

Meanwhile, a single US president in a single term can probably do more either to advance or to retard economic literacy than an army of economists can do in a lifetime. Presidential education sometimes works wonders. Fiscal policy was liberated from a crippling mythology by President Kennedy, and the economy boomed. Deregulation of air and truck transportation moved from economists' dreams to political reality thanks in no small measure to the effective ways in which Presidents Ford and especially Carter (a Democrat yet!) sold the case to the American people. President Reagan's indictment of the unfair and hideously complex tax system had been made a thousand times before. But when it came from his mouth, the words rang louder. President Clinton was dubbed the "explainer in chief" by President Obama. All that helped.

Unfortunately, the nation's bully pulpit is used as often to deceive as to enlighten. Such as when President Johnson insisted that America could have both guns and butter without aggravating inflation. Or when President Reagan assured America that a supply-side miracle would produce a balanced budget even with falling tax rates and rising defense spending. Or when President Clinton sold NAFTA as a huge job creator. (Good policy, bad argument.) Each such episode sets back the cause of economic literacy.

And now we have President Donald Trump, who has ratcheted up the problem several levels. Not only does he deny fundamental economic ideas such as the gains from international trade, but his claims often defy logic (example: his "terrific" health care plan was going to cover everyone at lower costs—how?) and reject even basic facts in favor of what we now (sadly) know as "alternative facts."

So the good and unsurprising news is that enlightened presidential leadership can and does lead to better economic policy, in part by harnessing the power of symbols and imagery to worthy ends. The corresponding bad news is that presidents are as likely to inscribe shibboleths as verities on their banners. So this road to better policy is easier to describe than to travel. We need good presidents. What else is new?

The second of the Three *Is*, ideology, is almost always a formidable foe of sound economic policy. To be clear, I do not believe that philosophical considerations and moral values should be banished from economic policymaking. Far from it. Many of the most profound economic issues have critical moral aspects. To cite just two current examples, think about reducing inequality or protecting the planet from ruinous climate change. Unfortunately, ideology often becomes the handmaiden of mythology. The problem with true believers is that they believe too easily.

Left-wingers who harbor hostilities to free markets want to believe that free trade is folly, that repealing Glass-Steagall caused the financial crisis, and that market-oriented approaches to environmental protection should be shunned. And so they do. Right-wingers want to believe that reducing tax rates on the rich will accelerate growth, that tax breaks for favored corporations will spur productivity, and that financial markets are stunningly efficient. And so they do.

But rigid ideological positions rarely lead to sound economic policies grounded in logic and fact—especially when valid but misplaced ideological concerns are applied to means rather than to ends. Pragmatists care less about whether a policy works by means that are labeled "pro-market" or "anti-market." They are more interested in knowing if it works at all and, especially, whether the economic benefits outweigh the costs.

Good economic policy exploits the market mechanism where it shines (like keeping trade mostly free and minimizing tax loopholes), helps it along where its flaws are easily remedied (like limiting pollution and fighting monopolies), and overrules it by government fiat where it fails (like distributing income fairly and keeping the banking system safe). Such eclecticism requires a results-oriented attitude that elevates facts and logic over myth and ideology. Unfortunately, too many people see the world through distorting ideological prisms and substitute incantation, or even "alternative facts," for rational debate.

Ideology dies hard. Across continents and over centuries, it has proven itself remarkably resistant to both logic and fact—especially when it's used as a smokescreen for promoting special interests. As Upton Sinclair sardonically noted, "It is difficult to get a man to understand something, when his salary depends on his not understanding it."

Fortunately, ideology is not always the enemy of good economics. Sometimes, by sheer luck, ideological crusades strike out in constructive directions. The strong lip service paid to free trade in the United States over many years has surely been a useful counterweight to all the special pleading for trade protection. It kept us (almost) in the vanguard of free trade for decades, though that has changed recently. Similarly, the American attachment to free markets has limited the spread of rent controls, even though tenants greatly outnumber landlords everywhere.

In some other instances, good economics triumphs by harnessing ideological appeal to its own advantage. Deregulation of trucking and air travel caught on in part because the idea appealed to both the populist, pro-consumer sympathies of the left and the right's adoration of the free market. It was also sold, rather misleadingly, as anti-inflationary at a time when inflation was running high.

But such events are serendipitous, not systematic. When they occur, the credit almost always goes to some astute politicians who seized the right issue at the right moment and knew how to market it. That's wonderful, but we cannot count on it happening regularly. The general rule is that good economic policy flourishes in a pragmatic atmosphere and wilts under ideological heat. But I have no recipe for cooling ideological fervor, and politicians often rise to prominence by fanning ideological flames.

The third and most powerful of the Three *I*s, interest groups, derives its power from the fact that economists and politicians work with profoundly different versions of arithmetic. Economic scorekeeping is simple, direct, and politically naive. If a proposed policy change promises, say, to cost ten million people $2 each while each of ten people stands to gain $1 million, it takes no great genius to calculate that the nation as a whole loses $10 million, net. Economists have a built-in hostility to such proposals. We cannot *prove* that each such idea is ill advised, for society may have some good reason to favor the ten winners over the ten million losers. Nonetheless, economists reflexively view such claims with deep suspicion. And we are confident that society will ultimately be poorer if it adopts such negative-sum policies repeatedly.

But only a dull economist with his hand on a calculator would fret over mundane arithmetic like that. Politicians have their hands on the political pulse instead, and receive entirely different signals. Who, after all, can get worked up over a puny $2 loss? Politicians understand that ten million tiny, quiet losers are a less potent political force than ten big, noisy winners—some of whom may give you large campaign contributions. Because so few effective political voices speak up for the broad national interest, negative-sum *economic* policies are often positive-sum *political* policies.

This little numerical example may seem contrived, but it is actually indicative of a deep-seated and pervasive problem: the two types of arithmetic, each logical within its own domain, frequently point in opposite directions. The strong political allure of protectionism derives precisely from this source. So does the pernicious politics of tax loopholes. In both cases, the benefits are concentrated, highly visible, and well understood, while the costs are diffuse, subtle, and barely visible—sprinkled like a light rain across the electorate, where it falls mostly unnoticed.

The conflict between political and economic calculus goes a long way toward explaining why economic logic so rarely prevails in Congress or in state legislatures. Policies that pair diffuse gains with concentrated losses make economic hearts beat with joy but may put political hearts into cardiac arrest. This being a democracy, such ideas are routinely rejected.

Part of the problem is that politicians in our great republic are myopic; their horizons are short in time and narrow in space. As David Stockman, Ronald Reagan's first budget director and a former congressman, put it years ago: "The politicians rarely look ahead or around. Two years and one Congressional District is the scope of their horizon."

Consider again the choice between free trade and protection. Quotas on textiles are likely to be good for textile workers in South Carolina but bad for consumers in every other state. Quotas on Japanese cars help Michigan but hurt most of the other forty-nine. Protection for the steel industry helps Ohio at the expense of states that buy steel rather than produce it. And so it goes, item after item, state after state. So South Carolina's congressional delegation wants textile quotas, Michigan's seeks automobile quotas, and Ohio's wants limits on imported steel. Soon the political logs are rolling. The vaunted art of compromise does the rest. It's all very democratic.

The process runs amok because no one pays enough attention to the economic well-being of the United States of America. No one dwells on the reality that caving in to one special pleader lowers our resistance to the next. If we would keep the national interest more firmly in mind, we would see that all protectionist measures, taken together, add up to a big net loss for the country as a whole. While some South Carolinians undoubtedly gain from the expanded employment and profits afforded by textile quotas, they lose when they pay more for cars, steel products, and so on.

Nonetheless, it remains in the self-interest of South Carolina, and therefore in the electoral interest of its congressional delegation, to seek protection for its textile industry. Likewise, any state can gain at the expense of the others if it succeeds in getting protection for its leading industries while out-of-state industries must fend for themselves. The joys of competition are particularly joyous when it is only the other guys who must compete.

Naturally, if every state and district plays the protectionist game, the country as a whole must lose. But try to explain that little piece of arithmetic to a member of Congress from a district whose principal industry is threatened by imports, and you will quickly understand the wisdom of the legendary former Speaker of the House Tip O'Neill's (D-MA) famous dictum: all politics is local.

The elusive missing ingredient is a sense of national community, a feeling that all Americans are in the same boat in the long run, a realization that it does no good *for the United States* if South Carolina or Michigan or Ohio reaps gains at the expense of its neighbors. Members of a family regularly resist temptations to advance their own parochial interests at the expense of the wider group—on the expectation that other family members will accord them the same respect. But members of Congress display such community spirit only at their electoral peril. We frequently witness cooperation in the national interest, sometimes even bipartisan cooperation, in foreign affairs or defense issues, where particularist local interests are far less significant. (One prominent exception: locating military bases.) But members of Congress rarely adopt the national perspective when economic conflicts arise. Patriotism apparently stops at the pocketbook's edge.

A senator is elected by the people of New Jersey, or Kansas, or Oregon. A member of the House is elected by people in the fourth district of New York, or the twenty-eighth district of California, or the twelfth district of Texas. No one should be surprised if elected representatives champion the causes of the folks who sent them. That is only natural, whether they are selflessly devoted to serving their constituents or selfishly devoted to promoting their own reelection. In either case, a legislator with a narrow constituency will instinctively favor parochial views over the national interest. If you doubt that, ask yourself why the US Navy has installations in Indiana and Tennessee. The problem is not that we fail to send good people to Congress. It runs much deeper than that. It's in our geography-based system.

Still, special interests do not *always* get their way. Pleas for trade protection are not always granted. Some tax loopholes are never opened; others are closed. Industrial polluters cope with onerous environmental regulations they bitterly opposed. Even though "that's where the money is," bankers were subjected to heavy regulation even before Dodd-Frank raised the regulatory bar higher. To understand why the interests of the majority do sometimes rule, we must look to the players in our political system who have *national* constituencies. That means, in the first instance, looking to the president.

The political perspective of the president differs fundamentally from that of members of Congress. Only he is elected by and responsible to all Americans. Even if narrow political self-aggrandizement is his only goal, the president is—or at least should be—chastened by the knowledge that only limited gains can be reaped by robbing one region to pay another. More likely, a president will have loftier motives—like a desire to serve the nation, or the constitutional duty to promote the general welfare, or concern for the verdict of history.

The institutionalized difference in perspective between the president and Congress is more critical in economic policy than it is in, say, foreign policy because the foreign policy interests of the various states and districts differ little, while their economic interests sometimes differ much. Someone once jokingly derided the members of a Senate committee as Senator Steel, Senator Chemicals, Senator Agriculture, and so on. There was more than a little truth to the insult. But rarely do such sobriquets apply to presidents. The job demands broader horizons.

In principle, the president is not the only political actor with a national constituency. The leaders of the two major political parties are forced by the laws of survival to worry about what the majority—albeit rejiggered by gerrymandering—thinks. Thus the much-discussed decline in the power of leaders, and the corresponding rise in congressional entrepreneurship, probably did little good for national economic policy. Similarly, the special responsibilities thrust upon the chairs of the key congressional committees demand a more national perspective—which they only sometimes supply. But they, too, have lost some power in recent decades. The federal courts should also serve the broad national interest, not the narrow interests of Illinois, or Kentucky, or Florida. We all know about our vaunted system of checks and balances. One thing it checks is naked pandering to particular industries or regions. One thing it balances is the public interest against the special interests. Madison got that part right.

The unsurprising conclusion here is that greater statesmanship—a focus on what's best *for the nation*—produces better policy. Statesmanlike behavior by political leaders nourishes, and is in turn nourished by, the public-spirited citizenship that is so vital if a democracy is to produce sound economic policy. Each contributes to the broader perspective we so desperately need.

But please don't misinterpret me. I am not arguing that our wonderfully pluralistic political system exquisitely balances special interests against the public good. On the contrary, interest groups, aided by politicians, fare much too well. And although statesmanship and public spiritedness reinforce one another nicely, so too do small-mindedness and pork-barrel politics. I am merely pointing out that there are some countervailing forces that keep the system from flying apart.

Can we do anything concrete to weaken the power of interest groups? Perhaps. After all, special pleaders do not *always* prevail. But all the potential answers lie in politics, not in economics. Economists instinctively champion the broad public interest and rebel against special pleading. It's practically a Pavlovian response. We do so even when the promised benefits from a policy, like a broad trade agreement, are diffuse and barely visible to the general public while the costs imposed on affected industries are concentrated and palpable—clear signposts of political losers.

Politicians see things differently. Naturally, everything must be *portrayed* as being in the national interest. But few politicians succeed for long without performing constituent service, which means focusing on the parochial interests of their state or congressional district. Unlike economists and other technicians, successful politicians never forget who sent them to Washington.

Ironically, both politicians and economists understand the essential truth of political cost-benefit calculus: policies that confer large and visible benefits on the few, paid for by small and mostly invisible levies on the many (such as special tax favors), probably win you more votes than they lose. Policies that hurt identifiable interest groups in order to sprinkle small, diffuse benefits on the amorphous public (like free trade agreements) are apt to be political losers.

But the two sides diverge sharply on the policy implications of that observation. Unless they are in the employ of special interest lobbies, economists invariably take principled if naive stands against special pleading. After all, it costs nothing to be noble if you never stand for election. Politicians, who do so regularly, are naturally less inclined toward self-sacrifice and more concerned with self-preservation. As I said, they hail from different civilizations.

Politics Matters—As It Must

The differences between good economics and good politics are basic and profound—and make life in Washington incredibly frustrating for an economic adviser. It is not that we policy wonks hold wrong-headed views on these matters. Mostly, I believe, we have it right. Politicians' time horizons really are too short. The substantive merits of a policy ultimately will matter more to the public than the slogans that helped sell it—because citizens will wind up living with the outcomes. (For a recent example, think about Obamacare.) The broad public interest really is more important than narrow special interests. Evidence normally beats hunches as a basis for policy formulation. All true. But the vagaries of politics often do not permit such tidiness of thought.

Formulating intelligent social policies that take proper account of the myriad of relevant factors is challenging enough in this complex world. Precious few policy analysts can do it well. Then layer on top of all that such "details" as political horse-trading, the frenzied pace of decision making, the need to generate ideas with superficial sound appeal, the maddening intricacies of navigating a path through a balky Congress, and more. Now you really have a tough problem, one that requires extraordinary perseverance and political horse sense.

But that's the nature of the game. Those seemingly extraneous political considerations are not extraneous at all because almost every significant policy decision is and must at bedrock be political in a democracy—which means that the *people* rule, not the *technocrats*. Politicians surely internalize the beliefs and aspirations of ordinary citizens far better than any group of technocrats can. If you rely on experts to take the case to the public, you are apt to be sorely disappointed.

Start with the role of slogans, which academics view with disdain, if not contempt. One implication of Madison's Curse is that prodigious political energy is required to get anything meaningful accomplished. You must somehow rouse the slumbering electorate and mobilize the relevant interest groups. In such campaigns—and they really are campaigns—slogans and symbols are more effective than learned dissertations, for mass politics displays little tolerance for complexity. So elected officials must care at least as much about what *sounds good* as about what *is good*.

Next, take those short time horizons. Politicians are surely guilty of myopic concentration on the here and now. In many meetings when I was in the Clinton administration, I muttered to myself, "There is no election next Tuesday." There wasn't. But the politicos often behaved as if there was.

On the other hand, however, we economists are often equally guilty of hypermetropic concentration on the distant future. Our particular brand of analysis is wont to focus doggedly on long-run consequences, to the exclusion of the many transitional problems that loom so large in the lives of ordinary people. As Keynes wryly put it, in the long run we are all dead, meaning that many of us will not live long enough to see the heralded "long run" arrive. So it is neither foolish nor selfish for voters and politicians to worry about what may happen in the next one, two, or five years. Economists sometimes miss that important though obvious point. And when they do, the policies they advocate may be political disasters.

Some economists have a second blind spot: distributional consequences. When contemplating changes in, say, tax, trade, or regulatory policies, economists generally think first—and sometimes last—about questions of efficiency. Will the policy make our market system function more or less smoothly? Will it raise or lower the gross domestic product? Is it a cost-effective way to achieve the stated goal?

These are all fine questions—and highly relevant, too. Politicians regularly squander the national treasure by ignoring them. But economic efficiency is not uppermost in the minds of the citizenry, nor therefore of their elected representatives. John and Jane Q. Public want to know who gets the gain and who gets the pain. They want to hear reasons why the losers from a proposed policy change should be asked to sacrifice for the good of the winners—especially if they may be among the losers. Some of the answers might be deemed acceptable; people are not always 100 percent selfish. But others will not be. Such questions are entirely legitimate, and economists who refuse to entertain them are not contributing to better economic policy. They are ensuring their own irrelevance.

So, for example, in selling international agreements that expand the realm of free trade—such as the late lamented Trans-Pacific Partnership—politicians understand that they must address fears of job loss and community disruption. (Who can forget that after Donald Trump's victory?) Economists may assure you that the new high-wage jobs created by enhanced export opportunities will outweigh the low-wage jobs lost to foreign competition. That's nice. But the folks who lose low-wage jobs in San Antonio will not secure new high-wage jobs in San Francisco. Why should these unfortunates be asked to pay the price? The case for free trade is not airtight unless something is done to compensate its victims—and it rarely is.

Similarly, economists who make elaborate efficiency arguments for switching from an income tax to a consumption tax, or who advocate privatizing Social Security, should pause more than they do to consider how changes like that would affect the progressivity of our tax-transfer system. (Each would reduce it.) The public will surely think such matters apposite.

While the analytical aspects of the calculus of pain and gain involve numerous difficult technical issues, they at least fall squarely within the realm of mainstream economic analysis. But when it comes to actually deciding *who* should reap the benefits and *who* should pay the bills, technicians must yield the floor to politicians. It is not for economists to say whether one group of people should be favored over another. That's for elected politicians.

Madison's Curse was not an accident. Our vaunted system of checks and balances was *designed* to be frustrating. American constitutional democracy is, in this respect, quite different from parliamentary systems in which the majority party can pretty much do as it pleases. No president of the United States ever has the kind of control that, say, a British prime minister with a working majority has. Even Lyndon Johnson, whose landslide victory in 1964 swept waves of Democrats into both houses of Congress, had to beg, cajole, and threaten the congressional barons. Even Franklin Roosevelt was thwarted by, among others, the Supreme Court.

Compromise is often said to be the essence of politics, and nowhere is that truer than in America. Major policy initiatives—say, overhauling the tax code or making large changes in Social Security—have traditionally required broad, bipartisan support. That tradition broke down in the 1990s, starting with Bill Clinton's first budget in 1993. It broke down spectacularly with Barack Obama's attempts to pass health care reform in 2010, and even more with Donald Trump's health care and tax proposals in 2017.

Bipartisanship means coalition building, vote trading, logrolling, difference splitting—and compromise, compromise, compromise. Policies that emerge from such political deal making are unlikely to follow the neat contours designed by economic technicians. More likely, they will be ungainly creatures whose central organizing principles are hard to discern, if any exist. Sort of like attaching the head of a horse and the tail of a monkey to the body of an elephant. But policy wonks must learn to live with such ungainly creatures, even if they never grow to love them.

For example, the Dodd-Frank financial reform legislation passed in 2010 was, in my view, a sterling legislative accomplishment. It fixed, or at least ameliorated, a long list of problems that had left us vulnerable to a devastating financial crisis. Yet it left the crazy quilt of multiple financial regulators largely intact. Why? Because both Representative Barney Frank (D-MA) and Treasury Secretary Tim Geithner decided not to start an unwinnable war with congressional barons who could be counted on to protect their home turfs. Similarly, if we ever get immigration reform, it will likely be forged in a series of political compromises with no coherent principles or philosophy. If the final products of such legislative battles leave some not-very-political policy wonks feeling frustrated, that's a trivial price to pay. The work of government must be graded on the curve.

While policy without politics is neither feasible nor desirable, politics comes in degrees. The trick for any society is to maximize the *high politics*—the mediation of competing interests and ideas—and minimize the *low politics*—politics as gladiatorial combat. This is something America has been doing poorly for years now, with the 2016 presidential campaign taking us to new lows.

High politics is what we were taught in civics classes. It is the politics of Roosevelt versus Hoover, of Lincoln versus Douglas, of Hamilton versus Jefferson (though those last two guys got pretty nasty). High politics is about clashes between competing philosophies and visions of government. It is about how the champions of alternative policies duke it out in the public arena. The combat may be rough-and-tumble—ideologically driven conflict can be particularly bitter and humorless—but the focus is squarely on the ideas.

However, purists and saints don't get elected, and successful politicians are neither. Political battles, like political motives, are apt to be less than pristine, political debates less than lofty. Message, parliamentary maneuvers, and raw political power all probably play bigger roles than expertise and evidence. Deals are struck. Logs are rolled. Compromises are forged. The whole process resembles a heavyweight boxing match more than the Oxford-Cambridge Debating Society.

Even when the politics sticks to the high road, the economic merits of an issue normally take a backseat in Washington debates.

Sometimes they are not even invited along for the ride. After all, economic policy has always been considered far too important to be left to the economists. Still, this situation is a good deal better than when low politics holds sway. Then the economic merits get treated like roadkill.

If high politics is like boxing, low politics—which is what crowds our TV screens and dominates blogs and Twitter feeds—is more like mud wrestling. Here, competing philosophies are smothered by political gamesmanship and name-calling. The contest among ideas degenerates into battles for partisan or individual advantage. Argument and debate give way to invective and lies. Legitimate mediation of competing claims turns into an unseemly squabble over who will feast at the public trough. It is not a pretty sight.

Gamesmanship has been elevated to absurd heights in contemporary Washington, where politics may eclipse professional football as the town's favorite sport. Political clashes nowadays are often not over ideas at all, nor even about policy. They are simply about winning and losing. Winning and losing *what* is considered less important than hurting your opponents. Here are two examples of this curious contact sport from the first term of the Obama administration.

With the economy nearly in free fall in early 2009, and the public terrified about what might come next, President Barack Obama followed his economists' sound advice and proposed a large fiscal stimulus—meaning more government spending and lower taxes—to boost demand and stem the economy's slide. It was his first major legislative proposal. Putatively, the president's party controlled both houses of Congress at the time. But the Democratic Party is congenitally fractious, as Will Rogers famously knew ("I don't belong to any organized political party. I'm a Democrat."), and the ever-present threat of a filibuster means that a "majority" in the Senate actually requires sixty votes. Furthermore, Obama had run as a postpartisan candidate, eager to paint America purple rather than red and blue. All this made political compromise the order of the day. Or so he thought.

In fact, congressional Republicans basically objected to everything but tax cuts, forced the White House to include more business
tax cuts than it wanted (even when they packed little stimulus punch),
and then voted against the bill anyway—almost to the person.* Apparently, the loyal opposition was more interested in tarnishing the
new president than in designing a better stimulus package. As Senate
Republican leader Mitch McConnell (R-KY) later admitted, his main
objective was to deny President Obama a second term.

Obama's second big initiative was the aforementioned health care
reform. Once again, the president entered the debate in a compromis-
ing mood, but the Republicans adopted the "just say no" (to everything) strategy they had used successfully to block health care reform
in the Clinton administration. This time, however, it didn't work because they were outmaneuvered by then Speaker of the House Nancy
Pelosi (D-CA), and a bill supported only by Democrats squeaked
through both the House and the Senate in March 2010. Nonetheless, Republicans arguably won the outside game by creating an anti-
Obamacare meme that resonated with (segments of) the public while
the Democrats were asleep at the message wheel.

The main point here is not that Democrats were right about health
care, but that Republicans never offered a serious alternative. They
just sought to hang a political defeat around the neck of the young
president. In fact, over the remainder of the Obama presidency, the
House voted to repeal Obamacare more than sixty times—a pledge
that was echoed prominently by Donald Trump in his campaign rhetoric. Yet by his inauguration day, Republicans (including Trump) had
never offered a single plan they preferred.

That plan arrived with a thud on March 7, 2017, but didn't
last long. The original Trump-Ryan plan to "repeal and replace"
Obamacare died in the House within days. Democrats didn't have
to lift a finger. The second try passed in May by an underwhelming
217–213 vote. Then it was on to the Senate, where Republicans could

---

*The package garnered just three Republican votes in the Senate and none in the
House.

never agree on the "replace" part, despite copious deal making and arm-twisting by Majority Leader Mitch McConnell—and several failed attempts, the last in September 2017.

I realize I'm sounding partisan myself here because, in these two examples, I cast the Republicans as the villains of the piece. But that's mainly because it was a Democrat who won the presidential elections in 2008 and 2012, making the Republicans the potential blocking party. But Democrats can and do play this game as well. Without really enunciating it as such, they played the "just say no" strategy effectively early in the Trump administration—beginning with his replacement for Obamacare, which struggled through the Republican-dominated House without a single Democratic vote and then died in the Senate. Democrats similarly opposed the broad attack on the social safety net proposed in the president's first budget. Neither was meant to help President Trump politically!

Low politics manifests itself in other unattractive ways as well—such as name-calling, personal attacks, and scandal-mongering. These tawdry aspects of contemporary political sport did not begin with President Trump, of course. As I mentioned, Hamilton and Jefferson really had at it. But the sport is growing nastier. Washington observers who are far more experienced than I report that the level of vitriol has been rising like the tide for more than two decades. One major effect of all this mudslinging is to make more and more viewers want to change the channel. Better to watch *Survivor*—it's kinder and gentler, and the rules are clearer. Or to elect a complete outsider with no political experience and no respect for political institutions—nor even any manners.

If you want to know why more and more of our citizens are tuning politics out, ask yourself this simple question: What do you think would happen to the national appetite for hamburgers if McDonald's and Burger King constantly bombarded us with ads condemning the other's products as vile and hazardous to your health, rather than extolling the virtues of their own? That, by the way, seems to be an apt metaphor for the 2016 presidential campaign.

But all this is surface stuff. Many of the truly deplorable aspects of low politics are kept off the TV screen and, indeed, are barely visible to the public at large. What happens in the shadows is known only to the participants: the politicians themselves, their staffs, and the K Street lobbyists.

Start with the zaniness induced by the congressional committee structure. The all-important House and Senate Appropriations Committees—the ones that spend our money—are divided into twelve subcommittees, each with jurisdiction over a portion of the budget. Did I say jurisdiction? When they can—less often now than formerly—the chairs of these subcommittees treat their bailiwicks more like private fiefdoms than public trusts. Presidents and even congressional leaders are expected to appear as supplicants bearing gifts, like medieval monarchs seeking the support of local knights and lords. Favors are dispensed or denied. Turf is protected. Just *try* cutting highway demonstration projects (have you ever seen one of those roads that leads nowhere?) or maritime subsidies.

The power wielded by certain members of Congress is sometimes quite amazing. And the public hardly knows it exists or who these people are. Neither, it appears, did the neophyte president Donald Trump before he met up with members of Congress—some from his own party—who opposed his agenda in 2017.

Then there is the public feeding trough, access to which is granted mainly to the politically powerful and well connected—and in a bewildering variety of ways. The accepted euphemism for such things is "members provisions," a sanitized phrase that translates roughly into highway robbery. Some popular examples are inserting tailor-made clauses into tax bills in the dead of night—and passing them without debate. Or writing special protectionist provisions into the 583rd section of a huge trade agreement. Or granting exceptions to regulations that, somehow, seem to benefit a single company. (Just a coincidence, of course.) The vaunted end of "earmarks" in 2011 did not do away with any of this; it just demanded more ingenuity.

My all-time favorite example was unearthed decades ago by Jacob Weisberg, then a reporter for the *New Republic*, while Congress was working on tax reform in 1986—ironically, one of the most principled bills Congress ever passed. On page 651 of a monstrously long draft, a list of exceptions to the general crackdown on abuse of municipal bonds contained a cryptic reference to "an area of a city described in paragraph (4)(C)." If you turned to that paragraph, you did not find the city's name, but you learned that it had more than 2.5 million inhabitants and an American League baseball team. Hmm. That left New York (the Yankees) and Chicago (the White Sox). More information awaited you in section 145(d)(3), if you could find it. (Try page 569.) It located the city in a state whose new constitution took effect on July 1, 1971. Bingo (if you were among the cognoscenti): the state was Illinois, and the city was Chicago.

What a surprise. Representative Dan Rostenkowski of Chicago then chaired the House Ways and Means Committee. Turning back to page 651, you found that the law exempted redevelopment projects approved before July 1, 1986, in a neighborhood that the city council declared to be blighted on November 14, 1975. Now how many projects do you think fit that description? Do you think the developers knew Dan Rostenkowski? Do you think any of them worried about the national interest?

I could go on and on with further examples, but I am a rank amateur in such matters. The real pros can, and do, run circles around me—and, more important, around the voters.

In the small, outrages like these are invisible to the average person on the street, who is unaware of the bizarre special interest favors that Congress routinely bestows. But in the large, people get the message. Some scams are unmasked by intrepid journalists, as in the example just above. Others get revealed by clumsiness or accident. A few come to light because of sheer chutzpah. As a result, people come to believe that unseemly shenanigans take place on a daily basis. The public may see only the tip of the iceberg, but that tip is big enough to convince most Americans that the governmental deck is stacked against them. "Rigged," if you like Donald Trump's word. And it is more than enough to turn people off politics.

My examples so far may give the impression that all this pilfering of the public purse emanates from Congress. Far from it. Many state legislatures are worse. And the executive branch knows how to play the game, too. In fact, unless the White House stops them, many of the departments and agencies of government misconstrue their mission as defending the vested interests of their constituencies against possible encroachment by—perish the thought!—the public interest. Here's an ancient example that I experienced firsthand in the early months of the Clinton administration.

Looking for budget cuts in 1993, we economists trained our eyes on (among other targets) maritime subsidies. The economics were all with us. The United States once had a large and thriving fleet of merchant vessels. But times had changed, and we no longer had a comparative advantage in this industry—to put it mildly. Other nations could and did provide commercial shipping services far more economically than we could. What remained of the US shipping industry was largely on life support—including generous subsidies from the federal government and restrictive legislation like the Jones Act (of 1920!) and cargo preference (which originated in 1904) that mandated the use of US carriers. The annual bill to American consumers ran into the billions every year to save a paltry number of jobs, making maritime one of America's clearest examples of what Europeans call "lemon socialism." It was protectionism at its worst.

Why, you might wonder, was the taxpayer being asked to shoulder such a burden? The putative answer was what it often is in such cases: national security. (Tip for taxpayers: Whenever you hear the phrase "national security," reach reflexively for your wallet.) The United States may have the greatest navy in the world, but the Pentagon feared it might not have enough shipping capacity should a major war break out—and I mean the old-fashioned kind that requires armadas of supply ships. Yes, Virginia, we may live in an age of electronic warfare, but your navy was afraid it didn't have enough frigates. The suggested solution? Keep the American flag flying over the decks of privately owned merchant vessels so the navy could commandeer them in time of need.

Okay, let's accept that. After all, ships actually were commandeered in preparation for the Gulf War in 1991. Besides, who were we economists to question the national security judgments of the Pentagon? So let's imagine a war massive enough to exceed the supply capabilities of the entire US Army, Navy, and Air Force and yet proceeding at such a leisurely pace that commercial ships can be refitted for military use in time. Even then, there must be *some* limit on the number of ships we need to hold in reserve for this purpose. At a large interagency meeting on the question in June 1993, I suggested a simple principle: the Pentagon's own estimate of its *maximal* requirement ought to be an upper limit on the number of vessels we even think about subsidizing. Surely everyone could agree on that.

Well, not quite everyone. The representative of the Department of Transportation reacted with horror. No, we need to maintain subsidies for at least ninety-two ships, not just for the thirty-four the Pentagon says it might require in time of war.* And besides, a couple of senators would be greatly distressed by the loss of jobs in their states—a fact they have already communicated to the president. You can probably guess how this debate turned out. Maritime subsidies survived. They are with us still.

Trade policy is another favorite conduit for doling out special favors. In the large, America before Donald Trump stood for free and open international trade. Not only did we talk the talk, but we were generally at the vanguard of multinational trade liberalizations from World War II until recently—regardless of whether the president was a Republican or a Democrat. Presidents Clinton and Obama, in fact, promoted trade steadfastly, despite much opposition from within their own party. When trade liberalizations succeed, they are almost

---

*The numbers are fictitious. They were classified at the time, and by now I have forgotten them anyway.

always in the broad national interest, even though some particular groups lose.

But American trade policy looks quite different when seen up close and personal. There, it seems, every plaintive industry seeking protection gets a sympathetic ear—at least if it has congressional patrons. (And don't they all?) It's one special interest provision after another. We may have entered into a free trade agreement with our northern and southern neighbors, but just let those Canadians try to ship us too many logs or those Mexicans sell us too many tomatoes. Quicker than you can say, "NAFTA," the administration will have the Commerce Department and the US trade representative on their backs with antidumping statutes, countervailing duties, laws against import surges, Title VII proceedings, section 22 actions, section 301 investigations, and so on. America's protectionist toolbox is generously equipped. And its use is, of course, dictated by domestic politics.

It's a nonpartisan affair, by the way. At least before President Trump, Republicans favored free trade more than Democrats. Yet it was Ronald Reagan who put a sharp limit on Japanese auto imports in the 1980s and George W. Bush who granted protection to the steel industry that Bill Clinton had earlier refused. Donald Trump, of course, pulled us out of the Trans-Pacific Partnership, began to renegotiate NAFTA, and blamed all manner of economic woes on "unfair" imports. It wasn't just China and South Korea. Even Australia, Canada, and Germany became—in Trump's mind—trade adversaries.

Bismarck's Sausages and Madison's Curse

Bismarck had a point—perhaps a better point than he knew—when he advised us not to watch either laws or sausages being made. By adding rank partisanship and political dysfunction to the system of checks and balances that Madison cleverly designed, the contemporary United States has created a recipe for stasis. Problems arise; solutions don't.

When you combine all that with the need for clever, if misleading, slogans and the Three *Is* (ignorance, ideology, and interest groups), you have a potent mix that can be lethal to sound economic policy, even when the policy *should be* nonpartisan. You have an environment in which politicians opt to use economists the way a drunk uses lampposts—for support, not for illumination. You have an atmosphere in which even good economic advice is met with political dissent.

Part of the problem, which I've mentioned but not emphasized thus far, is that politicians are myopic; their time horizons are too short. It's true. But economists' time horizons are probably too long. Might there be a golden mean? We'll search for that in the next chapter.

Chapter 3

Lost Horizons?

Timing is everything.

—Anonymous

The year 2010 was a landmark year for economic policy.

In March, after a fiery and highly partisan debate, Congress passed and President Obama signed into law the Patient Protection and Affordable Care Act. The ACA, establishing what came to be called Obamacare, made several major changes in America's health insurance system—most prominently, bringing many previously uninsured Americans under the umbrella of health insurance. From its passage until early in Donald Trump's term, repealing Obamacare became the mantra of the Republican Party.

In July, Congress passed and President Obama signed the Dodd-Frank Wall Street Reform and Consumer Protection Act, which rewrote many of the rules governing America's financial system in the wake of the financial crisis. Once again, Republicans were almost united in opposition. Ever since then, much of Wall Street and many Republicans have tried repeatedly either to weaken or repeal Dodd-Frank—with some successes. Early in his presidency, Donald Trump promised, quite nonspecifically, to "dismantle" Dodd-Frank, though no one quite knew what that meant.

In November 2010, Republicans won a smashing midterm electoral victory, acquiring an overwhelmingly Republican House and leaving the Democrats with only a razor-thin majority in the Senate—which they subsequently lost.

Now here's your political test question. (Don't worry, you'll get it right.) Had President Obama and congressional leaders postponed the votes on health care reform and Wall Street reform until the new Congress was seated in January 2011, would either bill have passed? The answer, of course, is no.

Not a very interesting thought experiment, you say? Well, that depends on which civilization you hail from. The conclusion that the two votes would have differed dramatically is entirely natural and obvious politically. But from an economic perspective, it is deeply weird. After all, nothing notable happened to either America's health care system or its financial system during the year 2010. So the substantive pros and cons of the ACA and Dodd-Frank hardly changed. Nor did the economic evidence germane to deciding—*on nonpolitical grounds*—whether to support or oppose either bill. Had the two laws been put to a vote of members of the American Economic Association before and after November 2010 (now there's a fanciful thought!), the outcomes would probably have been about the same.

The point of this thought experiment is simple: timing can be everything in politics—2011 was not 2010.

The Long and Short of It

It is a commonplace that politicians have excruciatingly short time horizons. While it is often said that they cannot see past the next election, the truth is far worse. The political pros who advise politicians often cannot see past the next public opinion poll, maybe not even past the next tweet. Their natural time horizon extends only until that evening's news broadcasts, if that long. But I have also noted that economists are often equally guilty of telescopic concentration on the distant future. They suffer from hypermetropia (farsightedness) rather than from myopia (nearsightedness).

For openers, standard economic analysis is wont to dote on long-run consequences, to the exclusion of many problems said to be "transitional"—and thereby belittled. Those transition costs, however, loom large in the lives of ordinary people. Would I lose my job to foreign competition—and perhaps be unemployed for a year or two—if the TPP (Trans-Pacific Partnership) was approved? Would tax reform reduce the value of my home or business? Not such little problems, really—and not very transitory.

It is true that the nation does not hold elections every Tuesday, and making policy as if it does courts economic disaster. But it is equally foolish to belittle the "short-run" effects of economic policies when the short run may last one, two, or even five years. If we are to bring political and economic civilizations closer together, one good place to start would be reducing the yawning gap between the time horizons of politicians and economists. If one is twenty-four hours and the other is twenty-four years, then we need to lengthen one and shorten the other—quite a bit.

Consider: Any economist worth his salt, and most who are not, can explain to you why freer trade is good for the nation as a whole. But truth be told, some people are likely to lose their jobs anytime international trade is liberalized. Those folks will suffer what economists call "transition costs" while they seek new employment. Compounding their difficulties, the evidence suggests that the jobs most such displaced workers eventually land will pay lower wages than the jobs they lost. Those people are right, not wrong, to fear trade liberalization. Economists often ignore that. Politicians do not.

Or take another example: Many economists favor a consumption tax over an income tax. They can explain to you at length (if your eyes don't glaze over) why the former is more *efficient* than the latter, and their arguments may be valid in the abstract. But real-world tax policy is not written on a blank slate. The transitional problems that would arise in replacing our current income tax with a consumption tax are monumental—enough to make a strong politician weep. For example, the value of assets like stocks, bonds, and houses might change dramatically.

The torrid pace of Washington life is a second way in which politics sometimes makes a hash out of rational policymaking. At times, the high-speed chase is unavoidable. After all, there really are emergencies now and then; sometimes there are deadlines to meet (*This bill must be passed before Congress goes on recess*); and political windows do open and shut. But all too often the people charged with developing policy options are forced to race toward deadlines that have been imposed artificially by message meisters. The predictable results are shortcuts, sloppy work, and errors.

Here's what David Stockman, Ronald Reagan's first budget director, said about how the pressure for speed tripped up the Reagan economic team in early 1981:

> Designing a comprehensive plan to bring about a sweeping change in national economic governance in forty days is a preposterous, wantonly reckless notion. . . . I soon became a veritable incubator of shortcuts, schemes, and devices to overcome the truth . . . that the budget gap couldn't be closed except by a dictator. . . . My expedients saw to it that critical loose ends were left unresolved everywhere. They ensured that the whole fiscal plan was embedded with contradictions and booby-trapped with hidden pressures.

Exactly twelve years later, I was in the White House when the Clinton administration took office. Did we learn from the procedural missteps of the harried Reagan team? No, we emulated their breakneck schedule by racing to meet a tight February 17 deadline that was in no way imposed by law. Why the rush? One factor was certainly that the Reagan budget had been presented to Congress on February 18. We would beat them by a day! Extreme haste naturally led to several mistakes—not to mention exhaustion for the economic team.

But, fortunately for President Clinton, and even more fortunately for the nation, none of those mistakes proved particularly serious or damaging.

A more recent example pertains to Congress rather than to the executive branch. In rushing through the text of the Affordable Care Act in 2010, Congress wrote—read carefully now—that subsidies could be given to enrollees who bought health insurance on "an exchange established by the state." However, states were given a fallback: if they didn't want to establish their own exchange, the federal government would do it for them. Did the legislative language really intend to provide subsidies only to citizens who bought their health insurance on exchanges established by *states*, excluding citizens who purchased theirs on exchanges established by the *federal* government? Of course not. It was just sloppy draftsmanship. Why in the world would Congress have wanted to make such a silly distinction? Nothing in the legislative history suggests that members did.

Nonetheless, a legal challenge that tried to use this shoddy draftsmanship to punch a gigantic hole in Obamacare went all the way to the US Supreme Court in 2015. There, Chief Justice John Roberts, writing for a 6–3 majority, reached the obvious conclusion that it was a drafting error, not something Congress had intended. (What were the other three justices thinking?) In a bit of judicial chiding, he opined that the maladroit wording "does not reflect the type of care and deliberation that one might expect of such significant legislation." Darn right. Had the Court read Congress's words literally, its decision might have gone the other way, taking Obamacare down with it. A close call.

Yet another poignant example came early in 2017, when House Republicans and the Trump administration decided they had to rush to redeem the campaign pledge to "repeal and replace" Obamacare. There were two big problems, however—both of which argued to slow things down. The first was that neither the Trump White House nor the House Republicans had a substitute plan at the ready. Whoops! You can't beat something with nothing.

Second, the plan that was hastily cobbled together in two House committees (under cover of darkness—literally) turned out to lack political support. President Trump and Speaker Paul Ryan (R-WI) suffered a political humiliation when they had to pull the bill in March rather than see it voted down on the House floor. A substitute measure passed the House in May. But when it came to the Senate, Majority Leader McConnell, after pulling his first version of "repeal and replace" (like Ryan), saw several replacements defeated in the Senate in July and September.

These examples notwithstanding, political experts will argue that the orderly, deliberative decision-making processes favored by technicians are apt to lead nowhere. You must seize the moment when the time is right, else political life may pass you by. Perhaps that is true at certain unusual junctures of history; political opportunity doesn't knock every day. But I do not believe that mad dashes toward artificially imposed deadlines generally produce good policy—whether judged on economic *or* political criteria. More often than not, haste makes waste not only economically but also politically.

The Tax Reform Act of 1986 offers a superb example of doing precisely the opposite. Despite the political tendency to rush things, the tortoise triumphed over the hare. The act was passed in September 1986—almost two years after the US Treasury issued its first comprehensive recommendations in a thick report nicknamed "Treasury I." That report, itself a product of over nine months of intensive work inside the administration, was followed by "Treasury II" and then by months of legislative to-and-fro. The whole process took over two and a half years from start to finish. But the end product was perhaps the finest tax bill Congress ever passed. It created a simpler, fairer tax code, lowered tax rates dramatically, closed numerous loopholes, and removed many near-poor taxpayers from the tax rolls entirely. It was worth waiting for. In stark contrast, President Trump and the Republicans rushed tax reform through Congress in 2017—with results that were less than stellar.

Sequencing Matters

There is a third, and quite important, aspect of scheduling in which politics rolls over economics: the sequencing of issues in time. Policy wonks rarely give this factor a second thought. But it is always prominent in political minds, and the politicians have this one right.

In the academy, issues are judged one by one, each on its own intrinsic merits. How unrelated matters are sequenced in time is irrelevant. After all, how could it possibly matter whether the government stakes out its position on a trade agreement before or after it deals with health care reform? Except in rare cases, the order of battle does not affect the substantive merits of the various cases and so cannot possibly affect the decisions—or so it seems in economists' way of thinking.

In fact, economists have a special name for a closely related principle of rational choice: the *independence of irrelevant alternatives*. Loosely speaking, this principle states that whether you prefer lamb chops to lobster or vice versa should not be affected by the presence or absence on the menu of some other dish that you would never choose, perhaps sweetbreads.

But the political world does not operate by such neat, rational rules. It uses an entirely different form of logic. Seemingly irrelevant alternatives turn out to be maddeningly relevant for a variety of reasons. One is logrolling: if my support for your bill hinges on your support for mine, it may be helpful to take up the two bills closely in time because "mine first, yours second" may not work in politics. And since the congressional machinery can cope with only a limited number of issues at once, this linkage may crowd other—even more "irrelevant"—issues off the legislative calendar entirely.

Here's a recent example. Around Thanksgiving of 2015, members of New York's congressional delegation thought they had an agreement that secured health benefits for first responders to the 9/11 catastrophe at the World Trade Center. They expected it to be attached to the omnibus spending bill that Congress needed to pass in December, and few members of Congress seemed opposed. Yet Senate Majority Leader McConnell stopped the train in its tracks. Why? Was he against helping the first responders? Probably not. But he wanted New York's senators and representatives to give him something in return. In the end, McConnell did get something Republicans wanted—lifting the forty-year-old ban on US exports of crude oil products—before he would allow New York's first responders to get their due. Were the two proposals linked substantively? Not at all. But sequencing in time and logrolling linked them politically.

A second reason has its origins in the need to husband valuable political capital. Presidents can augment their stock of political capital with a series of legislative victories or fritter it away in a string of defeats. Even a bruising battle that ends with a win can leave a residue of ill will that hurts later. Most legislative victories enhance the president's political cachet, thereby easing the way to subsequent victories. Every loss or pyrrhic victory squanders some precious political capital and makes achievement of the president's remaining agenda more elusive. So presidents and congressional leaders care mightily about the sequencing of issues in time, as they should.

Accidents of geography also intertwine issues that seem intrinsically unrelated. Remember Tip O'Neill's famous dictum that all politics is local. Members of Congress are experts on what will please and displease their constituents. If the voters of, say, Iowa are being asked to swallow some bitter bill, their representatives in Congress may insist on sugarcoating it with some kind of goody—such as larger ethanol subsidies.

I came to appreciate the importance of sequencing by watching from a front-row seat as the agenda of the first Clinton administration unfolded. It was decided early on that the budget, which included a great deal of new policy, had to come first—even though we knew it would encounter fierce political resistance. At one point prior to the president's first big economic address, Hillary Clinton and leaders of the health reform effort argued for bundling a health care proposal into the already crowded budget package. They had two reasons. One was fear that the large expenditure of political capital needed to pass the budget would damage the chances for health care reform. The other was the parliamentary fact that a budget reconciliation bill, unlike ordinary legislation, cannot be filibustered in the Senate.

They were right on both counts. But the idea of melding health reform into the budget legislation was quickly rejected by the economic team and President Clinton for a simple reason: no health care plan was ready yet. It was a good reason, but the decision to wait probably damaged prospects for health care reform in 1993 enormously.

At that point, the scheduling contest shifted to health care versus the North American Free Trade Agreement. With NAFTA in some political danger, it would clearly take a major effort by President Clinton to push the treaty through. More political blood would doubtless be spilled in the process, further diminishing the chances for health care reform. A battle royal ensued within the administration over whether health care or NAFTA would be next out of the chute. For a variety of reasons, including the mundane fact that NAFTA was scheduled to start in January 1994, the decision was made to move NAFTA first. Health care reform would have to wait again, even though it was the president's top legislative priority.

In the end, the fears of the health care team proved amply justified. The president *did* expend a great deal of political capital on NAFTA, and that *did* hurt the chances of passing health care reform—which ultimately failed.

For all these reasons and others, political logic can give rise to something that is completely ruled out by Aristotelian logic. Economists call it *nontransitive preferences*. Suppose a consumer prefers pizza to hot dogs, and prefers hot dogs to tofu, then—to economists' way of thinking—we know for sure that she prefers pizza to tofu. That's called *transitive preferences*, and it's one of the most basic axioms of rational choice. If preferences aren't transitive, who knows what will make consumers happier?

But that neat axiom of choice doesn't apply to politics. Because of logrolling, or accidents of geography, or the vagaries of congressional scheduling, it is not uncommon to find politicians favoring Policy A over Policy B, favoring Policy B over Policy C, and yet still preferring C to A. To a strictly logical economist, that's befuddling. But to a skilled politician, it may all make sense.

Room in the Middle?

Can anything close the gap between the ultra-short time horizons of politics and the ultra-long time horizons of economics? Well, maybe. Getting politicians to focus on the long run is not as hopeless as it may seem because it does not require them to peer all that far into the future. It certainly does not ask them to adopt the excruciatingly long time horizons that typify economists' thinking. Those are rather too leisurely for politics.

Just for a moment, suspend disbelief and suppose that the extreme myopia that pervades modern politics is actually a tactical error. Suppose behaving as if there is an election every Tuesday is not as smart politically as politicos seem to believe. Then sound policy has at least a glimmer of hope. After all, politicians are among the most adaptable of God's creatures. If they can be persuaded that current political practices are counterproductive, they will change their ways—not because they have suddenly become idealists, but because they want to win elections.

What, then, is the basis for my audacious claim that adopting a longer time frame might actually be good politics? The answer lies in a mundane fact: a presidential term lasts four years, making that a uniquely sensible, even natural, time horizon for many political decisions. At least early in a president's term, the president and his political advisers should focus on what the economic situation will look like three or four years down the road. Yes, midterm elections come every two years—that's too bad. But the big events in US politics are the presidential elections.

Happily, four years is more than long enough for most economic policies to have substantial effects. Long after the spin and counterspin have been forgotten, voters will be living with the consequences of policy decisions made two, three, or four years earlier. Perhaps without even knowing it, they will render their verdict on those policies—or rather on the *results* of those policies—when they go to the polls. The political implication is clear: even the most cynical political technician should focus on the next presidential election—which may be years, not weeks, away. Except when elections are around the corner, the newspaper headlines, blogs, and polling results of the week really won't count for much on election day.

Unfortunately, too few political pros seem to have internalized this lesson. In fact, most of them instinctively reject it. Almost all politicos need corrective lenses to improve their long-distance vision. Examples in which short time horizons have led to poor public policy abound. Here are two.

The federal budget deficit ballooned alarmingly in the early years of the Obama presidency, for two main reasons. One was the whopping-big recession, which reduced tax receipts and increased expenditures on programs like unemployment insurance and food stamps. The other was a long list of antirecessionary policies, of which the most notable ones were bundled into the American Recovery and Reinvestment Act—the large fiscal stimulus that Congress passed in February 2009.

Regardless of the reasons, which I would argue were good ones, the sheer size of the resulting deficits alarmed many Americans. After all, running budget deficits of 10 percent of GDP is something we associate with Greece or Argentina, not with the United States. A strong political backlash against such large deficits ensued, and the direction of American fiscal policy quickly turned from being more expansionary (meaning more spending and/or tax cuts, which support job creation) to being more contractionary (meaning less spending and/or higher taxes, which destroy jobs).

Importantly, it was the *timing* that was off, not the policy objective. Deficits near 10 percent of GDP are indeed far too large. They are unsustainable and *must* be reduced. But not necessarily in 2010 and 2011, when the unemployment rate averaged 9.3 percent. Under political pressure from budget hawks, Congress shifted fiscal policy toward smaller deficits much too quickly. By late 2012, US policymakers were even toying with the idea of going over what was then called "the fiscal cliff"—a combination of spending cuts and tax increases that would almost certainly have pushed the economy back into recession (but which, fortunately, was avoided at the last minute).

Most economists think the ill-timed "fiscal drag" that resulted from shrinking the deficit too soon slowed economic growth markedly in 2011, 2012, and 2013. And perhaps the saddest part was that the lion's share of the super-sized deficit was going to disappear anyway as the economy improved and the stimulus money ran out. Bad policy was fostered, in part, by myopia.

My second example is more generic. Budgetary scorekeeping by the Congressional Budget Office often rules the Washington roost. Nonpartisan technicians tell Congress what its spending and taxing proposals are likely to do to the budget deficit, and the CBO's estimates are normally taken seriously. That's not an inherently bad idea; Congress has amply demonstrated the need for external budgetary discipline. But senators and representatives of both parties are pretty adept at manipulating scorekeeping rules, and some of those manipulations reflect the short time horizons I have been talking about.

Years ago, when budgeting was on a one-year-at-a-time basis, this was easy as pie. To illustrate, one frequently proposed suggestion for producing scorable savings for *this year's* budget was to pass a law giving holders of appreciated assets strong incentives to realize their capital gains now rather than waiting. For example, suppose Congress enacts a statute lowering the top rate on capital gains from 20 percent to 10 percent *for one year only*. If a number of people holding accrued capital gains cash out during what amounts to a "tax sale," the rate cut will actually *raise* revenue immediately. Of course, such short-run revenue gains come at the expense of future revenue losses; capital gains taxed this year will not be taxed in the future. But the latter would fall beyond the one-year budget window and so would be ignored by annual scorekeeping.

Such accounting legerdemain is harder to pull off when the CBO is scoring proposals over five years (as it used to) or ten years (as it does now). But it is still possible. President George W. Bush's 2001 tax cuts were scored within the ten-year budget window. By no coincidence, all the tax cuts were legislated to disappear conveniently after nine years, recording a mythical zero as the revenue loss in the tenth year (2011) and nothing after that. No one really believed that would happen, certainly not President Bush. And it didn't. But the CBOs scorekeepers in 2001 had no choice but to accept the statute as legislated. They don't second-guess Congress.*

President Trump's first budget submission took this chicanery to a much higher level. It included the "supply-side" growth benefits ascribed to tax cuts—themselves a big stretch of the imagination—and the additional revenue such magnificent growth would bring it (over $2 trillion within the ten-year window). But it conveniently "forgot" to net out the revenue losses from the tax cuts themselves. This convenient omission enabled Budget Director Mick Mulvaney to claim budget balance within ten years. It was breathtaking.

The point of these tax-window examples is the same: favorable scorekeeping that reduces the deficit within the budget window can make some pretty awful long-run policies look superficially attractive in the short run. To economists, a far more sensible way to do scorekeeping would be to track the *annual* costs of any budget change *when fully phased in*. But try selling that to your representative, who is serving a two-year term.

---

*A bit of congressional arcana is relevant here. The so-called Byrd Rule prohibits budgetary items in a reconciliation bill from increasing the deficit *beyond* the budget window, e.g., in the second ten years. Making the Bush tax cuts permanent would have run afoul of that, too.

The Social Security system doesn't have this problem; it is blessed with a naturally long time horizon that *should* make reform easier than most politicians realize. For purposes of assessing long-run solvency, which is Social Security's current problem, what happens in the next year or two doesn't matter—*literally*. The natural time horizon for coherent Social Security analysis is at least decades, and probably generations. So the politician's normally short time horizon should be lengthened to correspond to the economist's naturally long time horizon on this issue. The two civilizations should not clash—at least not over time horizons. Concretely, it is perfectly responsible behavior, not a pusillanimous dodge, for Congress to legislate savings in Social Security (whether they be benefit cuts or new revenues) that don't start for many years. More than that, it's good economics, for we don't want to pull the rug out from under the feet of people nearing retirement.

Yet economists and politicians don't see eye to eye on this issue. Why not? Perhaps it's because many of today's politicians are too young to remember the early 1980s, when Social Security came much closer to going broke than it is today. With their backs to the wall because the trust fund was running out of money, President Ronald Reagan and the Congress appointed a distinguished bipartisan commission chaired by economist Alan Greenspan. (Yes, the same guy who later ruled the Federal Reserve for over eighteen years.) When the Greenspan Commission issued its report in January 1983, its recommendations both touched the alleged "third rail" of American politics by cutting Social Security benefits (for example, by making some of them taxable) and broached the dreaded *T* word by raising taxes (even though Reagan was an avowed tax cutter). Two political sacred cows got slaughtered at once. Perhaps even worse politically, the ensuing congressional debate also raised the normal retirement age from sixty-five to sixty-seven.

Lots of political poison, it would seem. Yet these recommendations sailed through Congress with amazingly little resistance. Why? Part of the answer is that both President Reagan and the Democratic

Speaker of the House at the time, Tip O'Neill, were back-slapping deal makers who were ready to compromise—and who were forced to compromise by the frightening prospect of the trust fund running dry. Another small part may have been a linguistic dodge: you don't have to call an increase in the retirement age a *benefit cut*, even though it is. Euphemisms sometimes help.

But the key ingredient in the secret sauce was deferring the pain. The payroll tax increases were gradual and small, phased in over seven years. The older retirement age came in much more slowly. *Nothing* was to change until the year 2000—which was seventeen years away at the time—and then the increase from age sixty-five to age sixty-seven would phase in gradually over the next twenty-two years. (Yes, we are still phasing it in!) You don't find many politicos worried about what's going to happen seventeen to thirty-nine years in the future. Yet that was fast enough to make the economics work. It can happen here.

Sizzle or Substance?

An important, and related, part of the central dilemma of policy-making in a modern, PR-driven democracy is that sizzle often sells better than substance in the short run, but substance, not sizzle, matters more in the long run. Where serious public policy issues are concerned, the economic equities of the case will eventually come shining through and overwhelm the cleverly crafted but long-forgotten messages that politicos devise. Even if only subconsciously, many people will perceive the benefits of sound policies and be distressed by the failures and costs of bad ones. And they will express their affection or disaffection when they go to the polls. Perhaps that is what Lincoln had in mind when he said you cannot fool all the people all the time.

To most politicians of the Internet Age, the Lincolnesque long run must seem an excruciatingly long time to wait. But sizzle sometimes gives way to substance much faster than that.

The first Obama administration spent countless hours in health care meetings worrying about their sales pitch, their congressional strategy, how to appease (or at least neutralize) the various interest groups, the timing of announcements, and so on—all the details that are the stock-in-trade of political pros. Either despite or because of all that effort, the plan made it through Congress by the skin of its teeth—albeit heavily revised, and only because of House Speaker Nancy Pelosi's political acumen—and was unpopular at its launch. (The infamous failure of the website healthcare.gov did not help.) But actual experience with the new health care system was going to get the public either loving or hating Obamacare over time.

This process had partly played out by the time of the 2016 election, and the experience was more favorable than unfavorable. Donald Trump ran and won that election on many issues; trade and immigration come quickly to mind. But among his campaign promises was repealing Obamacare and replacing it by "something great." On assuming office, however, he and his fellow Republicans were surprised at the resistance they encountered. Obamacare had "suddenly" become popular. When they tried to repeal and replace it several times in 2017, they failed.

So part of the solution to political myopia, and not an impossible part, is to put corrective lenses on the eyes of the political "experts," who must learn to look ahead to the next presidential election—not just to the next news broadcast. As their time horizons lengthen, they will automatically attach less importance to sizzle and more to substance.

Or will they? Remember, political leaders tend to be people of action. They will feel uncomfortable patiently awaiting the state of the nation four years hence. Nor will their constituents be pleased if such farsightedness gives the impression of inattention. There *are*, after all, public opinion polls to contend with every week, pesky news broadcasts every night, the minute-by-minute jury that tweets all day (and night) long, and of course, midterm elections. Fortunately, a sharp focus on long-run *economic* consequences does not necessarily undermine the case for short-run *political* action. In fact, the unforgiving nature of the American political calendar makes the two consistent.

Three stark facts shrink what I call the "policy phase" of any administration to roughly its first eighteen months. First, the wheels of Congress grind excruciatingly slowly. With rare exceptions, major policy initiatives that fail to emerge from the White House pressure cooker within the first twelve to eighteen months after inauguration day stand little chance of enactment. After that, the approach of midterm elections marks the onset of the political silly season—and thus the end of the serious policy phase of most administrations. After the midterms, of course, it's all presidential politics all the time. Second, once significant economic policies are enacted into law, they invariably take substantial time to implement. Third, still more time elapses before they have significant effects on the economy.

The consequence is sobering. The Constitution gives each newly elected president a four-year term. In practice, however, he has barely more than a year to develop the core of his economic agenda. (Small stuff can come later—maybe.) After that, natural political rhythms take over, and legislative windows start closing. With just twelve to eighteen months to work with, there is ample reason to hurry.

Expert politicians will feel intuitively the urgency to act quickly. But in doing so, they should keep their eyes trained on the future consequences of present decisions. This month's policy decisions will ultimately matter much more than this month's message—regardless of whether outcomes are scored on economic or political criteria. In both realms, actions last longer than words. Maybe that is what Keynes had in mind when he declared that ideas rule the world.

The Nonpendulum Theory of Politics

There is another critical aspect of timing that economists often fail to appreciate but politicians don't. Circumstances that foster legislative success come and go, and some astute politician must be there to seize the moment before it passes.

- Ronald Reagan correctly assessed that the time was ripe for massive tax cuts in 1981—and that he could roll the Democrats, who would normally have objected to enormous tax cuts tilted so lopsidedly to the rich.
- In the spring of 1986, Senator Bob Packwood (R-OR) turned a sow's ear of a tax bill into a silk purse of tax reform by changing course abruptly. The main reason was that Packwood saw his reelection chances in jeopardy.
- Bill Clinton read the antideficit message in voters' support for Ross Perot in 1992, and concluded that he could turn deficit reduction into a political winner in 1993—which he proceeded to do.
- Barack Obama guessed correctly that he could push health care reform through a balky Congress in 2010—and that it might be his only chance.
- Donald Trump, running for president in 2016, sensed that many Americans were fed up with international trade and globalization in general. So he ran the most protectionist campaign anyone could remember—and won.

In all of these cases and others, astute politicians took risks that paid off handsomely.

An equally keen sense of timing is necessary to recognize when circumstances are *not* propitious. Sometimes the timing is just not right, even if the cause is just and the policy is well designed. The master politician knows when to hold back. It is an important talent, for a policy initiative can be severely damaged or even killed by rushing it to the fore before its time. Unlike salmon, major legislation rarely swims upstream.

Let's go back to one of the examples just mentioned. Was the time really ripe for health care reform in 2010? We know that President Obama won a legislative victory that had eluded presidents since Harry Truman, and we know that he probably would have lost the battle had he waited another year. But we also know that in order to push health care so early, the new president had to put a number of other pet issues, including climate change, on the back burner.

Many people also believe that devoting so much time and energy to health care diverted the president's attention from fighting the terrible recession. As one White House aide later admitted, "No one thought we would have to take every element of the administration and dedicate it to health care both publicly and privately, which is what we ended up having to do." In a famous incident, Obama's first secretary of the Treasury, Tim Geithner, told his boss, "Your signature accomplishment is going to be preventing a Great Depression," to which Obama responded, "That's not enough for me."

It wasn't. But was President Obama's decision to move health care reform early in his first term right or wrong? Historians will likely debate that question for decades. But regardless of the answer, the sequence of events illustrates an important generic issue that scientists call *path dependence*. In plain English, path dependence means that where you wind up depends on the path you take to get there. The hand of history is not dead.

At first, that idea may seem axiomatic. Doesn't the path always influence the final outcome? Doesn't history always matter? The perhaps surprising answer is no.

Consider, for example, the final resting place of a pendulum that is set in motion by a push. The ultimate resting point—what physicists call the *equilibrium* of the system—is always at the bottom of the arc, meaning that it is *independent* of the path traversed in the interim. Shove the pendulum left or right, vigorously or gently, once or twice, and it always comes to rest in precisely the same spot. Or take a more homely example: the final outcome of an agreement to meet a friend under the Biltmore clock in Grand Central Station at seven p.m. is not affected by the paths the two of you take to get there—provided, of course, you both make it.

Most of the models we economists teach our students are *not* path dependent. As you may remember from college, we tell beginning students that the equilibrium price in a free market is where the supply and demand curves cross, regardless of the adjustment path the market takes to get there. None of these three examples—the pendulum, the meeting, or supply and demand—exhibit path dependence. In each case, all roads lead to the same Rome.

But other systems *are* path dependent. Depending on how you start the journey, you may wind up in Rome, Italy, or Rome, New York. One well-known scientific example is evolution. Because of the vagaries of mutations, Darwinian natural selection does not lead to a predetermined "equilibrium" outcome. Had a series of random biological events over many millennia turned out differently, we humans might look quite different from the way we do. Similarly, some systems in physics and economics exhibit path dependence.

One oft-cited example is the standard QWERTY keyboard. Look at yours. The ten letters across the top row spell QWERTYUIOP. This arrangement, which dates from the 1870s, is dictated neither by the alphabet nor by ergonomics. In fact, one major selling point of the design was that it placed all the letters needed to spell TYPE-WRITER across the top row—which helped Remington's early salesmen impress customers by rapidly banging out the name of their new product. An alternative keyboard configuration known as the Dvorak Simplified Keyboard was patented in the 1930s. Although it produced demonstrably faster typing, it never caught on. Why not? Because QWERTY had gotten there first and commanded the market. It was a sheer accident of history. Had we been luckier, the top row of your keyboard would now read DHIATENSOR and people would type faster—or so the story goes.

A more recent historical example was the competitive war between VHS ("video home system") and Betamax technologies for the VCR market, which began in the 1970s and lasted a quarter century or so. Many technologists thought Betamax had the edge. But VHS won the competitive race through strategies like better marketing and cleverer licensing arrangements. A pendulum would, I suppose, have selected Betamax.

Political and bureaucratic outcomes are strongly path dependent because the game of politics is played with rules that are in constant flux. Timetables and sequencing matter. Quirks of history push decision-making processes in different, sometimes surprising, directions. Personalities and group dynamics change. All these things and more can leave lasting imprints. The path influences the ultimate policy because, unlike the pendulum, there is no natural resting place.

I do not, for example, believe it was in any way preordained that Hillary Clinton's health care plan had to lead to naught in 1994, Barack Obama's effort in 2010 was bound to succeed, and Donald Trump's attempt to "repeal and replace" Obamacare in 2017 was doomed to failure. Nor do I believe that the impasse between President Obama and the Republican Congress inevitably had to produce a government shutdown in October 2013 but not in December 2015. That is the way things actually turned out. But in each case, it is easy to imagine different processes producing totally different outcomes. That's path dependence.

If this discussion of path dependence seems overly wonkish and unimportant to you, rest assured that it is not. Politicians take path dependence for granted; it's an obvious, and obviously important, aspect of the world in which they live. In a path-dependent system, timing may indeed be (almost) everything. Equilibrium is the alien concept.

To economists, it's just the reverse. They think first—and maybe even second and third—about the equilibrium state where, e.g., supply equals demand, unemployment is at its "natural" rate, and tax changes have been capitalized into real estate values. To them, path dependence is the unusual, maybe even uninteresting, exception.

Oddly, they are both right—and both wrong. In political matters, path dependence is more than just a norm; it's close to a law of nature. So politicians, naturally, live in and think about transitions all the time. To them, equilibrium is an abstract concept, close to meaningless. But in many economic matters, equilibrium states really are important. They are not just "academic" because most real-world economic systems tend to move there—eventually—as in the supply-and-demand example. Politicians who ignore the long-run equilibrium are setting themselves up for some unpleasant surprises.

The payroll tax for Social Security makes a wonderful example. If, say, Congress were to raise only the employer's share of the tax, leaving the employee's share unchanged, workers would get off scot-free for a while. Neither their pretax wages nor their tax payments would change. But both economic logic and supporting research show that the situation would be fleeting—it's not an *equilibrium*. Once labor markets adjust, pretax wages would fall, and workers would wind up bearing the full burden of the tax hike. But try explaining that to voters, and therefore to politicians. It's all a bit subtle for a bumper sticker.

This fundamental difference in perspectives makes communication between economists and politicians difficult. It is one reason why politicians often find economic analysis more useful for support than for illumination. It is often why sound advice is greeted by dissent.

When the Time Is Ripe

While timing may be everything, getting the timing right requires a rare blend of luck and skill. For starters, you may need patience—lots of it. Like ancient Rome, good economic policies are not built in a day. They may, in fact, take a decade or more to develop and blossom.

A problem must first be recognized and acknowledged. Unfortunately, denial seems to be a powerful human instinct. So policy wonks trying to call attention to an economic problem may find themselves whistling in the dark for quite a while. But they should keep at it, for the intellectual spadework must be done. It helps a lot if expert opinion has reached a rough consensus prior to any serious attempt at political action.

Next, ordinary people—which basically means politicians and their constituents—must be persuaded that this rough consensus is roughly right. Remember the Colson Principle: "When you've got them by the _____, their hearts and minds will follow."* If you can convince the voters, the politicians will follow. But if people aren't convinced that a problem exists, it will be hard to persuade their politicians to adopt solutions.

Finally, you must tolerate the inevitable false starts, and you may have to fend off some egregious quack remedies. Churchill allegedly said that you can always count on the Americans to do the right thing—after they have tried everything else. That about sums it up.

The 1986 tax reform, which I've lauded as an example of policy success, passed through each of these stages on the way to the promised land. Specialists had been singing the same hymn for years: broaden the base; lower the rates. Volumes of research had been published on the distorting effects of our complicated, loophole-ridden tax code. Ideas for reform were abundant. Indeed, the US Treasury had published a comprehensive *Blueprints for Basic Tax Reform* as early as January 1977—seven years before Treasury I emerged. Importantly, the public was fed up with tax laws that were terribly complex, patently unfair, and frequently seemed to let the wealthy off the hook. (Does that sound familiar?) Many unlovely (except to lobbyists) tax bills had passed Congress before President Reagan embraced the cause. But even then, with the backing of a politically powerful president, it took almost two additional years to get a watered-down version of tax reform through Congress.

Now think about global climate change, where policy success in the US has been elusive and where—at least politically—the time seems not yet to be ripe.

Lots of scientific and economic spadework has been done over the years. It is by now well established that the world has a huge problem. And economists are pretty much agreed on the right solution: taxing

---

*Charles "Chuck" Colson was a close aide to President Richard Nixon, known then for occasionally blunt language.

carbon emissions or, alternatively, creating a "cap-and-trade" system, which is almost the same thing. So the first stage, where the experts do their work, is pretty much done.

But for years, maybe for decades, the dominant strand of thinking—if you want to call it thinking—in popular and political circles was denial. Is the planet really warming? (*Wait, aren't winters still cold?*) Even if so, does human activity have anything much to do with that? (*Humans did not cause the Ice Age.*) Even if so, maybe there is not much we can do about it—except at enormous cost. (*King Canute could not command the tides.*)

We now seem to be moving into the second stage, where most of the public is convinced that climate change is a serious problem, that at least some of it stems from human activity, and that we humans should do something to mitigate it. No bipartisan *political* consensus yet exists, however, in the United States. Instead, while the Democratic Party appears ready to take action, most Republicans seem stuck in the denial phase. President Trump even had the comic audacity to claim it was all a hoax. Let's see. A hoax perpetrated by thousands of scientists in dozens of countries for decades?

Economists have a remedy for climate change at the ready: a corrective tax on carbon. But that solution uses the *T* word, which most Republicans still treat like poison and which most Democrats still dare not utter—perhaps because they fear voter reaction to higher energy prices. In short, when it comes to mitigating climate change, we may already be too late *scientifically*, we are definitely ready to go *economically*, but the time is not yet ripe *politically*. Indeed, when Donald Trump became president, he quickly rescinded several executive orders by which Barack Obama had hoped to meet the US commitments under the Paris Climate Accord. Then, in May 2017, he pulled us out of the Paris Agreement entirely, thereby breaking ranks with 194 other countries. So we stand here, doing next to nothing, as the earth gets warmer.

Can the Twain Really Meet?

Something may be nagging you about my proposal to close the gap between long economic time horizons and short political time horizons by focusing on full four-year presidential terms. It is true that four years is long enough for most economic policies to do their work. But what I've offered as the "natural" political time horizon—the end of the president's term—is four years away only on inauguration day. Then it begins to shrink. By a year before the next presidential election, the time horizon is down to 365 days. By a month before, it's only 30 days long.

All true—but not as bad as it sounds. Remember, I have argued that the serious policy phase of any presidential term lasts no more than eighteen months—at the end of which the presidency still has two and a half years to run. Once the next presidential election grows closer than that, the nation is entering the political silly season anyway, which stacks the deck against any major domestic policy initiatives. Try to think of a major domestic achievement that came in the last year of a president's term.

The upshot is that the inexorable shrinkage of the natural political time horizon between one presidential election and the next may be a *nonbinding* constraint. It is present, to be sure. Nothing sensible will get through Congress in an election year. But it is irrelevant because other constraints limit policymaking even more severely. You better get it done in the first eighteen months.

Important as it is, however, the clash between the short time horizons of politicians and the long time horizons of economists falls short of a full explanation of why the two groups inhabit such different civilizations. Nor would bringing the two time horizons closer together solve the Lamppost Theory problem. There is much more to the story, as the next chapter shows.

Chapter 4

Madison's Curse Meets Madison Avenue

All politics is applesauce.

—Will Rogers

President Obama's health care proposals put administration economists in a ticklish situation in 2009—strikingly similar to one faced by President Clinton's economists sixteen years earlier, when I was one of them.

Among the more politically damaging criticisms of using a government mandate to expand health insurance coverage was the charge that forcing either employees (as in the Obama plan) or employers (as in the Clinton plan) to purchase insurance would destroy jobs. The accusation had superficial plausibility because mandating significant health care expenditures as a condition of employment is akin to raising the payroll tax and, for very-low-wage workers, to increasing the minimum wage. Economists in both administrations made this point *internally*, as part of their efforts to tweak the plans in ways that would minimize any job loss.

As usual, the truth was "two-handed." There were also valid arguments why Obamacare might be expected to *increase* employment. Successful medical cost containment would reduce the financial toll the health care industry was levying on the rest of the economy, thereby spurring employment growth outside the health sector. Increased health insurance coverage would create many new jobs in the health care industry itself. Furthermore, near-universal coverage would reduce "job lock," whereby fear of losing health insurance coverage keeps people in jobs they would rather leave.

What, then, were administration economists in 1993 and 2009 to do? Serenely turn the other cheek and answer the one-handed criticisms with two-handed, objective truth? That's what academics do, but it would have given aid and comfort to the opposition. Act like advocates in an adversarial proceeding? Most of the politicos and spinmeisters pushed for that. They wanted to counter spin with spin by denying that *any* jobs would be lost as a result of health care reform. Don't even think about it! But the economists argued that such a claim flunked the laugh test. After all, there were valid reasons to think health care reform might either increase or reduce employment.

After what I assume was a heated internal debate, the Obama team opted for a middle ground—if you are pretty generous in defining "middle." The executive summary—which is all anyone ever reads (if that)—of a Council of Economic Advisers report on health care reform in June 2009 included the following bullet point:

> Slowing cost growth would lower the unemployment rate consistent with steady inflation by approximately one-quarter of a percentage point for a number of years. The beneficial impact on employment in the short and medium run (relative to the no-reform baseline) is estimated to be approximately 500,000 each year that the effect is felt.

That sounded pretty good—if it didn't lull you to sleep, which may have been its prime purpose. Only if you read all the way to pages 35–36 of the report did you encounter a brief section entitled "Potential offsetting effects," which began by admitting that "not all of the effects of health care reform would necessarily work in the direction of raising labor supply," and went on from there.

Thus the CEA adroitly managed to support the administration's policy, to get very little press attention, and yet to maintain its credibility by recognizing some arguments on the other side—but only if you looked hard for them. Perhaps not intellectually pure. Certainly as much support as illumination. But a lot better than undermining the administration's policy by stepping on the message.

This little example illustrates one of the central problems of policymaking in our democracy—and the central theme of this chapter. The American system of government, which was carefully designed to make it hard to change anything, frequently becomes adversarial when anyone tries to effect change. So policy wonks pursuing reform need lots of help from politicos, especially from spinmeisters, to accomplish anything. In fact, efforts to get a policy initiative enacted look a lot like political campaigns—replete with hoopla, slogans, and gimmicks. Instead of objective analyses of pros and cons, the public is more likely to hear pros perpetrating cons. Economists are not terribly useful in such debates. Often, the best thing they can do is get out of the way.

Madison's Curse Revisited

Blame it again on James Madison and Co. As we were all taught in grade school, the Founders created a unique form of government with multiple checks and excruciating balances. They did so for a good reason: to make it difficult for government officials to exercise power over the citizenry. Tyranny might have been fine for the mother country in 1787, but not for the brand-new United States of America.

Madison and his friends succeeded, maybe beyond their wildest dreams. The Constitution they wrote has given us what may be the most hamstrung form of government on the planet. It's the little government that couldn't, because it was too tied up in knots.

To be sure, the US Constitution is a remarkable document that has served the republic well. But it has a dark side. One distinguishing characteristic of the American style of government is that it is strongly biased toward the status quo. The Constitution created—by design—a form of government that is conservative in the deepest, nonideological sense of the term: it strongly resists change. Machiavelli understood the essential idea in the sixteenth century: "For the initiator has the enmity of all who would profit by the preservation of the old institution and merely lukewarm defenders in those who gain by the new ones." But Madison did him one better.

Resistance to change has both advantages and disadvantages. On the one hand, the American system embodies extremely strong safeguards against *errors of commission*—which have served us well. Rarely does the US government embark on massive, ill-considered social crusades. (Prohibition comes to mind as an exception.) On the other hand, it has almost no safeguards against *errors of omission*. So while our national government finds it devilishly difficult to get anything done, it finds it amazingly easy to let nagging problems fester and grow.

To pick a fairly mundane example, compare the British and American ways of accomplishing something that every government must do: passing an annual budget. In Britain's highly disciplined parliamentary system, the chancellor of the Exchequer submits the budget on, say, Wednesday. The parliament then debates the budget perfunctorily for a few days (if that) and passes it, generally with minimal amendments. No fuss, no muss, no bother—and, of course, none of the checks and balances that we Americans prize. The prime minister has his or her way.

Things are quite different in the United States. A few days? Rather, it takes the better part of a year to legislate each year's budget. And sometimes we never get it done—as in 1995 and 2013, when parts of the US government shut down spectacularly, leaving passport applications unprocessed and tourists stranded at the Grand Canyon. Here briefly, and omitting many gruesome details, is how the budget process is supposed to work.

The president submits his budget proposal—everyone knows it's just a proposal—to Congress in early February. (President Trump didn't submit his first budget until May.) It is first considered, separately, by the budget committees of the House and Senate, which are supposed to report out budget resolutions outlining the main features of the budget by April or early May. This deadline is often missed.

Then it is on to the floors of each chamber, where separate budget resolutions are supposed to pass, with a conference committee ironing out any discrepancies before additional floor votes in both the House and the Senate. All this is supposed to happen by summer; in reality, it may not happen at all. Meanwhile, the White House is in constant negotiation with the leaders of both chambers over differences between the president's budget and the House and Senate resolutions—because everyone knows that the budget resolution is far from the final word.

Once the resolution is agreed to, supposing that happens, the budget moves down two separate tracks. The programs that need annual appropriations (called "discretionary spending") are divided into twelve categories, each to be acted on by its own subcommittee of the Senate or House Appropriations Committee. Yes, that's twenty-four subcommittees in all!* The rest of the budget—a vast mélange of all entitlement programs plus anything having to do with taxes—is handled by the Finance Committee in the Senate and the Ways and Means Committee in the House. The budget resolution gives these two powerful committees only vague, nonbinding guidelines. And the chairs of all the committees zealously guard their legislative fiefdoms. So, in a real sense, much of the budget work starts over from scratch.

When and if all these committees report agreements that hit the targets set forth in the budget resolution, each chamber is supposed to vote on as many as twelve separate appropriations bills plus one huge bill that bundles all changes in entitlements and taxes together. The

---

*The reality is even more labyrinthine. In many cases, there are separate authorizing committees to establish and/or change programs in addition to the appropriating committees that come up with the funds. It is not uncommon for spending to be authorized but not appropriated. Less commonly, appropriations are made without authorizing legislation.

political battle over this so-called (and badly misnamed) reconciliation bill can be the biggest and most contentious battle of them all.

Then guess what? If the House and Senate versions of several of the thirteen bills differ, as many as thirteen conference committees must go to work ironing out the differences. If and when they succeed, new floor votes are required in both chambers. That's the climax of the whole process, and it is sometimes quite dramatic. In August 1993, for example, the first Clinton budget—having already been changed in a thousand ways—passed by a single vote in each chamber of Congress, with Vice President Al Gore's vote needed to break a 50–50 tie in the Senate. Since then, the budget has rarely been passed by the October 1 start of the fiscal year—and often never passed at all. In December 2015, when Congress "made history" by passing the budget on December 18, a mere two and a half months after the fiscal year had started, there were congratulations all around. (Congress did not do so well in 2016 or 2017.)

Finished? Maybe not. While all this is going on, there are also parallel—sometimes seemingly endless—negotiations with the White House over what the president will or will not sign. In a good year, all the points of contention get settled amicably, and the president is prepared to sign what Congress sends up. That's what happened in 2015. Then it's on to the Rose Garden for proper photo-op etiquette: smiles, handshakes, and souvenir pens.

But as with wines, not every year is a good year. In bad years—which have become the norm—the president may veto several of the bills that arrive on his desk, in which case yet more negotiations ensue. In 2016, Congress never passed a budget. The House and Senate avoided a government shutdown only by agreeing, at the last minute (almost literally), to a stopgap resolution to keep the government running until April 2017—at which time, under a new president, Congress passed another "continuing resolution" that kept the government open for business through the end of the fiscal year (September 30). It looked like a shutdown was looming then, but President Trump cut a controversial deal with the Democratic leaders of Congress, "Chuck and Nancy" (Senator Charles Schumer and House Minority Leader Nancy Pelosi), to keep it open until December.

Exhausted? So are the president and Congress by the time it's all over. By then, the Office of Management and Budget (OMB) is deep into the spadework for the following year's budget.

Salesmanship Matters

Did Madison really intend to hamstring the US government this severely? Well, he's not around to tell us. But while he did know about pamphlets and debates, we can be pretty sure he didn't know about their steroidal descendants: talk radio, cable TV, the Internet, and Twitter.

One source of frustration to economic advisers is the incredible amount of time and energy devoted to message. When I joined the new Clinton administration in January 1993, I started out with the typical academic's prejudice against this vaguely disreputable activity. But I soon learned there is a good reason for the preoccupation with message. Let's start there.

When economists discuss policy issues in the classroom, they are usually careful to outline the pros and cons of various approaches. After all, there is rarely one clean, right answer. That's fine when you are addressing students who are compelled to sit there for an hour listening, taking notes, and knowing they may be examined on the material later. But in the real world of markets and politics, people with short attention spans and much else on their minds are half-listening, at best. If you transmit a complex message, your audience may not receive it.

That is one reason why messaging is such a vital and delicate art form in a vibrant democracy. People in public life must care as much about what is *heard* as about what is *said*. They must craft their words so that listeners receive the right message. Among other things, they must keep their messages short, clear, and punchy because political discourse has limited room for complexity.

It's a fine line to walk, to be sure—and a perilous one. If you are concerned with intellectual honesty, the absolutist dictum "the truth, the whole truth, and nothing but the truth" is the only safe haven. Once you depart from it, you are on the proverbial slippery slope. Even with the best of intentions, a slip in the direction of spin is all too likely—especially when your opponents are spinning furiously in the opposite direction.

Academics and other technocrats are predisposed by both inclination and training to look askance at messaging. It's an unsavory activity suitable only for the vaguely disreputable. (Would you like your son or daughter to grow up to be a spinmeister?) And, believe me, a close-up view of a message mill in full throttle is not a pretty sight.

The Council of Economic Advisers, where I once worked, is located within the White House complex. Though it's a distance from the vortex of the message tornado, both literally and figuratively, it is close enough to feel the swirling winds every day. Inside the administration—any administration—the council is normally viewed as a sanctuary for academic economists whose political ears, if not made of tin, certainly have less than perfect pitch. Since the CEA cannot be trusted to stay "on message," it is kept under constant surveillance by the message police. Donald Trump went even further early in his term: he went many months without even appointing a CEA!

One of my regular tasks at the CEA in 1993 and 1994 was to participate in early morning conference calls as each new piece of economic data was released—an almost daily occurrence. The ostensible purpose of these calls was to discuss the content of the statistical release and decide on the administration's message for the day. That way, we could all "stay on the same page." But I always suspected that these calls had a hidden agenda: to ensure that we economists did not stray off message—a place you were never supposed to be.

The academic's snooty attitude toward message is a purist's point of view, however. It leaves out something vitally important: that message is an indispensable part of government in our great democracy.

You want to be truthful, sure. But a poorly chosen message can be distorted and spun against you.

The American system of checks and balances provides maddening roadblocks at every turn. Designing a good policy is just the first step, and rarely the most difficult one, along the tortuous road toward turning a policy idea into reality. You must then build a political coalition to get the necessary legislation enacted—and that means *selling* your policy to audiences both inside and outside the Beltway. Like it or not, message is the way official Washington communicates with the outside world and, in particular, how it enlists the support of the electorate.

That candidates are sold like hamburgers has long been a commonplace of American politics. Congressional, gubernatorial, and presidential campaigns are orgies of advertising. But in recent decades this practice—with all its virtues and vices—has spread to the selling of policies as well. Any realistic effort to approve a treaty, to reform health care, to overhaul the tax code, or to restructure entitlements is likely to resemble a full-scale political campaign—complete with message meisters, staged media events, war rooms, rapid-response teams, field organizers, and political consultants.

Such campaigns to win over public opinion may seem peculiar, since no vote of the electorate is ever required to move a bill through Congress. The right place to "campaign," it would appear, is on Capitol Hill, not on the Internet and TV. Nonetheless each side in a major policy debate expends enormous amounts of time and energy building grassroots support—or tearing down the other's. The reason is painfully obvious: many members of the House and Senate determine their positions on issues by watching the prevailing political winds.

Should we deplore that practice? A purist might say yes. Members of Congress should use their knowledge and best judgment and, when necessary, behave like a bunch of "profiles in courage." That's a nice image, but the reality is rather more complex. Paradoxically, there is truth in each of two diametrically opposed views of the role of message in our form of government.

One is associated with P. T. Barnum: there's a sucker born every minute. This view casts a jaundiced eye on all the hucksterism, which it sees as deceiving the public more than enlightening it. It's been said that you can fool most of the people most of the time, and that's good enough for politics. Political spinmeisters, it appears, live by this dictum.

But there is another view of the matter, one that can rightfully trace its roots to Thomas Jefferson. (Rather better lineage than Barnum, I'd say.) Among those self-evident truths of which Jefferson wrote so eloquently was that "governments are instituted among men, deriving their just powers from the consent of the governed." Catch that last phrase: *the consent of the governed*. Isn't that what grassroots campaigns are pursuing, albeit in a less than high-minded fashion? America may have the most democratic form of government of any major country on earth—complete with all the joys and frustrations that brings.

So which view of message is more descriptive, Jefferson's or Barnum's?

Spin Wars

The preoccupation with message certainly has its downside. One reason was mentioned earlier: slogans and shibboleths often sell better than messy, complex realities. Ideas that *sound good*—especially in eight-second sound bites—may not actually *be good*. This unfortunate fact opens the door to the P. T. Barnums of the world, who seek not to inform but to deceive—and to manipulate public opinion. Much political spin is so misleading that it resides just inches away from outright lying; some of it crosses that line.

Spin is nothing new, but modern media-centered politics has raised it to an art form—and to a profession. Spin doctors swarm around major speeches and other political events like bees around honey. They ply their wares on news broadcasts, on the apparently endless parade of political talk shows, via Twitter and targeted email, and in the blogosphere. The doctors of spin exemplify the idea of politics as sport so well that they are veritable human metaphors.

But no social phenomenon, not even political spin, should be judged solely by its worst manifestations. Some massaging of the message is inevitable in any society that is not populated by angels and saints. After all, it is only human nature to promote the virtues of your plan and downplay its vices, especially when the other guy is spinning madly against you, perhaps none too scrupulously. The trick is to avoid a race to the bottom in which truth is left at the starting gate.

After serving at the CEA for a while, I developed what seemed to me a workable—albeit less than lofty—principle for defining the limits of spin. I used to tell the staff that we should always tell the truth and nothing but the truth, but not necessarily the *whole* truth. Exposing the weak points in our arguments should be our opponents' job, not ours—especially when dwelling on such details might step on the administration's message.

One example of this principle, if you are generous enough to call it a principle, was illustrated at the start of this chapter in discussing possible job loss and the marketing of Obamacare. But there was more to the story.

In February 2014, enemies of the plan received an apparent gift from a Congressional Budget Office report that was portrayed as estimating that health care reform would cost more than two million jobs. Republicans had a field day trumpeting this conclusion. But it wasn't what the CBO actually said. Almost immediately after the partisan attacks began, CBO director Douglas Elmendorf refuted the claim that the ACA was a job killer. He explained that a number of American workers might *voluntarily* reduce their hours of work, perhaps by retiring, because they no longer feared loss of health insurance. That's something positive, he insisted, and very different from being fired.

It sure is. But was it different enough in the world of political messaging? As two *Politico* reporters noted at the time, "The Republicans just got a big gift from the Congressional Budget Office: It's going to be a lot easier for them to call Obamacare a 'job killer.'" The reporters noted correctly that "CBO said it's in large part about the number of hours people choose to work, not actual job losses." But then they went on to add, poignantly and correctly, that "what matters politically is how the numbers look in attack ads. And in this election year, '2 million lost jobs' is a Republican ad-maker's dream." Indeed it was.

I have emphasized that there is often a huge chasm between policies that sound good and policies that actually are good. But political discourse thrives on—indeed requires—simple slogans. Hence politics often leads to what I call the T-shirt mentality: to be marketable in the political arena, an idea must be short and snappy enough to be emblazoned on a T-shirt—or on a baseball cap. (Example: "Balance the budget!"). But any economic idea expressed that tersely is almost certainly wrong; there are always qualifications. (Example: You don't want to force budget balance during a recession.)

Sometimes the political slogan is an artificially selected number that somehow takes on a mystical aura. One clear example is the number zero, as in balancing the budget. A federal budget deficit of exactly zero is not a sensible goal in an economy that grows from year to year. Corporate debt grows larger every year. So does household debt, partly because there are more and more people. Why shouldn't government debt also grow? The correct analogy to a balanced budget in a *growing* economy is a deficit just large enough (and just small enough) to keep GDP and the public debt growing at the same rate. By no coincidence whatsoever, stabilizing the debt-to-GDP ratio is the budgetary goal most commonly advocated by economists.

But what a horrible slogan! Imagine a political message contest between "Balance the budget!" and "Run a deficit just large enough to keep the debt-to-GDP ratio constant!" The latter might just as well save its exclamation point. It loses.

One of the more curious aspects of spin wars is what I call "dueling experts"—the use of recognized outside authorities to render allegedly disinterested judgments on competing policies. The practice is curious because knowledgeable Washington veterans all realize that mass media, grassroots organizing, and raw interest-group politics will determine the end result—regardless of expert opinion. They also know that the chosen experts are rarely, if ever, truly neutral third parties.

Nevertheless, each side in an issue campaign normally seeks outside experts to verify that its positions are kosher—or to attack its opponents' positions. Competing validators, you might call it. Or using lampposts for support. Examples are legion. Just watch the op-ed pages of the *New York Times*, the *Washington Post*, or the *Wall Street Journal*. Or read influential magazines like the *New Yorker*, the *National Review*, or the *Atlantic*.

Ironically, open letters from dueling experts were de rigueur during the 2016 presidential campaign, even though expert opinion was being trashed by then-candidate Donald Trump. In late September, his campaign released a letter slamming Clinton's economic proposals signed by 305 "of the country's most prominent economic theorists and practitioners." (Actually, I never heard of most of them.) A little over a month later, the Clinton campaign responded with *two* letters—one signed by 370 prominent economists (I was one of them) and the other, more exclusive letter signed by twenty past winners of the Nobel Prize. By any reasonable standard, Clinton had the higher-quality lists. But did any voters care?

A second huge problem created by the spin wars is the fixation with polling. Public opinion polling may be a good way to test-drive your message, though even here push-polling is designed to produce misleading results. But polling is an atrocious way to formulate public policy. If you pay attention to actual polling data, rather than to spinmeisters' creative interpretations thereof, what you often find are utter confusion and lack of knowledge. Let me illustrate with a few examples.

As late as October 2015, only 21 percent of Americans thought the US economy had "completely" or "mostly" recovered from the Great Recession. But the objective truth was that it had. Some 44 percent told pollsters that we had "only somewhat recovered," while an amazing 34 percent said we had "not really recovered at all." Not recovered at all? Yes, some people were still doing badly, but that's always the case. The nation as a whole had recovered so much that the Federal Reserve was thinking about raising interest rates to slow the forward momentum a bit—which it started to do that December. Should the government have bent to public misperceptions and promulgated aggressive antirecession policies, such as easy money and tax cuts in October 2015? Certainly not. But poll respondents would have applauded such actions.

Or take another example: polling results consistently show that Americans have a totally distorted view of how much the federal government spends each year on foreign aid—which just happens to be their least favorite expenditure item. Should the budget-cutting ax therefore be wielded ruthlessly against foreign aid, thereby pandering to mass public opinion but saving a comparative pittance? Of course not. And presidents didn't—until Donald Trump.

Or consider one of the most contentious design elements of health care reform, mentioned earlier: whether the government should achieve universal coverage by requiring either *employers* (Bill Clinton) or *individuals* (Barack Obama) to purchase health insurance.* In the Clinton case, our side opted for an employer mandate despite urgings from me and others that the individual mandate (later chosen by Obama) would work better. Why? Largely because it sounded like our plan "made businesses pay," whereas an individual mandate "made people pay." It also did not help that the ultra-conservative Heritage Foundation was pushing an individual mandate at the time. It was guilt by association.

But the Clinton administration's choice led the health care plan straight into huge, and ultimately fatal, problems. For one thing, it set the small business lobby 100 percent against us, and the National Federation of Independent Businesses and related organizations proved to be a formidable lobbying force. For another, it forced the health

---

*The third way to ensure universal coverage, a Canadian-style national health plan financed by taxes, was ruled out early by both administrations.

care task force to invent one Rube Goldberg contraption after another to provide subsidies to small businesses, which allegedly could not afford health insurance, when our real goal was to reduce the cost of policies bought for low-wage workers. If those sound similar to you, stop and think about "struggling" small businesses like hedge funds or boutique law firms.

The Clinton effort to design subsidies for small businesses was wasteful, expensive, a public relations disaster, and ultimately impossible. But we sure tried! Sixteen years later, the Obama administration made the opposite choice—subsidies would go to low-income *people*, not to small *firms*—and won despite bitter political opposition.

So polls are the bane, make that *a* bane, of the policy wonk's existence. But polling is not the only way message tramples substance—or tries to. Here's an old and slightly absurd example where spin failed.

Just before President Clinton's first big economic address in February 1993, the White House held what amounted to a pep rally in the auditorium of the Old Executive Office Building. The putative purpose was to launch the Clinton budget and explain it to the many high-ranking officials who knew little or nothing about the young administration's first big policy rollout. Up to that point, the planning had been pretty much limited to the economic team.

The star of the show that day was neither the secretary of the Treasury nor the head of the National Economic Council, but rather a delightful and quick-witted young Texan named Paul Begala. Yes, the same guy you now see regularly as a TV commentator. Along with his partner James Carville, Begala had been instrumental in the 1992 campaign but held no official position in the administration. Nonetheless, he was the designated message man that afternoon.

In tones a Texas preacher might recognize, Paul explained that this was not a *deficit reduction* package. ("That's news to me," I murmured to a colleague seated next to me. The economic team had been working nonstop on deficit reduction for six exhausting weeks.) It was, he insisted, an *economic growth* package, and we were *never* to call it a *deficit reduction* package. Never! At this point, I thought about my mother slapping her ten-year-old son and warning him, "If you say that filthy word again, I'll wash your mouth out with soap!"

To help us along, Paul gave us a slogan to use in selling our deficit reduction—er, economic growth—package to the public: "This is change. This is good." Catchy, huh? Elegant in its simplicity. Two masterfully composed sentences, each of only three syllables, and yet pregnant with nonmeaning. I felt uplifted. Were we all now supposed to chant "Hallelujah!" and dance toward the exits? Wearing a pin-striped suit, rep tie, and wingtips, somehow that didn't feel right. So I walked out shaking my head instead of shaking my arms.

Postscript: About thirty seconds after the president finished delivering his masterful speech on the economic program, media commentators everywhere were talking about his "deficit reduction package." Well, even the best spinners can't win 'em all.

Two Different Worlds

Barnum had a point, but there is also a nobler and more benevolent role for message in our democracy, one more consistent with Jeffersonian principles. To put it plainly, the governed cannot give their consent if they haven't a clue about what is going on. Someone must explain the issues to ordinary citizens. Who will that be?

Here technicians and experts labor under a severe disadvantage, for the public neither draws inferences nor makes policy judgments the way we do. Economists, at least those with no ax to grind, take positions on policy issues after weighing economic analysis and statistical evidence—and then consulting their value judgments. As an illustration, consider a basic question that has been debated in Washington for decades (and still is today), one that frequently divides Republicans from Democrats: Should the federal budget deficit be reduced?

The first step toward answering such a question is analytical; call it "theoretical" if you like. Deductive reasoning is used to think through the likely implications of any proposed decrease in the deficit, including the important question of whether we cut the deficit by spending less (and if so, on what?) or by taxing more (and if so, which taxes do we raise?). To most economists, the strength of the economy will be among the leading considerations. If the economy is booming, then raising taxes or cutting expenditures may make sense. If a recession looms, the same policies may court disaster.

Next, economists bring empirical evidence to bear on the issue: What can historical and other data tell us about the likely magnitudes of the effects of lower spending or higher taxes on, say, GDP, employment, interest rates, and inflation? Here, statistical inference and modeling are likely to play crucial, if not dispositive, roles in molding expert opinion.

Finally, we trot out our value judgments. Some economists will be more favorably disposed toward deficit reduction if the higher taxes are on the rich and the spending cuts are on unjustified subsidies. Others think upper-bracket tax rates should not be raised because of daunting incentive effects, and favor less spending on entitlements. When it comes to value judgments, economists and other citizens stand on equal footing, for training in economics does not sharpen your moral sensibilities. Unsurprisingly, liberal economists tend to worry more about distributive consequences than do conservative economists.

This approach sounds incredibly neat and tidy. It is not always practiced as preached, of course. Nor does it lead all economists to the same conclusion, because we have different value judgments and because the theoretical and empirical evidence is often equivocal. Nevertheless, the common approach that economists share does narrow the range of disagreement. And we all speak a common language. Unfortunately for us, however, the body politic neither speaks this language, nor understands it, nor shares our way of thinking about social policy. What economists find natural, ordinary citizens often find strange. Our advice frequently elicits dissent—or even bewilderment.

Perhaps most fundamentally, the concept of economic efficiency is foreign to most voters. What's more, I suspect that few people would place it high on their list of priorities, even if they understood it. Instead, the average voter is viscerally concerned with *fairness*—which is a terrible blind spot for some economists.

Furthermore, economists and other analysts tend to think *abstractly* and *generally* about social policies, whereas ordinary citizens think *concretely* and *specifically*. To an analyst, the right sorts of questions are: "What will deficit reduction do to capital formation and GDP?" or "How would this change in Social Security influence national saving?" But these are cold, bloodless questions that carry little meaning for the average voter. He or she is more likely to wonder: "How would this affect me—or Aunt Nellie?"

An even more dramatic difference in perceptions arises when it comes to weighing statistical evidence. Economists, like other scientifically minded people, not only believe in but *rely on* statistical inference. Maybe too much. We are trained to ignore "anecdotes," sneer at "stories," and dote on means and standard deviations instead. But John and Jane Doe are rarely persuaded by statistics, which they neither understand nor trust. Personal experience counts for much more, as does whether a particular argument "sounds right."

Uh oh. There we go again. As I have emphasized several times, what *sounds right* can be quite different from what *is right*. That's a big problem. Personal experiences and those of friends and relatives are poor substitutes for statistical evidence. Unfortunately, most of the citizenry knows nothing of statistics, believing instead in what I call "proof by example." A particular type of operation is deemed to work because it cured Uncle Max. Never mind that a study in the latest *New England Journal of Medicine* says it's an expensive placebo. A Ford is considered "a good car" because your brother-in-law's lasted fifteen years. Who needs *Consumer Reports*? The stock market is seen as a "good (or bad) investment" because your neighbor made (or lost) money in it. You don't have to study articles in the *Journal of Finance* to decide.

On all these counts and more, the typical citizen sees the world quite differently than economists do. If we economists stubbornly stick to our own language and frame of reference, we can talk ourselves blue in the face without persuading anyone. (In fact, we do that.)

But politicians are not handicapped by training as technicians or analysts. For better or for worse, they generally share the people's attitudes, not the economists', on all these matters. They don't understand either economic theory or statistics. They naturally think about fairness before efficiency. Their world is full of anecdotes and stories, and they are convinced by examples. They may actually know Aunt Nellie or Uncle Max! And they have a strong sense of what sounds right to the voters.

So who do you think is better suited to carrying the message to the public?

Using the Bully Pulpit

If you live in the country, the incessant din of chirping crickets is omnipresent, except in winter. You get so accustomed to it that you barely hear it. If you live in a busy city, the clatter of traffic never stops. You get used to that, too. The corresponding background noise in Washington is the endless cacophony of political messaging, which wafts all over town. It emanates from the White House, the Capitol, all sorts of government agencies, and countless lobbying and interest groups—a thousand points of noise, you might say. Save for the message meisters, who listen with professional interest, the cognoscenti tune most of this out. The person on the street barely hears it, having developed a natural immunity—just like to cricket chirps or traffic.

But one particular type of political message is special. It rings far louder than all the others, commands a vastly greater audience, occasionally rivets the nation, and sometimes even alters the course of policymaking—not to mention the course of history. I refer to the heavy artillery of political message: the major presidential address.

These are staged events, to be sure, explicitly designed to produce sound bites and photo ops. They share much of the hoopla and manipulative trappings of a Hollywood extravaganza. They have more than their share of spin. But do not dismiss them as mere pep rallies staged by immature adults. In fact, major presidential speeches and similar media events are big deals that influence the political game on many levels.

Most obviously, they help set the national agenda. Significant policy initiatives are rarely launched or even gain important political impetus without a strong push from a presidential address—or, of course, a presidential campaign.* Especially when an administration is young and its agenda not yet firmly established, different constituencies within the administration will lobby hard to get the president to make a major address on their issues. If he does, they are cheered and energized. If he does not, they fear, their issues may drop off the agenda.

On September 9, 2009, less than eight months into his first term, President Obama delivered a nationally televised speech to Congress on the need for health care reform—not on, say, climate change or immigration policy or income inequality. His speech received huge attention and kicked off a heated debate on health reform—both inside the Congress and outside it. About six months later, after much political sound and fury, the president signed the Patient Protection and Affordable Care Act of 2010 into law.

I don't mean to imply that the path from the president's speech to enactment of the ACA was easy, straightforward, or in any way inevitable. It was none of those. (Remember the nonpendulum theory.) But it was no coincidence that health care passed while, say, climate change went nowhere in Congress.** Agenda setting matters, and no one can set the national agenda quite like the president of the United States.

---

*I speak here and throughout of *presidential* speeches. Very rarely, a speech by another political figure—such as a congressional leader—can have such an effect. *Very* rarely.

** The president later took a number of major steps through executive action. But when Donald Trump succeeded him, most of these executive orders were overturned.

Inside the administration, the approach of a major presidential address has a way of concentrating minds and serving as a focal point for staff efforts. (*This has to be ready before the president's speech.*) On the Hill, a big speech may be viewed with anticipation (*Once the president has spoken, we can really get the ball rolling*) or foreboding (*The president is going to beat us over the head tonight*)— depending on party affiliation. Presidents often use such occasions to prod Congress to act. In the hinterlands, landmark events like the State of the Union address are among the rare instances in which a significant share of the television audience turns away from sporting events and sitcoms and actually pays attention to political discourse. A few even stop texting.

Enormous amounts of time and energy are appropriately lavished on the preparations for such rare addresses. Speechwriters and spin-meisters hone the message. Policy people submit ideas and check the many drafts for accuracy. Politicos fret over the timing, the setting, and the audience. (Don't compete with Monday Night Football!) Media specialists dote on the lighting, the sound, and the colors of the president's shirt and tie. Cabinet officials and other designated spinners are armed to the teeth with bulleted talking points and prepped for the pre- and post-speech spin shows. And much, much more.

It's easy to poke fun at these spectacles, for, at some level, they surely constitute political theater of the absurd. But there is a serious side as well. Americans are not a very political people, and our citizens are almost innately cynical about all things political. They are also preoccupied by a thousand other pressing matters, like earning a living, finding a babysitter, or taking the kids to soccer. So the body politic rarely finds either the time or the inclination to tune in to the political debate. The rare moments when it does are therefore precious opportunities for small-*d* democrats to communicate with the electorate.

Such moments are not to be squandered, and politicians understand that. A well-timed, well-crafted, and forcefully delivered speech by the president of the United States, beamed into tens of millions of living rooms from the Oval Office or from the well of the House of Representatives, can invigorate the president's team, sway public opinion, and create a political force that puts pressure on Congress—all at the same time. A dud or a missed opportunity can let the air out of the incipient balloon.

Presidents therefore have a unique ability to educate the public or to mislead it, to galvanize the electorate or to lull everyone to sleep, to break through the inertia that is the essence of American government or to be entrapped by it. Theodore Roosevelt famously said that the president speaks from a "bully pulpit," a phrase with pretty clear religious overtones. If that was true then, in the days before radio and television, think how true it must be now, in the age of instant mass communications and social media. Amid the seemingly unending din of tweets and posts, the presidential bully pulpit stands out.

So those who ascend the national bully pulpit, and lesser political pulpits all over America, bear a special responsibility. As the principal points of contact between the government and the governed, they shape retail politics. Will they sell substance or sizzle? Will they keep message in its place, or let it run roughshod over substance? Can they stay on the high road if their opponents insist on traveling the low road?

The low road, the one with an excess of sizzle and spin, is by far the easier route. Unsurprisingly, it is also the road most commonly traveled. The central reason, it seems to me, was mentioned earlier: complexity is a hard sell, especially when attention spans are short and trust in government is lacking. Simplistic remedies and snappy slogans that sound right, being easier, enjoy a huge strategic advantage. In fact, it's a lopsided battle. When sensible but complicated solutions to social problems get into the political ring with sound bites, the referee is likely to stop the fight in the early rounds with the policy wonks bleeding profusely.

Examples abound. Consider a policy that virtually all Americans favor, at least since the financial crisis and probably even before: ending the "too big to fail" doctrine, the notion that the government will bail out any financial giant that threatens to go under. With the possible exception of some big bankers, nobody likes bank bailouts. Yet variants on too-big-to-fail were used to justify government rescues of Bear Stearns, Fannie Mae, Freddie Mac, AIG, and others (but not Lehman Brothers) during the crisis. Those bailouts may have been necessary to limit the collateral damage—look what happened when Lehman failed. But most Americans hated them, still view them as policy disasters, and don't want to see such bailouts ever again. The Obama administration and members of Congress knew all this when they sat down to write what became the Dodd-Frank Wall Street Reform and Consumer Protection Act of 2010.

And in fact, Dodd-Frank *did* abolish "too big to fail." The problem is that most people don't know that because the law did so in a complicated way that is difficult to understand—especially for a public that was (and still is) bombarded by claims that "too big to fail" lives on, while the Obama Treasury barely tried to explain why that claim was wrong. Specifically, Title II of Dodd-Frank created something called Orderly Liquidation Authority (Are you nodding off yet?), which gives regulators, led by the FDIC, the ability to lay sick financial giants to rest gradually and gently—rather than let them die in violent spasms, the way Lehman did.

The key word here is *liquidation*, a polite term for financial death. Interestingly, the Obama Treasury in 2009 had recommended giving regulators a choice between *liquidating* an ailing bank and *resolving* it, which means keeping it alive, though in modified form. Congress, however, firmly rejected the resolution option. Sick financial giants would not be rehabilitated; they would die. That's the law.

Unfortunately, it took the FDIC and other agencies about three and a half years to translate Dodd-Frank's grant of Orderly Liquidation Authority into specific rules and procedures, which it named the Single Point of Entry approach (don't ask) and published for comment only at the end of 2013. Trust me (I won't bore you with the details), it's a pretty good plan, though no one really knows how it will work in practice until it gets put to the test.

Finally, just in case something goes wrong, Section 214 of Dodd-Frank (Caught you napping again!) states clearly that "taxpayers shall bear no losses from the exercise of any authority under" Title II. Let me repeat that: *no* losses, as in *zero*. How can that be enforced? Should the orderly liquidation of a firm's assets leave a hole that the Treasury must fill temporarily, the law provides that paying the Treasury back "shall be the responsibility of the financial sector, through assessments."

Got all that? I didn't think so, and that's the problem. It's a pretty complicated message. Compare the preceding paragraphs to misleading rants that the too-big-to-fail doctrine lives on, or that going back to the 1930s separation of commercial and investment banking under the Glass-Steagall Act will somehow set things right. (Will someone please explain how?) Now you see how accurate-but-complicated messages are at a severe disadvantage when competing with inaccurate-but-simple messages.

A second example, which comes up again and again, is the rationale for reducing the federal budget deficit. Over the years, both Democratic and Republican politicians have been guilty of selling deficit reduction as a *job creator*—or, what amounts to the same thing, attacking deficit-increasing fiscal policies as job destroyers. The truth is closer to "it all depends"—which ranks pretty low in the pantheon of sound bites.

Whether smaller or larger budgets deficits are better public policy at any point in time depends on a myriad of factors, including whether the economy is booming or stagnating and the size of the preexisting public debt, relative to GDP, at the time. (Now, there's a snoozer.) But the fundamental reason to favor lower deficits in the long run is neither to create jobs nor to destroy them. It's to boost real wages.

Come again? The reasoning is somewhat involved, so please bear with me. (Political debate, of course, won't—which is my point.) Smaller deficits mean that the federal government borrows less. Reduced federal borrowing should lead to lower real interest rates, which should, in turn, promote higher levels of business investment.

As businesses invest more, workers get more, and newer, and better capital to work with. So their productivity on the job should rise and, with it, real wages. End of (long) story.

But what about jobs? Should deficit reduction be expected to have much of an impact on total employment? The answer is no, provided the Federal Reserve does its job, for in normal times the Fed has primary responsibility for managing short-run variations in the size of the GDP and therefore of total employment.

When I was in the Clinton administration in 1993, our carefully honed deficit-reduction message, the product of a tug-of-war between the economic truth squad and the political message police, respected this underlying reality—if you listened carefully. (Thank heaven, most people didn't.) Our claim—now pay attention, please—was that the US economy would create eight million new jobs in four years *with our program*. We were careful not to claim that the economy would create eight million *additional* jobs *because of our program*, which would have been a terrible exaggeration. But neither did we bother to mention that the economy was also likely to create close to eight million jobs *without* our deficit-reduction program! Well, that seemed like an unimportant detail. In any case, our message was certainly less misleading than the Republicans' nearly hysterical claims that higher taxes would throw the US economy into a tailspin.

A similar dialogue arose in 2009, when the Obama administration recommended a large fiscal stimulus package consisting of higher federal spending and tax cuts—as a way to "save or create" millions of jobs. Because the economy had so much spare capacity at the time, their claim of job creation was eminently reasonable. Nonetheless, the Republicans, led by then Speaker of the House John Boehner (R-OH), branded the increases in federal spending as "job killers," even though it was not clear how that could happen. When the government spends more, it does one of three things: It puts people on the government payroll. Or it buys products from private businesses (computers, aircraft, and so forth), which in turn hire more workers. Or it makes transfer payments to people (Social Security, unemployment benefits, and so on), which enable them to spend more money on private products, thereby creating more jobs. How can any of this *kill* jobs?

To be sure, more federal spending is not always the right answer. There are legitimate reasons to oppose particular spending programs. They may be wasteful (too many highways in West Virginia), useless (bridges to nowhere), foolish (President Trump's voter fraud commission), or simply too expensive. They may get the federal government involved in activities that are better left to state and local governments or to the private sector. They may balloon the budget deficit when it should be shrinking. And so on. There are many potentially valid arguments against any particular sort of government spending. But the claim that it "kills jobs" is not one of them.

A Hopeful Hypothesis

Is all lost? Must the spin wars continue the race to the intellectual bottom, leaving the truth behind like roadkill? Must Barnum's suckers outnumber Jefferson's consenting governed? Must politicians worry more about being "on message" than about being truthful? Modern American history suggested affirmative answers to all of these questions even before the 2016 election. Now such answers may seem axiomatic. They are certainly what most politicians appear to believe.

But I have an iconoclastic theory of the future of political message, one that points precisely in the opposite direction. It is based on the time-tested economic principle that scarcity creates value, which fades away as a commodity becomes too abundant. The surplus commodity I have in mind is political spin, which has proliferated at an alarming rate since about 1980. At first, it worked splendidly. President Reagan's handlers were justly celebrated as masters of the art. (Reagan's television skills didn't hurt, either.) But that was then, and this is now. After more than three decades on a diet of heavy political spin, the American people, I believe, have had their fill. They hunger for the commodity that is currently so scarce: straight talk.

According to this admittedly speculative hypothesis, politicos have carried the fine art of spin well past the point of diminishing returns. Voters have grown to be weary of, jaded with, and distrustful of the whole business, which they increasingly view as a con game. They eagerly await unconventional politicians who will speak to them plainly, like the folks they deal with every day, not like spinmeisters reading talking points from teleprompters. Such unconventional politicians would, of course, need to hone their messages carefully, for all the legitimate reasons discussed in this chapter. But they would sharply delimit the realm of spin and would talk to the public the way ordinary people converse across a kitchen table, not the way most politicians talk when the klieg lights go on.

Can I prove that this hypothesis is right? Certainly not. The vast majority of political experts—there's that oxymoron again—will assure you that I am dead wrong. That alone makes straight talk a risky strategy. But think back to the 2016 presidential primaries, when Senator Bernie Sanders (I-VT) showed astonishing political appeal and property magnate (and TV celebrity) Donald Trump triumphed over sixteen competitors. Sanders, who hailed from a state with three electoral votes, was seventy-four years old, a self-proclaimed socialist, and not even a Democrat. Trump, who was not obviously a Republican either, gained fame as a foul-mouthed billionaire who fired people on TV. Those were winning formulas?

But Sanders and Trump had one thing in common: when they spoke, their words sounded like what ordinary people (albeit people with chips on their shoulders) might say, not like poll-tested prose that emerged from spin machines and was transcribed onto teleprompters. Could that have been why so many voters were seduced by Sanders and taken in by Trump?

Of course, the plain-speaking President Trump has gone way beyond political spin to "alternative facts," aka lies. But, gradually, the American public seems to be seeing through that fog—and not liking what they see. In the next stage of political talk, might we be blessed with plainspokenness that is actually truthful? At least we can hope.

The Media as Intermediaries

My hopeful—and hopefully not fanciful—hypothesis that there is a strong latent demand for straight talk from politicians faces several daunting challenges. One is that every communication requires both a sender and a receiver. Only a few politicians, and essentially no economists, have the privilege of communicating directly with a broad swath of the American public. All others must go through the media. So to this crucial intermediary I now turn.

Chapter 5

The Media Are the Messengers

The poet was right: can't live with them,
or without them.

—Aristophanes

The first presidential debate between candidates Hillary Clinton and Donald Trump in late September 2016 was a mega-media event, with a TV audience rivaling—well, *almost* rivaling—the Super Bowl. Yet virtually all political experts agreed that what would matter most for the election was not the substance of the debate itself, which polling showed that Clinton won handily, but rather the snippets that the media would repeat over and over again in the days following the debate—in TV clips, news stories, tweets, blog posts, and the like.

As it turned out, the week following the debate was packed with potential blockbuster stories about Trump, including a report that his business had violated the US trade embargo of Cuba in 1998 by exploring a possible business deal there (a violation of federal law), news that his foundation failed to meet the requirements for soliciting donations from the public (a violation of New York State law), and a revealing peek at his 1995 tax returns. But the story that hogged that week's media attention was none of these. It was his derogatory statements about Alicia Machado, who had been Miss Universe 1997— whom he had called, among other things, "Miss Piggy" (thereby insulting all overweight people) and "Miss Housekeeping" (thereby insulting all Latinas).

It wasn't exactly edifying. Nor did it convey much information about the issues of the day. But it was an apt metaphor for press coverage of the whole campaign: it sold newspapers, attracted TV audiences, and sparked numerous "discussions" (to use an overly polite word) on Twitter, on Facebook, and in the blogosphere. Who really cared about the tax treatment of "like-kind" real estate sales anyway?

Media in the Middle

Aristophanes wrote the words of this chapter's epigram in the year 411 BCE—way before the existence of mass media. He was referring to the complex and sometimes tempestuous relationships between men and women—as seen through the eyes of men, of course. But the thought applies equally well to the complex and sometimes tempestuous relationships between government officials and the press—which we must now define broadly to include websites, blogs, and even Facebook posts and Twitter feeds.

The press can make life miserable for people in high places, and it sometimes interferes grotesquely with governmental processes. The prolific leaks from the early Trump administration were just an extreme example of something that happens constantly. So it is plain that public officials cannot live very well *with* the media. But, at its best, the press holds government actors accountable and is the essential conduit of information to millions of citizens who otherwise would have no idea what their government is up to. (Both of these apply in the Trump case, too.) So officeholders obviously cannot—or rather should not—live *without* the media, either.

True, prominent politicians do get opportunities to speak directly to the people on occasion. "Going around the media" it is called. The president of the United States can perform this maneuver almost any time he pleases, and President Trump makes extraordinary use of this privilege—especially on Twitter, where, conveniently, you don't have to answer any questions. Other leading elected officials get similar, if lesser, opportunities now and then.

But direct communication from most politicians to citizens is sporadic and intermittent at best. And even when they speak "directly" to the people, their words are at best heavily edited and at worst turned into sound bites by reporters and editors. It is a rare occasion indeed when a political speech is broadcast in its entirety to a wide audience. Think of the president's annual State of the Union address. Now try to think of another example. Twitter and streaming videos, trendy as they are, remain pretty imperfect substitutes for network TV coverage—except perhaps for President Trump, whose every tweet, it seems, gets displayed prominently on national TV news.

So politicians and top government officials have no choice. If they want to be heard, they must deliver their message through the media. The rules of the game are simple: the officeholder speaks to reporters, who raise questions but then communicate at least parts of the message—faithfully, we hope—to millions of viewers, listeners, or readers.

Economists and other unelected experts who serve in government—even in high places—virtually never speak directly to the general public. Who would listen, anyway? I was vice chairman of the Federal Reserve Board in 1994–1996, and in that capacity delivered numerous speeches. But all of them were to relatively small audiences (never more than a thousand people), and those that were on camera were headed for the likes of Reuters TV or C-SPAN, maybe to CNBC, but certainly not to NBC or Fox News. (The networks exercised good judgment there. Most of my speeches were deadly dull.) So the main way for a nonpolitical officeholder to get his or her message across is to present it first to the media for digestion and filtering—and then hope for the best. As one media scholar poignantly observed years ago, "If a tree falls in the forest, no one knows about it unless a journalist hears it."

He might have added: "and chooses to report it." For the press is much more than a passive conduit. Most obviously, reporters, editors, and producers are obliged to *select* what to report, what to ignore, and how much attention to lavish on each story. A fallen tree is news only if the press decides it is, and it's the same with economic policy. That aspect of editing is, of course, a necessary and proper part of journalism. Without some prior selection and filtering, our newspapers and TV news broadcasts would just bombard us with a cacophony of information and disinformation—sort of like the blogosphere, or the social media barrage.

But the role of journalists goes further. Reporters do not just transmit information; inevitably, they also *interpret* it. Once again, this interpretive role of the press is neither nefarious nor inappropriate. After all, most readers and viewers are not specialists; they need someone to put the news, including the economic news, into context for them—to *explain* it. Furthermore, citizens of a vibrant democracy should not accept the statements of public officials at face value. The interpretive role of the press is not only inevitable but entirely legitimate, probably even essential, and—when done competently and honestly—almost certainly in the public interest.

But it can be abused. We have all read newspaper stories and seen television reports in which the line between fact and opinion—the *reporter's* opinion—is all but invisible. Much of cable "news" is like that: it's all opinion, all the time. Many critics have suggested that Fox News is neither fair nor balanced. And then there are websites like Breitbart, where "fake news" was apparently invented.

But even balanced news can be extremely unfair, and very misleading, when the media succumbs to *false equivalences*. One such example was mentioned in Chapter 1. There I noted that the 1981 "supply-side" idea that lower tax *rates* might actually produce more tax *revenue* had the support of perhaps eighteen economists and was opposed by about eighteen thousand. Wanting to sound unbiased, the press dutifully reported that economists were divided on the issue. Divided? When the division is a thousand to one, reporting that economists are "divided" doesn't inform the public; it misleads them.

This tendency to indulge in false equivalences is one of the main reasons why bad ideas keep bouncing back to haunt us. During the race for the presidency in 2016, even Donald Trump, the non-Republican Republican, felt obliged to advocate a massive, budget-busting tax cut. It's what Republicans do. People were, apparently, supposed to believe that this mammoth tax cut was consistent with his pledge to balance the budget in short order—or even to pay off the national debt within eight years. (He actually said that.) New math? No, it was nonmath, a real whopper. But the media barely called him on it.

Once elected, Trump set out to make good on his tax-cutting pledge—sort of. In April 2017, his administration produced a one-page outline of a tax plan. Well, actually, the single page was mostly blank space. If you omit the hortatory language at the top and bottom, there were exactly 107 substantive words about tax reform. (I counted them.) A month later, when the Office of Management and Budget released the president's budget, it omitted the tax plan entirely! Whoops, they just forgot, I suppose. But they remembered to include the presumed growth benefits from tax cuts. Curious. Finally, in late September, the administration offered an eight-page document that was far less sketchy than April's one-pager. This document still left out many crucial details—such as what loopholes it would close to make room for the promised tax-rate cuts. These were filled in later as tax bills progressed through the House and Senate.

The problems caused by false equivalences are not limited to economic policy. One disconcerting meme of the 2016 campaign was the frequent observation that prospective voters didn't trust either Hillary Clinton or Donald Trump. Maybe that's why turnout was so low. But here's how *New York Times* columnist Tom Friedman characterized the situation during the campaign: "All lying in politics is not created equal. . . . What is grating about Hillary is that her prevarications seem so unnecessary and often insult our intelligence. But they are not about existential issues. As for Trump, his lies are industrial size and often contradict each other. . . . There is no theory behind his lies, except what will advance him."

So, for example, one candidate makes a somewhat dubious claim that the State Department allowed her to keep her emails on a private server, while the other candidate claims, preposterously, that he'll make Mexico pay for a multibillion-dollar wall. Or one candidate won't provide transcripts of her (almost certainly unremarkable) speeches to Goldman Sachs, while the other refuses to release even a single tax return. These are *not* equivalent, and treating them as such doesn't illuminate; it distorts.

An objective standard of what Stephen Colbert dubbed "truthiness" is hard to devise. Perhaps the closest we can come is PolitiFact's tabulation of statements by candidates Clinton and Trump, each rated on the following truth scale: True, Mostly True, Half True, Mostly False, False, Pants on Fire. Here was the scoreboard on the Sunday prior to the election, based on over six hundred statements:

	True or Mostly True	Half True	Mostly False or False	Pants on Fire
Clinton	50%	24%	24%	2%
Trump	15%	15%	53%	17%

Hillary Clinton's ratings were not quite up to George Washington's (alleged) standard. But treating them as even remotely equivalent to Donald Trump's was, well, a "Pants on Fire" untruth.

All that said, the press should not and does not exist to serve the interests of public officials, be they elected or appointed. Ideally, it should scrutinize the actions of the government and single-mindedly serve the interests of the governed. But a third interest sometimes creeps in, distorting the outcomes: the fourth estate's own self-interest. In fact, many thoughtful observers worry that the weight of this third influence on press judgments is both large and growing. TV news, for example, increasingly resembles entertainment. And how else can you characterize talk radio—not to mention many "news" websites?

To start, consider some of the implications of the seemingly mundane fact that virtually all newspapers, magazines, and television and radio stations are private businesses, in it to make money. (PBS and NPR are wonderful exceptions, as are public-interest websites like ProPublica.) There's nothing wrong with that per se. But like corporate giants in many industries, the largest media companies are prominent, powerful, and politically well connected. It is a sad but true fact that their corporate agendas may coincide only loosely with the public interest, if that. CBS's Les Moonves, for example, raised a lot of eyebrows when he declared in early 2016, referring to Donald Trump's surprising successes in the Republican primaries, "It may not be good for America, but it's damn good for CBS."

Yes, the mainstream media giants are powerful. But in a world in which smart phones threaten to get more eyeball time than TVs, these same media outlets are under siege from new competitors like websites, Twitter, and Facebook. To a news executive, loss of viewers, listeners, or readers is a catastrophe in the making. To a politician, life without media exposure is unthinkable. So there is potential for a symbiotic swap here. Donald Trump, the great audience booster, understood that better than anyone ever had before.

Nor are private agendas limited to the companies. Many prominent media personalities are independent entrepreneurs with goals of their own, including both fame and fortune. If you are an aspiring (or actual) media star, getting your face in front of millions of people may be seen as more important than getting the story right. Remember, the first rule of publicity is: just spell the name right. Star journalists who appear regularly on TV not only command enviable salaries but are in constant demand on the lecture circuit—where speaking fees of $50,000 and more are now commonplace. It gets worse. In recent years, several defunct politicians have transformed themselves into ersatz "journalists," earning both high salaries and outsized speaking fees.

Does any of this matter? Does the lure of lucre cloud the judgment of journalists or influence the content of their reporting? Well, you be the judge. But given a choice between spending another day digging into the gory details of some obscure tax break and speaking at the annual convention of the National Association of Meat Loaf Lovers for $50,000, which would you pick?

Some thoughtful observers have long worried that the whole process might be—or might appear to be—corrupting. NBC's Tom Brokaw once derided the practice of taking large speaking fees as a "white-collar crime," a "crime," of course, that is not limited to journalists. Years ago, Ted Koppel, then a star on ABC, stopped giving speeches for money because he became concerned that his credibility as a journalist was being threatened by the appearance of conflict of interest. "Nobody out there who makes a normal salary is going to hear that amount, and realize that it was paid for a day's work—to put it generously—and believe that there wasn't something else that was purchased for that price." Just ask Hillary Clinton, who for months fended off repeated criticisms of her high-priced speeches for Goldman Sachs. And beyond appearances, it's pretty hard for an investigative reporter to be too critical of a company that pays him or her handsome speaking fees. That's just human nature.

The Principal-Agent Problem

So journalists and their corporate bosses might be sullied by the chase for money. What else is new? So might almost everybody else. What follows from this mundane observation? Surely not that members of the press should take vows of poverty. Reporters, editors, and news anchors are not and should not be expected to be saints. The key questions are: To what extent does the self-interest of the press clash with the public interest? Do journalists face the right incentives, meaning incentives that induce them to serve the best interests of the public at large?

Perhaps surprisingly, economic analysis suggests some answers to these questions because economists have lavished a great deal of attention on an intellectual problem of just this sort. We call it the "principal-agent problem." The generic idea is this: Often an individual (the "principal"), lacking either the time or the expertise, hires someone else to serve as his or her *agent* in a transaction. Some common examples are the real estate agent who (you hope) tries to get you the best price for the house you want to buy or sell, the independent insurance agent who (you hope) shops around for the best policy, and the financial adviser who (you hope) unearths the best investment deals for you. But what if they don't? What if their decisions, supposedly made in *your* best interest, are distorted or even dominated by *their* best interests? That is the essence of the principal-agent problem.

The most compelling and economically important example is probably the potential conflicts that arise between the interests of owners and managers of large corporations—a problem that economists have studied for generations. Here the stockholders are the principals, and the company's top executives are the agents. The managers are supposed to pursue the best interests of the shareholders. The question is: Do they? Most economists would answer: not necessarily. If, say, executive compensation and prestige are tied to a firm's *size*, while the value of the firm's shares is tied to the firm's *profits*, then managerial decisions may favor size over profits—to the detriment of shareholders. For example, top managers may pursue mergers and acquisitions that make the company bigger even if they drive down the price of its stock.

How can such principal-agent problems be overcome, or at least mitigated? While there is no magic bullet, economic theory has identified a number of possible remedies, three of which also apply to the case of a high government official (the principal) who must use the press as his agent to communicate with the public.

The most direct solution to the principal-agent problem, where it is feasible, is to use appropriate (and sometimes imaginative) *financial incentives* to align the agent's interests with those of the principal. This is the remedy most often suggested for the manager-shareholder problem, for example. One widely adopted but incorrect solution was to pay top executives mainly in stock options, so the managers would pursue the shareholders' goal: higher stock prices.

What was wrong with that idea? This is not the place for a lengthy disquisition on the theory of managerial compensation. Suffice it to say that options do not fully align the interests of shareholders and managers. For example, once share prices fall well below the "strike price" of an option, stockholders lose dollar-for-dollar from any further price declines, but option holders may lose little. Option holders also have a much stronger upside than stockholders when share prices rise. Granting managers shares of *stock*, rather than *options*, is a better way to align their interests with those of shareholders. And companies are starting to turn in this direction.

Drawing an analogy from control of a corporation to the problem faced by a politician dealing with the press may seem a stretch. After all, the press is not in the employ of the government. But start by asking this simple question: Do the interests of the two parties coincide? Not likely. The politician wants his message communicated to the voters accurately, sort of, though with the friendliest possible spin. The reporter wants his story displayed prominently—on page one or on the evening news, which probably requires conflict, controversy, or sensationalism.

Is there any way for a public official to "pay" a journalist to behave better? Unfortunately, if the official is not too scrupulous, there is. By selectively leaking information, a government official can pay the reporter off in the coin of the journalist's realm: scoops.

I will return to the unseemly subject of leaks presently. For now, let me just observe that this solution is widely employed in Washington. It is, in fact, how some of the town's most astute political players acquire their famously good press. The deal is straightforward: you scratch my back by leaking information, and I'll scratch yours with laudatory press coverage. When you read a puff piece about some savvy but highly principled Washington player who always seems to make the right moves, chances are you are reading a paean to a chronic leaker. From the point of view of the public interest, however, these incentives are perverse.

A second approach to the principal-agent problem identified by economic theorists is to have the principal closely monitor the behavior of the agent to make sure the agent behaves properly. This particular solution is rarely promising in the shareholder-manager case because ordinary stockholders have neither access to the necessary information nor time to process it. (Very large shareholders can do better, and some do.) Keeping a watchful eye on the realtor who is selling your home is more practicable, though still difficult.

Can a government official look over a journalist's shoulder in a timely fashion—say, before the newspaper is printed? No, you say, that would violate freedom of the press. That's mostly right, but less intrusive press policies fall well short of censorship. For example, back in my day as vice chairman of the Federal Reserve Board, I sometimes insisted—as a condition of granting the interview—that the reporter check quotes with me before using them. And that meant checking not just the precise words but also the context. (This idea hardly originated with me.) While this weaker form of monitoring does not always work, it can be effective if you are dealing with a scrupulous reporter who wants to get the story right.

Perhaps the subtlest cures for principal-agent problems in economics arise when the parties believe the transaction is likely to be repeated time and again. Then they have strong incentives to develop a cooperative working relationship, built on mutual trust, from which both can benefit in the future. Think about it. The principal wants to minimize opportunistic behavior by the agent, such as earning more commission by getting you to overpay for a house. If the agent believes there is more profitable business down the road, she will be less inclined to seize such opportunities when they arise.

Does a similar idea apply to dealings between high government officials and the press? You bet it does. Journalists who cover, say, the White House, the Treasury Department, or the Federal Reserve want to return to the same sources over and over again. Since access to high-ranking officials is a precious commodity, especially if the officials will agree to on-the-record interviews, reporters have powerful incentives to cultivate long-term relationships. That means, among other things, playing it straight, respecting confidences, and not sensationalizing stories.

On the other side of the bargain, government leaders, whether elected or appointed, know they will be encountering the same group of journalists over and over again. If the officials are deceptive or unresponsive, the reporters may grow hostile. (Remember Sean Spicer?) But if officeholders are receptive and accessible, reporters may reciprocate with complimentary coverage. In the worst cases, bargains become Faustian in the way noted above: swapping leaks for puff pieces. But in the best cases, such deals can mean an exchange of truth by the politician for accuracy by the journalist, with the public winning on both sides. Making it all work is a tricky business, however.

One specific technique I found useful several times while vice chairman of the Fed was this: when a reporter wrote a particularly inaccurate or hostile story, I would put him "in the penalty box" for a while—meaning that I would refuse to let him in my office or to take his calls. Now put yourself in the position of a journalist assigned to cover the Fed. If your access to the vice chairman disappears, you have a problem—especially if he is still talking to your competitors. The offending reporters usually got the message, and things improved once their "penalty time" was served.

You cannot apply this strategy indiscriminately or ham-handedly. The small number of reporters I tagged for a penalty knew very well how they had earned it. (I told them.) The technique also depends critically on developing a long-term relationship that both parties prize. It is unlikely to work if you are a lame duck. Nor is it effective with hit-and-run reporters out for a single story.

What I have said so far casts government officials in the role of "principals" striving to make ornery members of the fourth estate behave properly as their "agents." That is a common view in government and politics. It is how the profession "spin doctor" got its name.

But the underlying reality is considerably more complex. In particular, the roles of principal and agent can be reversed. Sometimes media representatives act more like principals, using public officials as agents to further their own careers. Media games like episodes of "he said, she said" and other manufactured or exaggerated conflicts are familiar examples—ways for reporters to manipulate public officials in order to burnish their resumes.

While it takes two to tango, either party can lead in this dance. Officeholders may dangle leaks in front of reporters to encourage friendlier coverage and flattering portraits. But reporters can also dangle puff pieces and just plain exposure in front of officials to induce them to spill the beans. Just as the desire to preserve and enhance a long-term relationship can help keep a headstrong journalist in line, so too can it persuade a government official to mug for the cameras.

The case of staged media events is particularly perplexing, since it is far from clear who is using whom. The top echelons of government obviously see such occasions as opportunities to sell their story to the public, using the news media as the indispensable intermediaries. But these same events invite the media to use the drawing power of leading politicians as stage props to help sell newspapers or boost TV ratings—as Donald Trump did so dramatically for CNN and Fox during the Republican primary debates in 2015 and 2016. So it can be a symbiotic relationship from which both parties benefit. Unfortunately, the public loses if it accepts these staged media events as reality.

So who is the principal, and who is the agent? Put differently, who's manipulating whom? The complex reality is that often both parties try to scramble into the driver's seat at once—which doesn't quite work. But one important element of asymmetry tilts the game in favor of the media: they are (more or less) part of the permanent Washington establishment, while almost all high officeholders, whether elected or appointed, are temporary help.

One consequence of this marked difference in job tenure is clear and compelling. A journalist's error of judgment or fact rarely does him or her lasting harm. At most, an obscurely displayed retraction may have to be printed—and often not even that. Pundits, in particular, can (and do) make egregiously wrong predictions or offer absurd analysis that will most likely be forgotten by the next Sunday talk show. For them, the game goes on.

But public officials are in a dramatically different position. A serious media dagger stuck between the ribs can kill or maim. Careers or even lives may be ruined. The game may end abruptly, with the government official's career carried out in a body bag. Yes, it's true that anyone in Washington can play this game—and many do. But it's a dangerous game for the officeholder, and a comparatively safe one for the journalist. *Caveat officio.*

The Ship of State Leaks from Everywhere

The nasty matter of leaks was raised earlier. One saying I heard early and often during and after my time in our nation's capital is that "the ship of state leaks from the top." It's true, but it tells only part of the story. The sad fact is that the ship of state leaks from the middle and the bottom, too.

In categorizing leaks, let's first exclude the accidental ones—as when a politician lets some loose words slip into an open mic. Embarrassing, to be sure, but it's the purposeful leaks that are more interesting. They can be usefully categorized by the following two-way classification: leaks can be authorized or unauthorized, and they can be malicious or not.

A leak is authorized if it has been approved by someone higher up the ladder. In the case of the administration, that may mean the president of the United States or someone acting on his behalf. In the case of Congress, which speaks with many more voices, it normally means someone in the congressional leadership.

Authorized leaks are a way of life in Washington. But, for the most part, they are not meant to be malicious. (There are, of course, notable exceptions.) Some such leaks are trial balloons intended to gauge public opinion or political reaction. Others are simply low-key ways to inform the cognoscenti without beating the drums and blaring the French horns. Still other authorized leaks may be presented as gifts to favored reporters—payments for services rendered, if you will, or perhaps advance payments on hoped-for services in the future. The journalists will naturally pride themselves on digging up every scoop through diligent and crafty reporting when, in fact, some were dropped in their laps. It's all good clean fun—at least most of the time. And in fairness to a number of fabulous reporters, some of the best stories are dug up by intrepid investigative reporting. We saw numerous instances of such top-flight journalism in the investigations of Russian influence in the 2016 presidential campaign, which transfixed political junkies in 2017.

The truly nasty leaks are the unauthorized ones. In Washington, people leak maliciously to the press for two main purposes—other than to curry favor with reporters. You can leak to damage an individual, or you can leak to damage a policy. Both varieties are so distressingly common that they are seen as part of the natural order of things inside the Beltway. Unauthorized leaks are one big reason why Washington is such a tough town. As a *New York Times* reporter put it some years back, "Information is both currency and weaponry in Washington, a means to create and pay debts, to reward friends and destroy enemies." Yes, *destroy*.

Consider first unauthorized leaks intended to damage a person. While they come in many varieties, two are classic. While I escaped my three-plus years in Washington relatively unscathed, and wasn't in particularly "political" positions, I nonetheless was the victim of both types.

The first type is designed to label you as *controversial*, which is about the last label you want when you hold a high position in government. Being controversial is just fine, indeed desirable, for an author, a professor, or a TV personality. Controversy draws attention. But it is potentially disastrous for, say, a secretary of the Treasury or a chair of the Federal Reserve—or, worse yet, for their deputies. Knowing this, your opponents in Washington may goad the press into thinking that something you said is controversial. Like most brave souls, the leakers usually unburden themselves under the cloak of anonymity. It happened to me.

The Federal Reserve's annual conference in Jackson Hole, Wyoming, held in one of the most beautiful spots on earth—Grand Tetons National Park—is a major international event for the economic cognoscenti. Central bankers from all over the world flock to this remote location each August. Economists vie for the coveted invitations. The media descend in droves. Wall Streeters, who used to attend, were unhappy to be banished from Jackson Hole conferences a few years ago. They look on with envy. In addition to the scenic splendor, it is a place for people to see and be seen.

The August 1994 symposium was on "Reducing Unemployment," and the organizers asked me, as the sitting vice chairman of the Fed, to speak in the closing panel. But thanks to one unscrupulous reporter and a malicious leaker or two, my brief and largely banal remarks created a sensation in the tiny corner of the world that fixates on the Fed.

Having joined the Fed in late June, I had made almost no public utterances up to that point but had participated in two interest-rate hikes. I was solidly aligned with the Fed majority on raising rates, but I wanted people to know that I still cared deeply about unemployment. The topic of the Jackson Hole conference made that a convenient platform for getting the message out. So I said out loud something central bankers rarely said in those days: that the Fed should strive for *both* low unemployment *and* low inflation.

I was deliberately sticking my neck out a bit. That part was premeditated; I am the stick-your-neck-out type. But there is no way I or anyone else could have anticipated the media firestorm that ensued. In fact, it probably never would have happened were it not for the irresponsible behavior of a single journalist, egged on by the whispers of a few senior Fed officials eager to put a knife in my back. (Only metaphorically, thank goodness!) One of the Fed's top bureaucrats, in particular, helped steam up the reporter by calling me an "outlier"—a statistical term for a data point far different from all the others. The idea was that a person with such deviant views did not fit in.

Really? As a matter of fact, the Federal Reserve Act *instructs* the Fed to pursue both "stable prices" and "maximum employment." That was the law of the land then, as it is now. The one hundred or so economists listening that morning heard nothing new or remarkable from me. (*Ho hum. Now let's go whitewater rafting.*) Neither did all but one of the dozen or so journalists present that day. But Keith Bradsher of the *New York Times* concluded that he had heard the makings of a Big Story. The late John Makin, an economist who witnessed what followed, later told an investigative reporter, "What got Keith Bradsher pumped up about writing the article was talking to people inside the [Federal Reserve] system." I subsequently confirmed this from several other sources.

Alas, August is a slow month for news. The next morning, the *Times* prominently displayed a piece by Bradsher which began, "Alan S. Blinder, the vice chairman of the Federal Reserve, publicly distanced himself from most of his colleagues today by saying that he believed that the nation's central bank should seek to hold down unemployment." Distanced myself? Did the others wish to violate the Federal Reserve Act? (No, they didn't.) Nonetheless, it was off to the races—or perhaps I should say to the gladiator pits. Bradsher's shabby reporting reverberated through the financial press for more than a month. I had both defenders and detractors. Yes, I became *controversial*.

It all reached a crescendo on September 7, when *Washington Post* columnist Robert Samuelson asserted that I had "bombed at Jackson Hole" and that "Blinder lacks the moral or intellectual qualities to lead the Fed," as if I were in line for the top spot. That hurt. Immoral? Beneath the intellectual standards of the Federal Reserve? Which was the deeper insult? A few days later, *Newsweek* carried the piece nationwide. It helped fan the flames.

I learned something from all this. It was not to keep my mouth shut nor to dissemble in public, for I concluded (after much soul searching) that doing so would be both profoundly undemocratic and a dereliction of duty. After all, I then worked for the American people, not the other way around. When you live in the kitchen, you better get used to the heat.

Nor was the lesson that my views on unemployment made me an "outlier." They didn't, as subsequent Federal Reserve actions amply demonstrated. In fact, the allegedly controversial views that I enunciated at Jackson Hole were conventional wisdom before the decade was out.

What I learned, instead, was an important lesson about survival in an entrenched and unaccountable bureaucracy: watch your back. From that day forward, I did.

The second sort of malicious unauthorized leak is meant to make you a lame duck before your time. The name of the game in Washington is power and influence—not money. And power and influence start to slip away as soon as you become a lame duck. You can practically feel it. People on the other side of a dispute know they will outlast you; with luck your replacement will take a friendlier position. And no one wants to swim upstream with a lame duck. Hence wise political appointees delay announcing their departures until just before they intend to walk out the door.

Unfortunately, your adversaries may be only too happy to lame-duck you too early. It's so simple. All they need do is spread rumors that you will soon resign (or be dismissed). I have a vivid, though not fond, memory of one such occasion.

At a dinner in Stockholm in August 1995, I was seated next to—of all people—the prime minister of Sweden when someone passed me an urgent note to call my office in Washington *at once*. Since the PM had just risen to speak, I could hardly bolt from my chair. So I slipped away as soon and as gracefully as I could and found a phone.

(My departure was apparently not very graceful; it precipitated considerable clucking around the table that US interest rates were about to rise.) When I got my secretary on the line, I learned that the wire services were reporting that I would soon be leaving the Fed to return to Princeton University.

This prophecy did in fact come true about five months later. But at the time, not even I knew whether I would be staying at the Fed or returning to the university when my term ended in February 1996. The decision was not imminent. It took a few frenzied phone calls and a terse (but unequivocal) press statement from the Fed to quash the rumor.

While leaks against people are unsavory, malicious leaks designed to harm or foreclose a policy option are more corrosive to our democracy. Fodder for such leaks is always abundant because the world is full of tradeoffs and budgetary constraints. Prospective changes in policy almost always involve gains for some and pain for others. A little bitter medicine normally accompanies the sugar. For example, a well-conceived tax reform plan will involve closing some tax loopholes in order to reduce overall rates, or raising some tax rates in order to lower others. Virtually all trade agreements damage some industries or regions while helping others. Any plan to put Social Security or Medicare on sounder financial footing will almost certainly hurt someone. I could go on and on.

The truth is that there is rarely, if ever, a free lunch in public policy—or anywhere else, for that matter. Policy changes invariably create both winners and losers. And that is what gives the malicious leaker the opportunity to blow a hole in an idea while it is still on the drawing board. For by selectively revealing a single aspect of a multifaceted plan—presumably the most politically damaging one—the leaker can draw attention to the plan's Achilles' heel, precipitate a media frenzy, and thereby perhaps kill the embryonic idea. Did you say health reform will be financed by new taxes? Impossible! The new budget will propose drastic cuts in farm subsidies? Totally unacceptable! You want to reform Social Security by reducing the benefits of seniors? Not on my watch! You can easily add your own favorite examples.

Because tradeoffs are a fact of life, political bridges like these must eventually be crossed before any policy change can be enacted into law. So, you might ask, what harm is done by premature disclosure? My answer is: plenty.

First, the administration or congressional committee will want to announce its plan as a coherent whole, complete with a message campaign that accentuates the positive and downplays the negative. The leaker rains on this planned parade by releasing one of the policy's least attractive aspects before the rest—and before the administration's message masters are ready. The idea is to try the plan in kangaroo court, where it will lose. President Trump's second attempt to replace Obamacare provided a perfect case in point. In mid-April 2017, well before the plan was released by the House Republican leadership, some leaker let it be known that the (then-secret) plan would allow states to dispense with "community rating." Sounds wonkish. But it meant that premiums would likely soar for sick people with preexisting conditions. Cruel—or as the president himself later called it, mean!

Second, many of the most politically unpalatable ideas considered by any administration (or by any congressional committee) never see the light of day—or at least would not do so without the unwelcome intrusion of some leaker. So malicious leaks weigh down incipient plans with extraneous political baggage—baggage they should never have to carry. An almost comical example of this arose in April 2017, well before even the sketch of the Trump tax reform plan was announced, when some anonymous leaker hinted that tax reform would include a value-added tax. That was never going to happen, of course.

Leaks are an unending source of frustration for government officials. When I served in the Clinton administration, there were times when I understood the dark impulse that led Richard Nixon to establish his infamous "plumbers" unit. (*Will no one rid me of these wretched leakers?*) But so what?, you might ask. No one promised high government officials an easy life. These are tough jobs for many reasons (long hours, low pay, high tension, and more); leaky plumbing is just one of them. Perhaps we should consider it part of the job description.

While containing some grains of truth, this cavalier attitude misses something important. The quality of policymaking is likely to suffer when unauthorized leaking impairs the ability to conduct a healthy internal debate, to think out loud and explore options that probably won't be adopted, to probe your policy's weaknesses the way a debater would. And when the policy development process is impaired, the main victims are the citizens, not the officeholders.

The health care process that I lived through in Bill Clinton's first administration was a quintessential example. The task force leaked like a sieve. We used to joke that it didn't matter if you missed a meeting, for you could always read about it the next morning in the *New York Times*. And policy formulation suffered for it—badly.

At one point, it was decided that the leaking had grown so intolerable that all meetings would thereafter be paperless. That meant that no documents would be circulated in advance, even though important and complex issues were to be discussed. The meetings went something like this: We would all take our seats in the room, and Ira Magaziner, who headed the health care reform task force, would start talking while his aides passed paper around the table. Often we found ourselves puzzling over complicated tables of numbers while simultaneously trying to absorb what Ira was saying. (Can you talk and chew over numbers at the same time?) At the meeting's end, all the paper would be scooped up—including things you never had a chance to read. As we left the room, we took away only what we could retain in our heads. Is that any way to run a task force? You bet it isn't.

The Federal Reserve is a notable and remarkable departure from the picture I have just painted. Far from being a normal part of everyday life, a leak at the Fed is viewed as both a serious breach of ethics, if not indeed a crime, and a blow to the integrity of the institution. Leaks on monetary policy, in particular, are rare enough to be newsworthy—as happened with a (presumably inadvertent) leak of market-sensitive information by then-president of the Richmond Fed, Jeffrey Lacker, that came to light in April 2017. (Lacker resigned.) Maintaining this high degree of confidentiality greatly facilitates internal debate and, potentially, leads to better decisions.

Let me not be misunderstood. I am not arguing for more secrecy in government. Readers familiar with my previous writings and public positions will know that I argued for greater transparency at the Fed long before that was fashionable. Withholding information in order to obfuscate, dissemble, or conceal decisions is both unconscionable and undemocratic. So is hiding from the harsh glare of public accountability. Remember, you're working in the kitchen.

My point is different. Metaphorically, it amounts to this: While early drafts of policy proposals should be private documents, final products should be public. For the sake of debate, policymakers should be free to stake out positions they may not entirely believe, to think out loud, to conduct thought experiments, even to explore slightly fanciful options. If the fear of leaks steals these privileges, debate is limited unhealthily, and the quality of decision making may suffer.

But early drafts are one thing and final products quite another. Almost all final decisions on government policy—including the reasoning and facts that support them—should be promptly and fully disclosed to the public. There are certain obvious exceptions to this rule, such as national security secrets and confidential information. But such items play small roles in the deliberations surrounding most economic policies.

If leaking reaches its nadir at the Fed's Foggy Bottom headquarters, it surely hits its zenith on Capitol Hill. The White House leaks, but Congress hemorrhages. This is more costly than is commonly understood.

In the American system of government, potential legislation needs to be *negotiated* between the executive branch and the relevant congressional committees. If it is not, Congress is all too likely to dispose peremptorily of whatever the president proposes—especially when the two branches of government are controlled by opposing political parties. That is Congress's constitutional prerogative. To minimize this ever-present hazard, the president or his top lieutenants should therefore consult extensively with congressional leaders as proposals are being crafted. Lower down the ladder, their staffs should confer frequently to iron out many details.

If too little of this essential interaction takes place early in the legislative process, the president's proposal may get a frosty reception when it reaches Capitol Hill. Thus, for example, Republicans complained loudly that they were not consulted about the composition of President Obama's original 2009 fiscal stimulus package, which was put together on a partisan basis by the White House and Hill Democrats. I have my doubts about the validity of this complaint. But it was made, and it was either a reason or an excuse for Republicans to dig in their heels. Similarly, when the House Republicans' first health care proposal was being designed in 2017, not only Democrats but even Republican *senators* were frozen out of the process. That was one reason it landed like a lead balloon.

When failure to prepare Congress hurts a proposal's legislative chances, two sorts of problems arise. First, prodigious amounts of hard work done inside the administration are likely to go for naught. This is both a shameful waste of scarce human talent and a strain on badly overworked White House personnel. Second, and much more important, the public is likely to witness—and to be repelled by—a repeated pattern of partisan bickering and frequent episodes of policy gridlock. Such political theater reinforces negative stereotypes about politics and alienates voters from their government. We saw the results when voters went to the polls in 2016.

So the conclusion seems clear: the White House and Congress should confer early, often, and at all levels. There is just one problem—and it's an insurmountable one. As soon as news of an administration proposal reaches Capitol Hill, it leaks immediately to the press. On the Hill, leaking is not a risk; it's a virtual certainty. When I

worked in the White House in the 1990s, we routinely viewed sending
a draft proposal to the House or Senate as tantamount to faxing it to
the *Washington Post*. And it's far worse today, with the twenty-four-
hour news cycle and the vitriolic relationship between Republicans
and Democrats.

The reasons behind the inveterate congressional leaking are, for
the most part, identical to those that motivate leaks within the executive branch: to curry (personal) favor, to damage a person, or to damage a policy proposal. But one further twist derives from the peculiar
sociology of Capitol Hill.

Any organization has a tacit (if not explicit) code of conduct that
defines acceptable norms of behavior. Unfortunately, the code that
prevails in and around the House and the Senate seems to omit the
admonition "Thou shalt not leak." Although unauthorized leaks are
all too common inside the executive branch, leaking is clearly viewed
as antisocial behavior. But on Capitol Hill, leaking is as normal a part
of everyday life as lunch hour and televisions tuned to CNN. To put
it mildly, there is no peer group pressure against leaking. Instead, in
a perversion of Descartes's *cogito*, the rule is: "I am; therefore I leak."

The Media as Intranet

One final and ironic aspect of the sometimes bizarre role of the media
in Washington life is rarely discussed. I have emphasized in this chapter that the press frequently erodes and sometimes destroys internal
debate. But there are times when policymakers use the media actively
to influence, or even to substitute for, such debate. In such instances,
the media—strangely enough—winds up intermediating among *in-
siders*, serving as an intranet rather than an internet.

This sort of thing happens quite a lot at the Federal Reserve,
though mostly not through leaks. The reason, I believe, is simple:
human nature abhors a vacuum. The full Federal Open Market Committee, which includes twelve Reserve Bank presidents from around

the country, meets only eight times a year, and the Government in the Sunshine Act prevents more than three Fed governors in Washington from meeting to discuss policy. So venues for debate are pretty scarce.

One way around this problem is to engage in debate through the media. So Reserve Bank president Smith may try to promote his hawkish views by giving a speech to the local chamber of commerce. The next day, some wire service may publish a dovish-sounding interview of Federal Reserve governor Jones in Washington. Unfortunately, this cacophony of seemingly conflicting opinions is more likely to confuse financial market participants than enlighten them.

Things are different inside the executive branch or Congress, where anonymous leaks, not stories with names attached, are the preferred vehicle for internal communication via the media. This practice reached epic proportions in the early months of the Trump administration, when many careerists in what then White House aide Steve Bannon derisively called the "deep state" and numerous White House staffers leaked massively against what they saw as ruinous presidential policies and practices. They saw it as cris de coeur. President Trump saw it as an outrage.

I have already dealt at length with leaks designed to discredit a particular policy. Here are some other common examples:

- The most time-honored case is surely the trial balloon. A policy option may be deliberately leaked to the press not to damage it, but to test its reception in the court of public opinion. Such trial balloons are so common that examples are hardly necessary. If you read the newspapers this week, you will probably find three examples.
- Another type of leak is designed to force the hand of some decision maker. A policy process may reach a stalemate because the person or people at the top (perhaps the president) cannot decide between two options. To move things off dead center and, not incidentally, to tip the scale in his preferred direction,

a leaker may slip a confidential memo to some reporter, or reveal one or more of the options under consideration, or simply make it known (or, if need be, make it up) that the president will decide the issue over the weekend.

- Sometimes the media serves as a convenient surrogate voice for officials working several levels down the hierarchy, who can't get their positions heard and can't get taken seriously by those at the top—or who may fundamentally disagree with what the boss is saying. An article in the *Washington Post* or the *New York Times* will get people's attention. The early Trump administration experienced this enough times to become obsessed with leaks.

- And the game is not limited to officials. Lobbyists and corporate PR firms are pretty adept at planting stories designed either to kill or to promote their favored policy option.

It's a curious business. Disputes and debates that ought to be held in private—sometimes within a single government agency—are instead aired in public. More open and inclusive internal processes should, in principle, minimize this problem. But, paradoxically, the virtues of inclusiveness are badly compromised by the propensity to leak.

To Speak or Not to Speak?

So every public official must face up to a question that is no more easily answered than Hamlet's: Should I speak to the press, or should I clam up?

On the one hand, holders of high public positions who want to communicate with the public have little choice if they want to be heard—even if it's via a Twitter feed. But I would take the point further: officeholders have a *duty* to communicate with the public, and unless you're the president, working through the press—which nowadays includes websites, blogs, and the like—is the only viable way to do so. On the other hand, anything you say can be, and not

infrequently will be, held against you. It's an inherently dangerous game, made worse by two unattractive features of Washington
reporting.

First, the Washington press corps, bless their hearts, has a way of
turning every dispute into a sporting event: it's Yankees versus Red
Sox, Ohio State versus Michigan, Christians versus gladiators. Who's
up? Who's down? Who's ahead? Who's behind? And above all, who's
knocking heads with whom? If you read the newspapers or blogs or
watch cable TV, you can hardly help coming away with the impression
that the essence of every Washington debate is the unseemly struggle
for political advantage. It's talk radio writ large.

Second, complexity doesn't sell newspapers, keep TV viewers
from changing the channel, or fit into a 140-character tweet. So reporters are deeply respectful of the KISS principle ("Keep it simple,
stupid"). Besides, it's a lot easier for reporters to give you the skinny
on who's up and who's down than to figure out—and then explain—
the essence of a complicated policy issue. Unfortunately, this institutionalized shunning of complexity poses a severe obstacle to reasoned
debate and policymaking.

Examples abound. Do you remember the debate in the 2016 campaign over the Trans-Pacific Partnership, a monumental trade agreement that President Trump cancelled in 2017? I didn't think so. The
issues were numerous, and some of them were stupefyingly complex.
There were serious arguments—intellectual, social, economic—on
both sides. But the amount of press attention devoted to these issues was negligible. Instead, Americans heard lots about partisan advantage, how the TPP was dividing the Democratic Party, and why
Hillary Clinton, while battling Bernie Sanders for the nomination,
switched from supporting the TPP to opposing it. Did I say *why*?
Check that. We heard *that* she switched positions. But her reasons—
and she did give them—got almost no press coverage. It was not a
very edifying "debate."

The 2017 congressional debates over what ultimately became the
Republicans' debacle over health care were better. At least the media

told whoever was listening what the CBO said about budget impacts and likely losses of coverage from various iterations of "repeal and replace." But only a little better. Far more attention was lavished on nose counts and gladiatorial combat.

So what's a poor public official to do? Speak to the press, or keep his or her mouth shut? If you're in the administration, you know you are playing with fire, but there really is no choice but to risk singeing your fingers a bit. After all, the White House is the political and media center of the universe. If you hold a high position there, you must cross your fingers, feed the hungry beast, and hope for the best. Either that or hide behind the drapes. What little personal judgment you are free to exercise is over how much, to whom, and when—and, of course, what you say. Your main concern is that your words not be put in the president's mouth, where he may not want them.

There is a lot more choice at the Federal Reserve, which is hardly a media center. Some Fed officials are loquacious, while others are tight-lipped. Years ago, when I was the Fed's vice chairman, I frequently mulled the merits and demerits of talking to the press—which was far less common in those days. One thing was never in doubt to me, however, even though some of my colleagues disagreed: the Fed has a moral obligation to explain its actions and thinking to the public. Because monetary policy decisions have major effects on the lives of millions of Americans, we the people are entitled to explanations. Fortunately, both Janet Yellen and Ben Bernanke believed that. Indeed, it's becoming accepted wisdom in the central banking world.

But there are clear hazards anytime a Fed official opens his or her mouth. Like accidentally roiling the markets with a snippet quoted out of context, as I did more than once. Like seeing your carefully crafted, two-handed answers bowdlerized or distorted, which I saw more than once. Like risking a knife in the back from an anonymous leaker (and I took my share). Silence is evidently the safer course.

But it is not the right course. As I saw it then and see it now, the public purpose—providing more information to the citizenry—far outweighs the private hazards. So, to me, there was really no choice. Duty took precedence over personal convenience. Not everyone at the Fed shared my opinion then, and some still don't. But the central bank became vastly more open and communicative under Chairs Bernanke and Yellen.

So the debate goes on. Is there a happy medium? Is there a right amount—and a right way—for top Washington officials to speak to the press? If there is, I never discovered it. Nor am I convinced that anyone else has, either—although some people clearly play the game better than others. As Aristophanes might have said, you can't live with the press, and you can't live without it.

Chapter 6

Murphy's Law of Economic Policy

If anything can go wrong, it will.

—Murphy

Murphy, of course, was an apocryphal engineer, not an economist. And variants on his justly celebrated law have been floating around for decades. About thirty years ago, I coined a specific version of Murphy's Law for economic policy:

Economists have the least influence on policy where they know the most and are most agreed; they have the most influence on policy where they know the least and disagree most vehemently.*

My new wrinkle called attention to one particular aspect of the general perversity of human life: the frequency with which bad economic advice gets accepted and good economic advice gets rejected— which is precisely what the Lamppost Theory predicts. I bring this up now because things have not really changed much since then. Murphy's Law is as true today as it was thirty years ago. Consider:

---

* Alan S. Blinder, *Hard Heads, Soft Hearts: Tough-Minded Economics for a Just Society* (Reading, MA: Addison-Wesley, 1987), 1. Parts of this chapter and the next borrow from the opening chapter of that book.

- Then as now, virtually all economists opposed farm subsidies. But those subsidies persist. (A strikingly similar story about maritime subsidies was told in Chapter 2.)
- Then and now, most economists argued that the tax-deductibility of mortgage interest was an inefficient and inequitable way to subsidize homeownership—and that our country probably overinvests in housing as a result. Since then, Americans have witnessed a stunning run-up in house prices followed by a frightening collapse that helped usher in the worst recession since the 1930s. Yet the mortgage interest deduction remains a cherished, and politically untouchable, feature of the tax code.
- Economists know (yes, *know*) that charging a fee to drive a car into Manhattan at peak traffic hours would reduce road congestion on that frequently gridlocked island. We knew this thirty years ago, too, but no such fee has been imposed.

I could go on. Murphy was smart.

The broad public, I think, is not surprised by the second part of Murphy's Law: that economists influence policy even when they don't know what they are talking about. They are surprised, instead, by the first part: that there are issues on which economists agree, are secure in their knowledge, and yet have negligible impact on policy. According to an oft-repeated quip (attributed, perhaps wrongly, to George Bernard Shaw), if all the world's economists were laid end to end, they would not reach a conclusion. Cute, but dead wrong. The truth is closer to the reverse. Not only are we a much less fractious bunch than is commonly supposed, but the degree of consensus among economists on many issues is astounding, maybe even appalling.

Agreement Among Economists

Various ad hoc surveys and questionnaires have documented this high level of agreement sporadically for decades. But since 2011, the University of Chicago's Booth School of Business has been collecting systematic data on the opinions of a panel of leading economists from top universities, as part of its Initiative on Global Markets (IGM). Here's how the panel's organizers describe their selection principles: "Our panel was chosen to include distinguished experts with a keen interest in public policy from the major areas of economics, to be geographically diverse, and to include Democrats, Republicans and Independents as well as older and younger scholars." In short, they look for diversity, not for an echo chamber.

Here are a few examples of agreement among economists from IGM surveys that might be stunning to the general public. Regarding the congestion pricing idea just mentioned, they asked panelists to agree or disagree with the following statement:

> In general, using more congestion charges in crowded transportation networks—such as higher tolls during peak travel times in cities, and peak fees for airplane takeoff and landing slots—and using the proceeds to lower other taxes would make citizens on average better off.

An astonishing 92 percent of the respondents either agreed or strongly agreed, and *none* disagreed. (The other 8 percent either did not respond, had no opinion, or expressed uncertainty.)

Here's another example. In October 2016, with the presidential campaign in high gear and protectionism very much in the political air in both parties, the economic expert panelists were asked whether they agreed or disagreed with the following statement:

> Adding new or higher import duties on products such as air conditioners, cars, and cookies—to encourage producers to make them in the US—would be a good idea.

Not a single economist agreed; most "strongly disagreed."

Economists are not this united on every issue, of course. They do, for example, come in liberal and conservative stripes and so disagree, for example, on how progressive the tax code should be. But that is precisely my point. On some questions, economists are like-minded, and on others they quarrel. Murphy was right on both ends.

It is pretty obvious that Murphy's Law of Economic Policy is a prescription for policy failure—unless, of course, economists are systematically wrong about everything. Imagine the state of the nation's physical health if a similar Murphy's Law applied to medical advice. We would assiduously follow our doctors' advice in treating ailments about which medical knowledge is weak and quackery abounds— such as curing the common cold or dieting to lose weight. But we would leave our children unvaccinated, bake in the sun without hats or sunscreen, and live on a diet of deep-fat-fried foods. (Whoops, some people do all those things. But most don't.)

We act differently, however, when dealing with our economic doctors. The great economist Paul Samuelson once sagely observed that "he who picks his doctor from an array of competing doctors is in a real sense his own doctor. The Prince often gets to hear what he wants to hear." In the realm of economic policymaking, America's elected officials have shown a remarkable propensity for ignoring expert opinion (*Who asked for that illumination?*) and hearing only what they want to hear (*Give me support instead*). No wonder so many economists walk around with little gray clouds over their heads, clouds that darkened in the Trump administration when the new president and his people either ignored or denigrated sound economics—and expertise in other areas, too.

One major thesis of this book is that the misuse and disuse of good economics in policymaking is not just a run of bad luck or random error. It's systematic. Economic policy choices are made by politicians, as they should be in a democracy. A tiny number of economists get to whisper—or sometimes shout—in their ears. But as Murphy's Law warns us, politicians do not accept or reject economists' advice at random. Rather, they choose the solutions they perceive to be good politics and reject the others. Sadly, however, good economic solutions often make bad politics—and vice versa. So policymakers routinely reject opportunities to better the lot of millions of people.

Murphy's Law Illustrated

A few examples will illustrate both the underlying truth of Murphy's Law and the critical role it plays in formulating economic policy. My first example is one we have encountered already in this book; its roots go back more than forty years.

One day in 1974, a then obscure but soon-to-be-famous economist named Arthur Laffer took a paper napkin in a Washington restaurant and drew a curve that was destined to become famous. It looked like a little hill. As the hill rose toward its peak, it indicated that increasing a low or moderate tax rate produces higher tax revenues, as is obvious. But as it descended, the curve suggested something less obvious: that raising very high tax rates might so discourage the activity being taxed that tax receipts actually *fall*.

The basic reasoning behind the Laffer Curve was incontrovertible. After all, if the income tax rate were 100 percent, virtually no one would earn taxable income, cutting tax receipts almost to zero. But then, in a remarkable leap of faith unsupported by evidence, Laffer convinced several influential journalists and politicians that the US income tax in the late 1970s might actually be on the downhill side of the Laffer Curve. In one of the greatest flights of fancy since Peter Pan, Laffer and Company began claiming that the US government could actually collect more revenue by *cutting* personal income tax rates, especially the top rate. This was truly the New Math: you can add by subtracting!

Laffer's inspiration must have been otherworldly, for there never was a shred of evidence in this world to suggest that the US income tax system was anywhere near the danger zone of confiscatory taxation, where lowering rates raises revenue. In fact, there was voluminous evidence to the contrary. So Laffer won few converts among his fellow economists—who, by the way, have not changed their minds since. In October 2011, with Washington focused on either ending or trimming the Bush tax cuts, the University of Chicago's expert panel was asked to react to this reverse-Laffer statement:

> All else equal, permanently raising the federal marginal tax rate on ordinary income by 1 percentage point for those in the top (i.e., currently 35 percent) tax bracket would increase federal tax revenue over the next 10 years.

In reaction, 93 percent either agreed or strongly agreed with this obvious proposition; not a single respondent disagreed. (Mr. Laffer is not on the panel.)

But so what? Murphy's Law holds that even strong agreement among economists has little influence—maybe even *negative* influence—on actual policy choices when the agreement runs against the political grain. Laffer's original flight of fancy took off when it captured the imagination of candidate Ronald Reagan in the 1980 campaign. And after Reagan's landslide election, supply-side economics—the doctrine that all good things happen when you cut taxes—became the official policy of the newly installed national government. Within months, Congress was joyfully participating in the mass self-delusion of the day by enacting gigantic tax-rate cuts, premised in part on super-optimistic forecasts (fantasies really) showing that the federal budget deficit would shrink nonetheless. A tsunami of congressional testimonies, op-eds, and speeches by spoilsport economists could not deflect the political joyride. As often, the most powerful kind of thinking proved to be wishful thinking.

You know the rest of the story. The supply-side boast was proven false, and the tax cuts blew a huge hole in the federal budget. But did supply-side economics meet the ignominious demise it deserved? Not at all. (Remember Murphy!) Large tax-rate cuts for top earners are the mainstay of Republican economic policy to this day. Even the renegade candidate Donald Trump, no orthodox Republican, advocated them as a candidate in 2016. Then, when he became president, he boasted about proposing "the biggest tax cut in American history."

My second Murphyesque example came at the start of the Obama administration. One line of attack on Mr. Obama's proposed stimulus bill in early 2009 was that it would *retard*, rather than stimulate, economic growth. Senator John McCain (R-AZ) opposed the bill on the grounds that "this is not a stimulus bill, this is a spending bill." How's that again? As we have seen, then Speaker of the House John Boehner reveled in calling the stimulus package "job-killing government spending." A curious verbal construct that. As pointed out earlier, even if you don't like the particular forms of government spending under consideration, there is no logical way for spending to *kill* jobs. Yet, according to Republican dogma at the time, total employment was supposed to fall if the stimulus bill was implemented. Never mind *how* they reached that conclusion. (Come to think of it, how did they?) The president's foes were seeking support for opposing Obama, not illumination.

The stimulus bill passed nonetheless, albeit barely. Did it work as expected? The IGM panel of experts thinks so. Here's a statement to which they were asked to react in July 2014, more than five years after the stimulus was enacted:

> Because of the American Recovery and Reinvestment Act of 2009, the U.S. unemployment rate was lower at the end of 2010 than it would have been without the stimulus bill.

The McCain-Boehner answer is no. But a landslide 82 percent majority of economic experts either agreed or strongly agreed with this proposition; only 2 percent (one person) disagreed.

But don't jump to the false conclusion that economic logic triumphed in this instance, for the victory was short-lived. The political tide turned sharply against "Keynesian" fiscal stimulus only a year or two after the stimulus passed—even though the economy was still in the doldrums and the budget deficit, though still huge, was shrinking.

Federal spending cuts and some tax increases lopped about a point to a point and a half off the GDP growth rate in 2011, 2012, and 2013. The Republicans, who took control of the House after the 2010 election, won that round of the political debate. But sadly, it wasn't just the Democrats who lost; it was the country.

My third example of Murphy's Law in action is with us still. When concern over climate change finally roused the public early in this century, economists were ready with both a diagnosis of the problem and a straightforward remedy. The underlying theoretical analysis had been developed almost a century earlier, was inscribed in virtually every introductory economics textbook, and was second nature to almost every economist. It had even notched a notable success years earlier in dealing with sulfur dioxide and the acid rain problem. It was just waiting to be applied to carbon dioxide and global warming. (Could two dioxides be that different, economically?)

According to this analysis, market economies emit too much CO_2 because people and businesses that burn fossil fuels need not pay for the damage the carbon inflicts on the atmosphere. The point is general. When users of some resource (say, coal) do not pay the full costs of using it, elementary economics tells us they will use too much. That defect in the market mechanism is the root cause of excessive carbon emissions, sulfur dioxide emissions, and many other environmental problems.

The cure is obvious: make fossil fuel users pay for the damages they inflict on the environment by, e.g., taxing carbon emissions. (Alternatively, the government could require them to buy tradable permits.) That may sound simple, and as straight economics it is. But carbon taxes have been anathema to American politicians. A small part of the reason is technical: it is sometimes difficult or impossible to measure emissions, and if emissions cannot be measured, appropriate assessments cannot be levied. But the biggest drawbacks to carbon taxes are political. Most politicians on the right recoil in horror at the mention of the *T* word—thinking that their constituents do, too.

Some politicians on the left view letting businesses "buy their way out" of pollution problems as of dubious morality.

Yet the evidence is overwhelming that the costs of reducing CO_2 emissions via a carbon tax are far lower than the costs of achieving the same reductions through direct controls. Not surprisingly, our expert panel displayed little disagreement when asked to react to the following statement:

> A tax on the carbon content of fuels would be a less expensive way to reduce carbon-dioxide emissions than would a collection of policies such as "corporate average fuel economy" require-ments for automobiles.

Ninety percent either agreed or agreed strongly; only 2 percent disagreed.

Economists ask why it is good public policy to make saving the planet from overheating far more costly than it need be by relying on clumsy command-and-control techniques rather than market pric-ing. We are still waiting for an answer. But our recommendations for carbon taxes go mostly unheeded nonetheless—and the menace of global warming grows.

The Roots of Murphy's Law

More examples could be cited—such as rent controls, farm price sup-ports, and many others. But enough has been said to make the point. Many of the truths that economists hold to be self-evident are mis-understood, ignored, or rejected by the body politic. Others, though well understood, are overwhelmed by the well-financed propaganda of vested interests. On the other hand, bad economic advice is some-times accorded far too much respect—especially in areas where our knowledge is shaky or where internal debate racks the profession. The sad consequence is that, in the policy arena, economics often puts its worst foot forward.

The roots of Murphy's Law run deep. Some were described in earlier chapters.

First, there is apparently something in the American character that rejects any remedy too complex to fit on a baseball cap. What, for example, could "Make America Great Again" possibly mean? But short snappy slogans are almost always wrong. H. L. Mencken understood that decades ago: "There is always a well-known solution to every human problem—neat, plausible, and wrong."

In economics, such faux solutions are typically based on gross misunderstandings of elementary economics, utter disregard for the facts, or both. Better policies, however, tend to be less crisply defined and full of qualifications. They are not easily summarized in five words or fewer, or in 140 characters, so they do not sell well in the political marketplace. If we are to improve our nation's economic policy, we must begin by admitting polysyllabic solutions. Unfortunately, average citizens have little incentive to educate themselves about economics, a subject that alternately perplexes them and induces slumber.

Sloganeering is just a surface manifestation of the much deeper conflict between good economics and good politics that is the focus of this book. Sound economic policies promote the broad national interest over narrow special interests. They often inflict costs on the few to secure benefits for the many. And those benefits may be apparent only in the long run; indeed, they may be so subtle that they are never apparent at all. Think about that for a moment as a politician might: Taking a long-run perspective. Opposing special interest groups. Favoring programs whose benefits, though genuine, are diffuse and hard to pinpoint. If you want to know how long a politician who does these things will survive in our system, ask Charles Darwin.

When sound economics and sound politics clash, few politicians will hesitate long before taking sides. The result is the epigram that led off Chapter 2: "On a number of issues, a bipartisan majority of the [economics] profession would unite on the opposite side from a bipartisan majority of Congress." And of course, politics, not economics, dominates economic policymaking. So we get constituency-based policies that routinely sacrifice the public interest to support one special interest group after another, members of Congress who care more about the well-being of their states and districts than about the well-being of the United States, and abysmal economic policies.

Not that economics is flawless. Our discipline is neither as sound nor as exact a science as we would like it to be. We are not the physicists, nor even the physicians, of society. But the undeniable fact that economists do not know *everything* does not mean that we do not know *anything*. Unlovely as it may be, economics does have something positive to offer society. Something limited, to be sure, but positive. Yet society has been unwilling or unable to accept much of the offering to date.

The offer stands, however. In the next chapter, I describe and advocate an approach to economic policymaking that is deeply concerned with both preserving and enhancing the efficiency of the market system and with improving the lot of society's least fortunate citizens. Some of these policies appear conservative by conventional labeling. Others appear more liberal. They all derive, nonetheless, from a coherent underlying philosophy, a vision of what economic policy could and should be. It is to that philosophy that I now turn.

Chapter 7

Wanted: Hard-Headed but Soft-Hearted Policies

Reformers have the idea that change can be achieved by brute sanity.

—George Bernard Shaw

Murphy was smarter than Shaw's reformers. "Brute sanity" isn't close to enough. But let's suspend disbelief for a moment and imagine that, somehow, we could overcome Murphy's Law and adopt better economic policies. What would those policies look like?

In the book mentioned in the last chapter, *Hard Heads, Soft Hearts*, I advocated an approach to economic policy that is "liberal" in both the eighteenth-century and modern senses of that word, an approach that I nicknamed "hard-headed but soft-hearted." I return to these ideas here because they are just as relevant today as they were thirty years ago. In fact, if bipartisanship had a pulse in America, I would call the approach bipartisan, because it defies traditional Democratic and Republican labels. Hard-headed but soft-hearted policies combine profound respect for the virtues of free markets (the hard head) with equally profound concern for those the market leaves behind (the soft heart). While many economists feel comfortable with this philosophy, it is apparently alien to most Democratic and Republican politicians—and to the public at large. So let me explain it.

137

The conservative state of mind creates a strong predisposition to go along with market solutions. It therefore leads—as if guided by an invisible hand, you might say—to the correct answer to many economic questions. The eighteenth-century liberal in me says that traditional Republicans (let's ignore Donald Trump for a moment) deserve kudos for defending free trade, for arguing that rent controls can ruin a city (only a Republican could love a landlord), and for reminding us that large budget deficits can be problematic (though Republicans seem to remember that only when a Democrat occupies the White House).

But the contemporary liberal in me says that Republicans are wrong to promote tax cuts for the wealthy again and again (is there no limit?), are putting the planet at risk by treating climate change as a hoax (and therefore opposing policies that would mitigate it), and are mean-spirited in their attitude toward the needy (was Scrooge a Republican?). How else can you explain the stubborn refusal of nineteen Republican governors to accept Obamacare's 2010 offer to pay almost the entire cost of making Medicaid more generous in their states?

Under traditional Democratic policies, sympathy for the under-dog is apparent, but the requisite economic calculations and respect for markets are sometimes underappreciated. In consequence, Dem-ocrats sometimes advocate well-meaning but romantic schemes that pay little attention to how high the bill might run, who would pay it, or what the unintended side effects might be. Unfortunately, having your heart in the right place is not good enough if you insist on lead-ing with your chin.

Several proposals from Senator Bernie Sanders's (I-VT) remark-able populist campaign in 2016 illustrate the point. Think, for ex-ample, about free college tuition at public institutions (who would pay the bills?) or a $15 per hour *national* minimum wage (even in Mississippi?). Sanders lost the nomination battle to the more mod-erate Hillary Clinton. But it was close. The fact that nearly half of Democratic primary voters supported a seventy-four-year-old self-described socialist tells you something about attitudes on the Democratic left.

That said, a soft heart does help. It was, after all, the Democratic Party under Franklin Roosevelt that gave us unemployment insurance, Social Security, federal deposit insurance, and more. It was the Democratic Party under Harry Truman that committed the government to the pursuit of full employment. It was the Democratic Party under John F. Kennedy and Lyndon Johnson that pushed through Medicare and Medicaid and declared war on poverty. And it was the Democratic Party under Barack Obama that took a giant step toward universal health insurance with the Affordable Care Act. These and other examples of soft-hearted social and economic legislation have made America a better place to live. Virtually all were opposed by the Republican Party.

In fact, Republican economics sometimes seems to go out of its way to be hard-hearted—if not indeed punitive—toward people who don't manage to rise into the upper 1 percent of the income distribution. In Donald Trump's memorably heartless phrase, they are "losers." Though crudely expressed, Trump's attitude was not new. Four years earlier, the presidential ticket of Mitt Romney and Paul Ryan had disparagingly characterized the beneficiaries of government programs as "takers" rather than "makers." Despite reams of evidence that trickle-down economics doesn't work for the lower 99 percent, Republicans continue to look back on the Reagan tax cuts as the closest thing ever to policy heaven. They are constantly on the prowl for ways to cut food stamps, Social Security, and Medicaid—even unemployment insurance. Since the ascendance of the Tea Party faction and Trump himself, Republican economics seems to have become even more hard-hearted and even more soft-headed—a veritable caricature of its former self.

To achieve the highly desirable combination of hard heads and soft hearts, we must join rational economic calculation and respect for markets with compassion for the underdog. That may sound harder than marrying a Hatfield to a McCoy, as both families may view the proposed union as getting into bed with a skunk. But if you step back and think about it dispassionately, the required changes in attitudes are actually not that great. More clear thinking and less ideological sloganeering—brute sanity, you might call it—would get us most of the way. We must start thinking with our heads and feeling with our hearts, rather than the other way around. I hope that's not impossible.

A Case Where It Worked

Actually, we occasionally manage to do it. For a case in point, let me take you all the way back to 1962. (Don't worry, the issue I am about to discuss is very much alive today.) That's when Milton Friedman, the great ultra-conservative economist, published a remarkable book called *Capitalism and Freedom*. Among the many pearls of policy wisdom contained in that slim volume was a novel suggestion that the United States might best alleviate poverty via something he called a "negative income tax."

The idea was simplicity itself: If a family's income fell below some low, legally established limit, call it $X, the federal government would give them cash to fill part of the gap between their income and $X. Because the government would be *giving* income rather than *taking it away*, Friedman called this transfer payment a *negative* income tax. These negative tax payments would decline smoothly as the gap between $X and the family's income closed, reaching zero when the gap reached zero.

The negative income tax (NIT) idea was hard-headed but soft-hearted because it sought to alleviate poverty while creating only minimal disincentives to work. The latter feature stood in stark contrast to many other antipoverty programs at the time (and still), which often placed extremely high marginal tax rates—sometimes over 100 percent—on the earnings of the poor. Imagine if your family's after-tax income *declined* as you earned more. Would you find working an attractive option? Gigantic marginal tax rates created a welfare trap; the NIT did not.

Friedman's plan appealed to both liberal and conservative economists. But was it just an ivory tower idea with no prospects for enactment? No. In fact, the United States now has at least two major antipoverty programs that closely resemble the NIT.

One is the Earned Income Tax Credit, which has been a part of the tax code since 1975. The EITC supplements the wages of low-income workers just like an NIT would—by adding income tax refunds ("negative taxes") to workers' earnings. EITC payments decline smoothly as earnings rise, just like an NIT. The only important difference between the EITC and the NIT is that Friedman's idea pertained to low-*income* people whereas EITC benefits go to people with low *earnings*. You must work to earn benefits.

The second well-known NIT-like program is food stamps, now officially known as the Supplementary Nutritional Assistance Program (SNAP). Food stamps originated in 1964 as part of Lyndon Johnson's War on Poverty, and two features make them almost an NIT. First, the value of the food stamps given to each family declines as the family's income rises—just like NIT payments would. Second, if food stamp benefits fall short of the family's total spending on food, as they commonly do, the restriction that the stamps be spent only on food becomes meaningless. Families want to use all their stamps to buy food, anyway—making food stamps equivalent to cash.

So the United States has, in essence, two NITs, and one of them commands broad bipartisan support. Presidents Ford, Reagan, Clinton, and Obama have all supported expanding the EITC. So even has House Speaker Paul Ryan (R-WI), who is otherwise not a great defender of the social safety net. It looks like an example of hard-headed but soft-hearted thinking at work.

The Hard Head: The Principle of Efficiency

The hard-headed but soft-hearted approach is founded on two overarching principles that should not be controversial but apparently are.

The first, the hard head, is that more is better than less. The second, the soft heart, is that the poor are needier than the rich.

The concept of economic *efficiency* is the essence of the hard head. Though economists eat, drink, and sleep efficiency, the concept seems to make everyone else drowsy. Our failure to explain why economic efficiency is so important has made it all but impossible to have a meeting of the minds with the body politic. It's a bit like trying to explain the joys of baseball to a person to whom America's pastime is foreign. (*Why did that guy just walk to first base?*) That intellectual barrier, in turn, helps explain why politicians do not seek much illumination from economists.

A simple test will tell if you are a good subject for conversion to the economists' way of thinking about efficiency. See if you agree with the following three propositions:

1. More is better than less.
2. Resources are scarce.
3. Higher productivity is better than lower productivity.

They all sound reasonable, right? Let's take them up in turn.

First, economists since Adam Smith have thought of economic systems as mechanisms for delivering the goods and services people want. If consumers would rather not have what businesses in a market economy produce, we certainly have been barking up the wrong tree for almost 250 years. But that seems unlikely. Although each of us can draw up a list of items we disdain, chances are that what is on my list will not be on yours. Were it otherwise, the shunned items would not find a market. Indeed, economists take the point further: catering to consumer tastes is one of the things free markets do best. No other system comes close.

Second, the earth has less land, labor, machinery, and natural resources than its inhabitants would like. If you doubt that, try asking owners of these scarce resources to hand them over for free. Resources are scarce because most people crave more goods and services than they have or can afford. Biologically, we humans can survive on little. Economically, however, our wants seem insatiable. Because our desires for smart phones, air travel, and jogging shoes can be fulfilled only by using resources like silicon, aluminum, and leather—plus the skilled labor of engineers, pilots, and designers—these resources are scarce, and hence valuable.

The third proposition is almost a corollary of the first two. Higher productivity means—by definition—that more goods and services can be produced from the same inputs of labor, capital, and natural resources. If the fundamental role of an economy is to produce more of the things people want, anything that conserves on the use of scarce resources is ipso facto desirable. Though less single-minded on this point, the broad public apparently favors higher productivity, too. After all, if we really wanted to make our economic system *less* productive, we could emulate the former Soviet Union. They really knew how to mess things up.

Yet the idea that higher productivity is better than lower productivity is *quietly* controversial. If you pose the question directly, hardly anyone will express a preference for lower productivity. As economic journalist Neil Irwin put it, "Efficiency sounds great in theory. What kind of monster doesn't want to optimize possibilities, minimize waste and make the most of finite resources?" But as he cautions, "the economic and policy elite may like efficiency a lot more than normal humans do." Yup.

Think, for example, about policy changes that are sold mainly as ways to "create jobs." There are two basic ways to create more jobs. The socially beneficial way is to enlarge the GDP so there is more useful work to do. The self-defeating way is to see to it that each worker produces less, so that more labor is required to produce the same bill of goods. This second route to job creation does boost employment (though probably temporarily). But it is the path to rags, not to riches. Yet many of the policies we unthinkingly adopt—such as special tax preferences, import quotas, farm subsidies, and many types of regulations—reduce productivity in precisely this way. They create *inefficiencies*.

So those are my three propositions, each of which should be noncontroversial: more is better than less, resources are scarce, and greater productivity is beneficial. I hope you find each of them agreeable, even banal. For if you do, you should be attracted to the economist's cherished concept of efficiency. If more is better than less and resources are limited, we should seek economic policies that make the economy more, not less, productive. We should proscribe waste. It's that simple.

But how do we recognize a violation of the principle of efficiency when we see one? Some waste is so obvious that it jumps out and bites you on the nose—such as featherbedding or stubbornly sticking with an older technology that is both inferior to and more expensive than a newer variety. But most forms of waste are more subtle.

Standard economic analysis proposes a simple conceptual test for ferreting out these more subtly wasteful activities. Just ask this question: Could economic activities be rearranged to make some people better off without making anyone else worse off? If so, we have uncovered an inefficiency.

Like the three noncontroversial propositions above, this test seems trite. It amounts to little more than the unanimity principle. If everyone agrees that an alternative economic arrangement would be better—or at least no worse—than what we have now, then the current situation can hardly be optimal. The appeal of this test for economic efficiency lies precisely in its banality. Who would be so boorish as to dispute a platitude? The amazing thing is that it gets us anywhere at all. But centuries of economic analysis shows that it does.

There is an important subtlety, however. When the test uncovers an economic inefficiency, it does not necessarily follow that the government should take steps to correct it. Why is that? The reason is that the fixes—such as changes in tax laws, regulations, or trade provisions—will probably hurt *someone*. So even though the new situation will arguably be superior to the old one, getting from here to there may be problematic.

That statement sounds paradoxical. If the economy is inefficient, shouldn't it be possible to set things right without harming *anyone*? The definition of efficiency suggests that. But serious problems arise in bridging the gap between the ideal and the real. Let me illustrate with a rare example, alluded to earlier, in which good economic advice was taken—in rank violation of Murphy's Law.

If you lived in the United States, especially the northeastern United States, in the 1980s, you heard quite a bit about acid rain; it was then considered one of the nation's major environmental problems. The acidic rainfall was caused mostly by emissions of sulfur dioxide, much of it from coal-fired power plants in the Midwest, which the prevailing winds carried eastward. Cumbersome regulations were not very effective in limiting it.

You don't hear much about acid rain anymore, however, because the problem was mostly solved—not through scientific breakthroughs, but mainly by applying straightforward economic logic. Economists argued then, as they typically do in pollution cases, that the *most efficient* solution was not detailed controls but rather putting a price tag on the pollutant. Make polluters pay, the argument goes, and they will pollute less. Almost all economists believe that. In the case of sulfur dioxide (SO_2), the Clean Air Act of 1990 authorized, and the EPA subsequently established, a market-based approach to reducing SO_2 emissions. The specific technique is called "cap and trade." The government sets a *cap* on the maximum amount of emissions (in this case of SO_2) it will allow, and then sells *tradable* permits to allow only that much pollution.

Because the permits are tradable, the market establishes the price. In the case of SO_2 permits, the main buyers were expected to be the coal-fired power plants that were emitting so much. That's been true. But it turned out that citizens' and environmental groups have also bought some permits and presumably not used them—thereby effectively lowering the cap below the government's target.

The program has been a phenomenal success. SO_2 emissions have dropped about 40 percent since the 1990s, and acid rain has declined even more. Furthermore, the costs have run only about one-quarter of what the EPA originally predicted. Cap and trade turned out to be both cheap (the hard-headed part) and highly effective in reducing pollution (the soft-hearted part). It has been lauded not only by economists but also by the EPA, the power-generating industry, and many environmental groups.

What accounted for this "magic"? The main answer is that the original situation, with both heavy pollution (because it was unpriced) and heavy-handed regulation that attempted to control it, was so inefficient that improvements were easy to come by. The status quo ante left lots of money sitting on the proverbial table. So the winners (e.g., the people suffering less from acid rain, and the power plants that reduced their compliance costs) could *in principle* have compensated the losers (e.g., plants whose compliance costs rose) and still have been left with net gains for themselves.

In practice, however, compensation was not offered in the SO_2 case, and almost never is. The reasons are hardly mysterious. Drawing up detailed lists of winners and losers, with dollar amounts for each, is a difficult enough task on purely technical grounds. When the issue becomes politically charged, as it inevitably will, the job becomes well-nigh impossible. Because politicians and bureaucrats are not eager to charge head first into a meat grinder, compensation is rarely even discussed, much less paid.

In many cases, though apparently not in the case of acid rain, this lack of compensation is a serious problem. Improvements in the functioning of the economy, such as cap and trade, make society as a whole better off. But they almost always hurt some individuals and some businesses. Since the sum of all the gains and losses is *positive*, not *zero*, the winners from an increase in efficiency can in principle compensate the losers. But no such compensation mechanism was set up in the case of SO_2 emissions. Nor is it usually.

The absence of any effective compensation for losers is one reason why so many economic inefficiencies persist. Any proposed change creates losers, who will howl—with some justification—that they are being victimized. Often their anguished cries fall on sympathetic political ears, and the proposed change is blocked by the unstated precept that government actions must never harm anyone *directly*. (Indirect harm is apparently quite acceptable.)

The growing hostility to international trade, the subject of the next chapter, provides a classic and important example. Any proposal to end the protection of a particular industry will make the economy more efficient and benefit consumers with lower prices. But it will hurt the affected businesses and their workers, who will call on their lobbyists and favorite members of Congress to defend their interests. And their complaints are legitimate. Protected firms and their workers really do suffer losses when forced to compete in the open market, which is why trade protection, once granted, is so hard to take away. But somehow the whole comes to much less than the sum of its parts. Amid all the special pleading, no one watches out for the national interest in expanding trade.

Let's generalize this point. The sorts of changes that our political system has the hardest time digesting are those where the benefits are *subtle*, *hidden*, and *diffuse* but where the costs are *obvious*, *visible*, and *concentrated*. Unfortunately, many policies that would reduce or eliminate inefficiencies have precisely this character. Farm subsidies are a great example. They are grotesquely inefficient but politically sacrosanct, even though roughly 98–99 percent of Americans wind up overpaying for food so that about 1–2 percent of Americans can enjoy higher incomes. But the losses to taxpayers and consumers come in small doses and relatively subtle forms—such as slightly higher food prices—while the gains to farmers are large and obvious.

Much the same can be said, though in the opposite direction, about the unpopularity of international trade agreements, such as the late lamented Trans-Pacific Partnership (TPP). There is little doubt that more open trade with eleven Pacific-Rim countries would have benefited the United States as a whole. But the efficiency gains would have saved the typical American consumer a comparative pittance—certainly far too little to move him or her to political action. (The International Trade Commission estimated real income gains after fifteen years of about 0.23 percent.) By contrast, the minority who would have lost from the TPP (e.g., industries that would have been hurt by international competition) knew exactly where their bread would have been unbuttered—and the magnitudes were large enough for them to exercise whatever political muscle they could muster.

Economists, like accountants, sum up the small potential efficiency gains over the more than 320 million Americans and conclude that the *net* social benefits from TPP's trade expansion would have been sizable. But political scorekeeping is starkly different because the losers scream while the winners stand silent. When our political system is asked to weigh concentrated and readily identifiable losses for a vocal minority against diffuse and hidden benefits for the silent majority, it doesn't hesitate long before siding with the minority.

Therein lies the main explanation for the political popularity of trade restrictions, farm subsidies, tax gimmicks, and many other policies that undermine economic efficiency. America's system of government by lobbyist guarantees us a form of taxation and representation that the founding fathers did not foresee: special interests get the representation, while the broad public interest gets the taxation.

The generic problem is that *economic* calculus and *political* calculus are profoundly different. Economic analysis based on the principle of efficiency often focuses on the long run and points to solutions that yield small benefits to the majority. But politics is dominated by short-run considerations and often favors solutions that help the minority rip off the majority. Democracy has been defined as a system of majority rule with respect for minority rights. These always struck me as fine principles. But somehow the right to fleece the public has crept into our economic bill of rights. If we are to pursue a hard-headed economic policy based on the principle of efficiency, we must get it out.

Wishing Won't Make It So

Pursuit of efficiency may be the defining characteristic of hard-headed economic policy, but it is not the whole story. For openers, hard-headed policy decisions must be based on *facts*, as best we know them. Admittedly, life offers few certainties, and the evidence on many economic questions is sketchy and controvertible. But that does not give anyone license to bend the facts to suit his or her preconceived notions—nor just to make them up. Sensible policies must be based on our best estimates of the relevant facts, imperfect as those estimates may be. If the White House and Congress become zones where "alternative facts" flourish, we are all in trouble.

Probably no president in history has demonstrated these perils to the commonweal better than Donald Trump. Consider: On February 27, 2017, Mr. Trump amazed Americans by informing them that "nobody knew that health care could be so complicated." Actually, *everybody* with even the slightest acquaintance with the issue knew that. As a candidate in 2016, he suggested that the United States might renegotiate its national debt like a failing casino. Really? He famously promised to build a high wall along the two-thousand-mile border with Mexico—a major engineering feat, to be sure, but never mind that. Did Trump even know that, for years before his election, more people crossed the US-Mexico border heading *south* than heading *north*? Or that NAFTA reduced Mexican tariffs a lot, but reduced US tariffs just a little? I could go on and on.

Hard-headed economic policies must also be based on sober *logic* rather than on wishful thinking. Much as they disdain "theory," practical policymakers need to *predict* the likely consequences of actions they might be contemplating. And predictions, more or less by definition, rely on theory. Yes, even sound economic analysis delivers poor forecasts now and then. But wishful thinking does a lot worse.

Supply-side economics is an outstanding—and, sadly, still current—example of what can happen when wishful thinking supplants logic and evidence. Back in 1980, supply-siders sold the public on claims with no factual basis. They believed what they wanted to believe and assured Americans that conventional economic analysis was all wrong. But wishing makes it come true only in fairy tales. Supply-side predictions in the early 1980s that saving, investment, labor supply, productivity, and GDP would all soar while the budget deficit shrank were proven to be spectacularly wrong; in each case, predictions from conventional economists came far closer to the mark.

Sadly, however, this poor track record failed to dissuade future Republicans, many of whom have stuck with supply-side nonsense despite a second failure in the George W. Bush administration. As recently as the 2016 presidential primaries, Republican hopefuls (not only Trump) were claiming, without apparent embarrassment, that low-tax policies would produce growth rates of 4 percent, 5 percent, and even 6 percent. The braggadocio declined a bit once Donald Trump became president. His first budget projected GDP growth rates of "only" 3 percent—a rate that virtually all economists branded as unrealistic.

Wishful thinking is not confined to Republicans. As mentioned earlier, Bernie Sanders excited his base by promising a $15 *national* minimum wage, large job gains from restricting trade, free tuition at public colleges, bigger Social Security checks, and other spending programs that were not paid for.

Finally, hard-headed economic policies must respect the laws of *arithmetic*. That would seem to be a minimal requirement for rational policymaking, one that would be accepted by acclamation. But some politicians bridle at the irritating strictures of arithmetic. After all, we Americans live in a great democracy where everyone has the right to be above average and people in the top 1 percent routinely describe themselves as "middle class." Thus President Reagan betrayed his math teachers, but not his political supporters, when he promised to cut taxes, raise defense spending, and yet still shrink the budget deficit in 1981. Candidate Donald Trump outdid Reagan in 2016 by pledging at one point not just to balance the budget but actually to pay off the national debt within eight years. This despite another round of massive tax cuts. Such promises cannot be redeemed with arithmetic; they require smoke and mirrors.

These, then, are the central ingredients for a hard-headed economic policy: respect for efficiency, attention to facts, logical rather than wishful thinking, and adherence to the laws of arithmetic. Simple and obvious, right? Yet our economic policy would be far better if these ingredients figured more prominently in the actual political mix.

The Soft Heart: The Principle of Equity

You can always tell a true liberal, even if you can't see his weak knees or his bleeding heart. Walk into a room where he is watching a football game and ask him which team he is rooting for. If his favorite team isn't playing, he will be rooting for the underdog. He may not really care who wins; he just roots for the underdog reflexively. This predisposition carries over to economic policy, where it leads liberals to favor soft-hearted policies that help society's underdogs.

A market economy can be thought of as a game with winners and losers in varying degrees. But the economic game is no more fair than a contest between the New England Patriots and your local high school football team. Some players take the field with built-in advantages.

Body size is less important in economics. But some of us are born into wealthy families, or with nimble minds that enable us to pursue lucrative and pleasant professions, or with the shrewdness and drive that make for success in business. Some are blessed with good upbringings that provide high-quality education and instill "the right values," meaning the values that promote economic success. These born (or bred) winners can be expected to do well in the economic game without any help from the government. Although some will fail, most will fare well under laissez faire. Neither Jeff Bezos nor Mark Zuckerberg needed handouts from the government to achieve enormous success—though attending Princeton and Harvard probably didn't hurt them.

Other, less fortunate people are born into poverty, or with less native intelligence, or into environments where education and economic success are neither prized nor expected. Some remarkable individuals overcome these disadvantages through sheer grit. Hats off to them. But most lack the ability to accomplish that feat. Without some kind of outside help, they may founder and live in penury.

That all men and women are not created equally equipped to play the economic game is obvious. Now comes the hard question, the one that separates the soft-hearted from the hard-hearted. Should society try to ameliorate the resulting inequalities? Should government try to help the underdogs?

The hard-hearted attitude holds that the wonderful market system that is so essential to our prosperity is exquisitely fragile. So we must not tamper with it to aid the underprivileged, the shortsighted, the indolent, or even the unfortunate. Let everyone compete on an equal basis, the argument goes, and let the chips fall where they may. If some of the players are disabled or injured, that's a shame. They must be left to limp along, for efforts to assist them would be futile at best and harmful at worst. This attitude has led conservatives over the years to oppose labor unions, Social Security, unemployment compensation, minimum wages, Medicare, Medicaid, Obamacare, and more.

And it seems to have hardened within the Republican Party in recent years. Its leading "thinker," Paul Ryan, who is now Speaker of the House, put it this way in 2012, when he was chairman of the House Budget Committee. After admitting that his vision of an "opportunity society" requires a safety net "for people who cannot help themselves, for people who are down on their luck, so they can get back on their feet," he added: "*But we don't want to turn the safety net into a hammock* that lulls able-bodied people to lives of dependency and complacency, that drains them of their will and their incentive to make the most of their lives" (emphasis added).

This was his rationale, I suppose, for recommending cuts in the US safety net so severe that liberal budget guru Robert Greenstein characterized Ryan's proposed 2012 budget as "one that, for most of the past half-century, would have been outside the bounds of main-stream discussion due to its extreme nature. In essence, this budget is Robin Hood in reverse—on steroids." Some hammock.

Greenstein represents the soft-hearted attitude; he wants to cushion the blows for those who play the economic game poorly or who cannot play it at all. That objective can be served by making the game less risky—which is the rationale for programs like Medicare, Social Security, and unemployment insurance. Or it can be done by making the victors share some of the spoils with the vanquished—via welfare benefits, public housing, Medicaid, and progressive taxation. Liberals generally favor such public generosity. But, of course, society as a whole has no external benefactor. Providing benefits to losers means that winners must foot the bill.

Which attitude is correct? Which more nearly captures the ethical notion of fairness? There are no objective, scientific answers to questions like these, any more than there is an objective, scientific answer to whether it is better to root for the Patriots or your local high school team. Liberals instinctively favor public generosity. Conservatives draw the line after equality of opportunity. But more than a knee-jerk reaction leads me and many others to find the soft-hearted attitude more appealing. A thought experiment will help explain why.

Picture this: A billionaire is walking down Manhattan's Fifth Avenue when a $100 bill slips out of his pocket and flutters to the ground. (It is critical to the argument that the $100 was not stolen.) Minutes later, a busboy from the South Bronx, on his way to work at the local McDonald's, picks it up. The billionaire has lost $100, and the busboy has gained $100. Is society as a whole better or worse off?

Most people will answer instinctively: better off. But there is no scientific way to prove that. The billionaire may have earned the $100 by playing the economic game fairly and well, and he may be extremely chagrined by its loss. Perhaps he was going to donate the $100 to charity. The busboy did nothing to earn the $100 and may not spend it wisely. (On a hammock, perhaps?) Besides, we have no objective system of weights and measures to balance one person's loss against another's gain. So no one can say for sure that the accidental transfer of $100 has made society as a whole better off.

Yet when an answer seems so right, it just might be. The billionaire, it is natural to suppose, is so wealthy that losing $100 is beneath his notice. That same $100 might feed the busboy for a week, and therefore be of immense value to him. So it seems reasonable to suppose that the billionaire's loss and the busboy's gain leave society as a whole better off. Liberals certainly think that way.

This example, of course, is contrived to elicit that response. Now let's make it less extreme. Same scene, but now suppose it's a lawyer earning $300,000 per year who drops the $100 bill, and a clerk earning $30,000 per year who picks it up. Is society better off now? You may hesitate longer on this one, but the same reasoning applies. If we believe that the poor are needier than the rich, then the $100 is worth more to the clerk than to the lawyer. Society is therefore better off for the accidental transfer.

From here, it is but a short hop to the fundamental argument for using taxes and government transfers to redistribute income. For suppose now that the government raises the lawyer's tax by $100 and cuts the clerk's tax by $100. Unless something is inherently distasteful about using the tax system (rather than random accidents) to redistribute income, or unless this transfer creates serious disincentives that damage the market mechanism—an issue we'll take up later— the conclusion should be the same. The transfer of income down the economic ladder makes society better off.

Many philosophers and economists have found this line of argument persuasive over the years. I call it the Principle of Equity. It is the intellectual foundation of the soft heart.

Of course, any system of taxes and transfers that redistributes income must—by definition—interfere with free-market outcomes, and therefore must be at least somewhat coercive. Just as liberals instinctively favor acts of public generosity, conservatives instinctively bridle at interferences with free markets—sometimes they say, "with freedom." Nature gave us both sets of instincts for good

Darwinian reasons; if used properly, each has survival value. As the planet's highest animals, we should take a balanced view that both prizes the wondrous achievements of the market and recognizes its limitations.

In 1776, at a time when some other wonderful ideas were also bursting on the scene, Adam Smith showed the world how free markets miraculously harness greed toward constructive ends. Capitalists, motivated only by self-enrichment, are led (by the hand of God, Smith subtly suggested) to invent new products, to fill unfilled needs, to find better ways of doing things—in short, to do many things that make society (and themselves, of course) better off.

He was right. As a mechanism for delivering goods and services to the people at the lowest possible prices, the market system has yet to meet its match. The market also makes the most of society's limited resources. A free market will assign the highest prices to the scarcest inputs, which will therefore be used sparingly by cost-conscious entrepreneurs. Items in abundant supply will be cheap, and hence used profligately. For the most part, that is as it should be.

But unfettered markets do not get everything right. Because clean air and water typically are available free of charge, an unregulated market invites environmental degradation, as we have seen. The market alone will not provide for the national defense. It will not prevent recessions. And most germane to the topic at hand, it will not—except by sheer coincidence—distribute income and wealth in accord with anyone's ethical conception of equity.

The market is designed for efficiency, not for fairness. Those who play the economic game and succeed become fabulously wealthy. Those who cannot play may starve. There is no mystery about why. For a capitalist society to prosper, it must have big winners. But playing the game well takes hard work and, sometimes, the willingness to bear great risk. To encourage daring individuals to grab for the brass rings, the prizes must be commensurately large—which can result in startling gaps between the rewards of the winners and the crumbs left to the losers.

In its relentless drive to squeeze all it can out of society's scarce resources, a literally free market shows no mercy, allowing even extreme deprivation. If there is to be mercy, it must be imposed from the outside—which is why governments in all capitalist societies redistribute income to some extent. In the early days of capitalism, redistribution was meager—such as almshouses for the poor—and left mostly to private charity. Think Dickens. But as capitalist countries matured and grew richer, they also grew more humane. More and more people came to believe that the penalty for economic failure was greater than the offense merited. *Public* charity emerged. We now call it the social safety net.

Government redistributive programs have increased over the decades—not just in the United States, but everywhere. And everywhere the drive toward more and more redistribution has generated controversy. In the United States, the controversy often runs along partisan lines—with Democrats generally promoting redistributive policies and Republicans generally opposing them.

In this respect, recent economic debates over taxes and the budget echo the past. It was the Democratic Party under Woodrow Wilson that gave us the progressive income tax. It was the Democratic Party under Franklin Roosevelt that ushered in myriad New Deal programs like Social Security and unemployment compensation. It was the Democrats under John F. Kennedy who pushed for Medicare and stronger antipoverty efforts, and it was the Democrats under Lyndon Johnson who enacted these programs. It was Democrats under Barack Obama who gave us what came to be called Obamacare.

The observation that Democrats have been more redistributive than Republicans does not tell us which party was right at which time. It simply tells us that the Democratic Party put more weight on the Principle of Equity. The attitudes of the electorate have changed from time to time. But compared to Europeans, say, Americans have generally preferred to sweep the income distribution issue under the rug—perhaps until recently. In the 2016 presidential primaries,

Senator Bernie Sanders gave Hillary Clinton a serious run for her money by making economic inequality his central issue. But this was the proverbial exception that proves the rule. Over the generations, Americans have shown little interest in inequality as an abstract issue.

Nonetheless, government policies have always redistributed income, and in many ways. In fact, *implicitly* redistributive policies like farm price supports, tariffs and quotas, and tax loopholes may redistribute more income than *explicitly* redistributive policies like welfare and food stamps. More often than not, these implicit redistributions are either capricious or go in the direction Robin Hood would have opposed. Because such policies simultaneously exacerbate inequality and reduce the efficiency of the market mechanism, both liberals and conservatives should condemn them. Yet too often, our interest-group-dominated political system embraces them.

Marrying the Accountant to the Social Worker

That's where some illumination might help. Here's an apolitical litmus test for weeding out at least some policy disasters. When an economic policy is proposed, first ask: Would this improve the efficiency of the market system? That is, would it give us *more* rather than *less?* If the answer is no, then ask next: Would the proposed policy redistribute income from richer people to poorer ones? If the answer is again no, the proposal flouts the principles of both efficiency and equity, and probably should be rejected.

Many policies that fleece the public to feed special interests would fail that simple test. For example, most protectionist measures redistribute income from the average consumer to wealthy capitalists and to workers with above-average wages while damaging efficiency in the bargain. Many egregious tax loopholes distort market incentives while lining the pockets of the rich.

The test also works in the opposite direction. If a suggested policy both improves economic efficiency and helps the less fortunate, it probably has merit. That's why so many economists of all political persuasions favor comprehensive tax reform and defend free trade. Our politico-economic system should have a built-in bias against policies that thumb their noses at both equity and efficiency and in favor of policies that further both goals. Instead, it now seems biased in the opposite direction.

To raise the quality of our national economic policy, we must marry the hard head to the soft heart, join the calculating accountant to the caring social worker. Conservatives must be persuaded to pay more attention to equity and to realize that intelligently designed policies that promote equality need not interfere unduly with efficiency. Liberals must gain greater respect for efficiency and learn that conservative means can be harnessed to liberal ends. If both would learn their lessons, we'd have a better chance of developing economic policies that are simultaneously rational and humane. At the very least, we should start rejecting policies that both harm efficiency and foster inequality—something we don't do now.

The principles of efficiency and equity are not only useful beacons for practical policymakers but also embody an element of political ideology. Our current approach to economic policymaking often sets one interest group against another: labor against capital, rich against poor, exporters against importers, buyers against sellers. To some degree, the interests of these groups do collide. That's life. But too often the *national* interest gets lost while special interests duke it out in the political arena, forgetting that the United States was founded, among other things, to "promote the *general* welfare." That phrase from a bygone day may sound corny from today's cynical perspective. But some things were seen more clearly in the 1780s.

For the hard-headed, soft-hearted approach to succeed, economic issues must be cast in a less adversarial mode. We must all recognize that the broad national interest is not a meaningless abstraction, but something concrete. At least sometimes, on some issues, we must be prepared to subordinate our narrow parochial interests to the common good.

The free-enterprise system is marvelous, but it cannot do everything. In particular, it will not guarantee distributive justice. To create an efficient but compassionate society, we must put reasonable redistributive mechanisms in place and then let the productive players slug it out with little or no protection from their rivals, whether foreign or domestic. Nothing is wrong with tough competition as long as the weak have some protection from the fallout.

But greater homage to the principles of equity and efficiency will not provide answers to all questions of economic policy. Many policies enhance efficiency but damage equity, or vice versa. For example, making the personal income tax more progressive, as many Democrats want, would reduce inequality but subject upper-bracket individuals to higher tax rates that distort incentives. Curtailing food stamps, as many Republicans want, would improve work incentives for the poor but also take from the have-nots to give to the haves.

When the principles of equity and efficiency conflict, we must supplement them with ethical judgments. Do the gains in efficiency compensate for the losses in equity? Or vice versa? On questions like that, reasonable people may disagree. Such judgments are inherently political. But keeping the two principles firmly in mind still helps. We need not summarily dismiss a substantially redistributive program just because it inflicts some minor harm to economic efficiency. We need not shun a significant improvement in economic efficiency just because it raises inequality slightly.

For decades, economists have emphasized the fundamental tradeoff between equity and efficiency: if society wants more of one, it may have to settle for less of the other. There is nothing wrong with this analysis. If our current economic policies were more or less right, we'd be facing this agonizing tradeoff every day. Policies that promoted greater equity (such as making the tax code more progressive or raising food stamp benefits) would harm efficiency, and vice versa. But as things stand today, we can often elide the tradeoff between equity and efficiency because of the low-quality base from which policy starts. We can concentrate on changes that enhance *both*.

I'd like to call such opportunities objective policy *improvements*. They should be noncontroversial because most people should accept the notion that more is better than less and the notion that the poor are needier than the rich. Yet real-world policy decisions often slap both principles rudely in the face. This book is meant to point toward a better way. Let's turn now to some concrete examples.

Chapter 8

Trade Disagreements

No one ever looks over their shoulder to see who lost their job because of protectionism.
—Ronald Reagan (1985)

Ronald Reagan, who spoke the words just above, was not on the ballot in the 2016 election, when free trade and globalization in general took a beating. Whether the issue was immigration, NAFTA, or trade with China, the American electorate—and especially the victorious Donald Trump—seemed to be in a very different place than virtually all economists (and Reagan).

Disenchantment with international trade started early. In the Democratic primaries, Hillary Clinton had to fight off a stern challenge from Bernie Sanders, the self-described socialist senator from Vermont, who was nearly as protectionist as Trump. In fact, while discussing trade agreements with the *New York Daily News* in April 2016, he said, "Well, if he [Trump] thinks they're bad trade deals, I agree with him. They are bad trade deals."

Clinton had supported NAFTA as First Lady and had called the Trans-Pacific Partnership "the gold standard" for trade agreements as secretary of state. She was certainly not as protectionist as either Trump or Sanders. As she noted correctly in the first presidential debate (and elsewhere), "we are 5 percent of the world's population; we have to trade with the other 95 percent." But Clinton was basically forced by the political winds to oppose the TPP unless it was modified to offer "a better deal" to American workers—whatever that meant. Her hostility to the TPP hardened as the campaign progressed. By August 2016, she was declaring, "I oppose it now, I'll oppose it after the election, and I'll oppose it as president." That didn't leave much wiggle room if she was elected.

Then, of course, there was candidate Donald Trump, who triumphed first over sixteen other presidential hopefuls in the Republican primaries and then won the general election despite losing the popular vote by almost three million votes. His vitriolic hostility toward both trade and immigration separated him from the pack— and from most of American history. He claimed America is a "loser" anytime a country runs a trade surplus with us, which is an absurd thought. And while his pledge to have Mexico pay for a wall across our southern border garnered the most attention, Trump also promised to renegotiate NAFTA and even to impose a 35 percent tariff on Mexican imports. For good measure, he threw in a 45 percent tariff against Chinese imports. Shades of Smoot and Hawley.*

Trump's antitrade, anti-Mexico, and anti-China rhetoric cooled down a bit once he assumed the presidency. In particular, his tone toward China softened for a while following a chummy April 2017 meeting with Chinese leader Xi Jinping, and the two countries announced a minor trade deal in May. Rewriting NAFTA proceeded at a snail's pace. Progress? Maybe. But before that, the president had picked a trade fight with—you'll never guess—Canada!

Neither Support nor Illumination

Probably no subject divides economists from politicians more deeply than international trade. Naturally, the politicians who were so

---

*The Smoot-Hawley tariffs were the US version of the worldwide trend to try— unsuccessfully—to "save jobs" during the Great Depression by reducing imports. The problem is that, when every country tries this, the whole world loses. History records Smoot-Hawley as one of the reasons the Depression lasted as long as it did.

hostile to trade in 2016 neither sought nor received much *support* from economists. (In my own role as an external adviser to the Clinton campaign, I tried to avoid talking about trade.) Nor did they seek *illumination*. Why such a sharp divide? I have pondered this question many times over the years, and this chapter is meant to get you pondering it, too.

Virtually all economists believe that a brilliant thinker named David Ricardo got the analysis of international trade basically right two hundred years ago when he published his famous principle of comparative advantage, which showed that nations fare better when they specialize in producing what they are best at—and then trade with each other. As an illustration of economists' near-unanimity about trade, the University of Chicago asked its panel of economic experts in 2016 whether:

An important reason why many workers in Michigan and Ohio have lost jobs in recent years is because US presidential administrations over the past 30 years have not been tough enough in trade negotiations.

There is little doubt that a majority of the political world agreed with this sentiment. In fact, Donald Trump claimed almost exactly what these words say, and he carried both Michigan and Ohio. But among the economic experts, a mere 5 percent agreed with the antitrade proposition, while 64 percent disagreed.

Ricardo did not get all the nuances, exceptions, and qualifications right in 1817; he left generations of economists lots of *i*s to dot and *t*s to cross. Yet his remarkable insight stands as one of the great achievements of the human mind. I begin teaching comparative advantage to introductory economics students at Princeton each year by telling them they are about to cross a great intellectual divide. On one side is the minority of people who understand the principle of comparative advantage. On the other side is the vast majority, who do not. Once you cross this divide, I assure them, you will never go back.

Ricardo's genius is best explained by examples. So let me invent one, involving two hypothetical countries that I'll call "the United States" and "China." (Okay, the example may not be entirely hypothetical.) Suppose the United States is particularly good at producing automobiles, and China is particularly good at producing toys. The basic case for specialization and trade is clear and intuitive: the United States should make the cars, China should make the toys, and the two nations should trade. That division of labor will make workers in both countries more productive and consumers in both countries better off. Simple.

But now change the story a bit. Suppose China can produce *both* autos *and* toys at lower cost than the United States. In this sense, American workers are inferior at everything. (I hasten to add that this is by no means true, though it reflects current fears.) If the two countries trade with one another, will all American workers lose their jobs to lower-cost Chinese labor? Many people reflexively answer yes. But Ricardo saw two hundred years ago that this "obvious" answer was wrong. Rather, free trade will drive workers in each country into the industry in which their nation holds a comparative advantage. A what?

Here's the basic vocabulary. Imagine the Chinese are just slightly more efficient than the Americans at manufacturing cars but vastly more efficient at manufacturing toys. Then we say that China has a *comparative* advantage in toy making and the United States has a *comparative* advantage in automobile making—in each case, compared to the other country. The basic idea is that any Chinese labor devoted to auto production could be employed more productively making toys, and any American labor wasted on toy manufacturing could be more productive building cars.

Under these circumstances, open markets between the two countries will push Chinese workers out of auto plants, as that business naturally migrates to America. The displaced Chinese autoworkers will find employment in the expanding toy industry instead. Across the Pacific, free trade will push US workers out of toy making and into automobile plants. Yes, it's true that China could manufacture its own cars a bit more cheaply than the United States can. But diverting labor to auto making would squander China's huge comparative advantage in toy making. So it makes economic sense for them to boost both their productive efficiency and their citizens' standards of living by specializing in toys and buying their cars from the United States.

If you're resisting this conclusion—as people have for centuries—try this more homely example on for size. Imagine that some high-wage professional, perhaps a doctor, also happens to be a whiz at cleaning shirts—even better than a professional dry cleaner. Should she wash and iron her own shirts at home? Or should she take them to the dry cleaner, thereby giving gainful employment to someone else, and concentrate on treating patients?

The answer, which is obvious to every doctor, is a straightforward application of Ricardo's principle of comparative advantage. The doc is slightly better at dry cleaning but overwhelmingly better at practicing medicine. So she should exploit her comparative advantage and leave the dry cleaning to someone else—which, of course, is exactly what doctors do. If someone suggested to the doctor that she "protect" herself from the "unfair competition" of "cheap dry cleaners," she might think about referring them to a psychiatrist. Yet somehow, when the exact same illogic is applied to nation-states, many people jump off the logical train. (*The Chinese are taking advantage of us with cheap labor!*)

Economists have had only modest success explaining Ricardo's insight for two hundred years. It is probably our profession's biggest failure. And unless and until we do a better job of persuading the electorate, we will never persuade the politicians—who know how to count noses. Right now, things aren't looking too good.

Why this centuries-long failure? One prime reason is that comparative advantage is counterintuitive; it seems to defy common sense. Common sense normally steers us in the right directions; it has Darwinian survival value. But comparative advantage is one of those rare exceptions that prove the rule. Here common sense often fails us. Isn't it obvious that cheaper Chinese labor will outcompete American labor in everything? No, it's not, but it takes some thought to see why.

Another crucial reason stems from people's resistance to unwanted change—and their appeal to the political system to block it. New trade patterns, whether caused by trade agreements or anything else, can cause major disruptions in people's lives. In our hypothetical US-China example, the inefficient American toymakers stand to lose a great deal from trade with China. Plants will close as Chinese toys flood US markets; workers will lose their jobs. So they have a lot to gain if they can persuade their government to protect them from "unfair" Chinese competition. The same holds for China's automakers, who might be wiped out by free trade with the United States. Each group will therefore trot out all sorts of bogus arguments—many of which we will dissect in this chapter—toward that end.

Moving from the hypothetical to the real, the emergence of China as a major player in world trade during this century has in fact cost many American jobs. It has also created new jobs for Americans exporting goods to China, but those are fewer in number. More important perhaps, they are *different* jobs for *different* people. As trade between the United States and China exploded, US job losses were concentrated among blue-collar workers without college educations and in localities where Chinese competition was most ferocious. New jobs did pop up around the country to serve the Chinese market, but they were mainly for highly skilled, college-educated workers.

When something like that happens, the losers from international trade will marshal whatever political muscle they have to block trade—which is far easier to do in a responsive democracy like ours than in an authoritarian state like China. That muscle was flexed in the 2016 presidential election, and it is central to this chapter. The best *economic* arguments almost always favor trade, but the most salient *political* arguments are often arrayed against it.

The Long and Short of It, Redux

Why? Let's start with an important point emphasized earlier: economists and politicians operate on different time scales, with the economists taking a much longer-term perspective. On few issues is this difference in time horizons as stark as it is on trade. But here, it turns out, the politicians may have a better case than most economists care to admit.

Economists like to focus on comparing equilibrium positions: Once all the dust has settled, is the economy better off or worse off because of trade? Ricardo established two centuries ago that the answer is almost always: better off. That's nice to know, but the dust may take a long time to settle. Too long for politics.

Consider again trade between China and the United States. American workers who lose their jobs in, say, apparel or footwear factories won't find employment in, say, the aircraft or software industries instantly or easily. Instead, they may face lengthy spells of unemployment, or even be forced to move to where the new jobs are. When they get those new jobs, the evidence suggests, most of their paychecks will be smaller than from their old jobs. Economists label these and related problems "transition costs," a term that clearly belittles them. Yes, these transition costs will eventually fade into history. But if you are a fifty-five-year-old American worker who loses his job in a shoe factory, the costs are not small, and the "transition" may last the rest of your working life. Economists too often ignore that. Politicians can't afford to—and don't.

Now let's broaden the example. The total number of manufacturing jobs in the United States has been declining for decades, dropping from nearly 20 million in 1979 to under 12.5 million today. (See Figure 8.1.) In some specific manufacturing industries, the declines have been spectacular. For example, the number of Americans employed in apparel making has dropped from about 900,000 in 1990 to barely 130,000 today. In primary metals, which includes steel, the drop since

FIGURE 8.1   US Manufacturing Employment, 1960–2017 (in millions)

Monthly data are for all manufacturing employees and are seasonally
adjusted. Source: US Bureau of Labor Statistics.

1990 is from nearly 700,000 jobs to around 375,000. Many people,
especially those who make apparel or steel, find numbers like these
alarming. Many economists don't.

Why such discrepant views? When a steel mill, say, closes down,
economists tend to view that development as inevitable—maybe even
beneficial to the whole economy since we have lost comparative advantage in steelmaking. But American steelworkers' lost jobs are, in
a literal sense, probably irreplaceable. If Joe gets laid off by the local
steel mill, he may never find work in a steel mill again. Furthermore,
the job he eventually does find will almost certainly pay less than what
he earned at the mill. So these costs won't seem very "transitional" to
Joe. And economists who use that language won't make much head-
way with either Joe or his representative in Congress.

Economists often accuse politicians of focusing myopically on
the short run, even when the short-run situation is unsustainable.

Realistically, manufacturing employment in the United States is never going back to twenty million, Pittsburgh will never be a steel town again, and the flat-screen televisions we buy will continue to be manufactured abroad. Everybody should understand that and act accordingly. Politicians who tell people otherwise are misleading them, creating false hopes.

But many economists are just as locked into the elusive long run, barely even considering the "transition costs" that are so palpable to real people in real time.

Who's got it right? Neither. A holistic—and realistic—approach to trade policy must balance long-run gains against short-run pain. But rather than engage in healthy debate, myopic politicians and hypermetropic economists mostly talk past one another.

Politicians Are from Venus; Economists Are from Mars?

The intellectual Berlin wall about trade extends beyond time horizons. Like all economic changes, new trade patterns create winners and losers—a simple observation that seems to weigh far more heavily on politicians, who home in on the politically connected losers, than on economists, who dote on the *net* of gains versus losses.

Remember, economists generically focus on *broad groups* of people who garner *diffuse* and *barely visible* gains from trade. Think of all those Walmart shoppers wheeling Chinese-made goods out in their shopping carts. In stark contrast, politicians often curry favor by securing *concentrated* and *highly visible* gains for comparatively small and *targeted* groups of people. Think of using trade barriers to protect steelworkers. To economists, politicians' attitudes look crass. To politicians, economists' attitudes look like political malpractice. No wonder the politicians don't seek illumination from economists.

Think back to our hypothetical China-US example. American toy buyers will save a few dollars here and there. Added up over hundreds of millions of purchases, this constitutes a tidy sum. But how many Americans will applaud their government for driving down toy prices?

How many will even connect the dots from freer trade with China to lower prices? In stark contrast, American toy companies and their workers, who are severely threatened by trade, will make their positions known to their politicians—loudly and clearly. So if you were an American politician, would you side with free trade economists or with protectionists who sound like Donald Trump?

Before you jump over to the protectionist side, however, let's remember that trade has upsides, too. In our hypothetical example, trade will create new jobs for autoworkers in the United States and for toy workers in China. In the real economy, freer trade overall (though not necessarily with China specifically) will create roughly as many new jobs in export industries as it destroys in import-competing industries. That's the point President Reagan was making in this chapter's epigram. And as an extra bonus for the United States, the jobs created by exports typically pay higher wages than the jobs destroyed by imports—estimates range from 5 percent to 18 percent higher.

Great. But all those wonderful new jobs created by trade will provide little solace to the workers who lose their jobs. And they will let their politicians know they feel aggrieved. Economists armed with spreadsheets and computer models may assure everyone that both the *average* American and the *average* Chinese will be made better off by trade. But politics doesn't work on averages. Rather, politicians hear from people with strong vested interests in whatever issue is on the table—especially from those who stand to lose.

Stick with that thought for a moment, for it points to another blind spot of (some) economists—a blind spot goes a long way toward explaining the negligible political demand for economic advice on trade policy. As I've observed before, efficiency-enhancing economic policies don't make *everyone* better off. More often than not, they create lists of winners and losers. It's nice to know that, in the case of freer trade, the list of losers is almost certainly shorter. But if you're on that list—as, say, US steelworkers have been for decades—you won't welcome trade openings. Should you just take one for the team?

Some hard-headed but hard-hearted economists answer yes. After all, they argue, stuff happens—and not all of it is good. Specifically, economic change is taking place everywhere, all the time, creating winners and losers with impunity. The Internet killed off most travel agencies. Amazon and others grabbed market share from conventional retail stores. Uber and Lyft have shaken the taxi and limousine industry to its roots. Such "creative destruction" is nothing new. Decades ago, air travel decimated long-distance passenger trains. Long before that, the automobile destroyed the horse-and-buggy business. And before that, electric lightbulbs meant lights out for candle makers.

Notice that in each of these cases the real culprit was improved technology, not international trade, and in none of these cases did governments intervene to stop the process. Why, many economists ask, should trade be treated differently? After all, expanding trade is very much like improving technology. In fact, the former is often a consequence of the latter. Think, for example, about the advent of commercial shipping several centuries ago, cargo aircraft almost a century ago, and the Internet about two decades ago. Trade will get another big boost if "beam me up, Scotty" teleportation ever gets close to reality. In fact, 3-D printing has already taken a step in that direction. Though Scotty can't beam up a colleague, he can get some handiwork delivered over the Internet.

Most of the manufacturing job losses depicted in Figure 8.1 are attributable to technology, not to trade. As productivity in manufacturing industries soared, businesses found they could produce a lot more goods with a lot less labor. Figure 8.2 is a stunner. It shows that the share of US *output* accounted for by manufacturing has barely changed since the 1960s, but the share of manufacturing *employment* has declined dramatically. Robots killed far more American manufacturing jobs than Chinese workers did. But while many people seek to block trade agreements, the ranks of the Luddites have thinned since the nineteenth century. Few people nowadays seek to impede the upward march of technology, even though technology destroys (and creates) vastly more jobs than trade does.

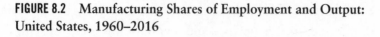

FIGURE 8.2 Manufacturing Shares of Employment and Output: United States, 1960–2016

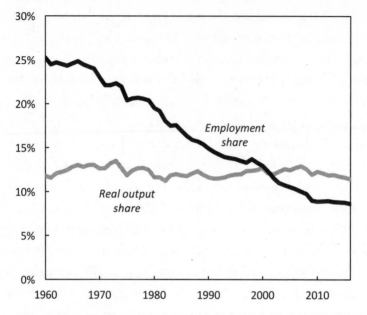

Output data are real value added in billions of 2009 dollars, adjusted using the chain-type quantity index. Source: Bureau of Economic Analysis.

Here's another fact about the US economy that may knock your socks off: roughly five million workers leave their jobs *each month*, either because of being fired or quitting, and a slightly larger number find new jobs, leaving the small net increment (say, a hundred thousand jobs or so) that we measure as monthly employment gains. Not even the most ardent protectionists claim that international trade accounts for more than a small fraction of that staggering job loss. Vastly more derives from technological change and the hurly-burly of competition. But technology and competition are widely applauded, as they should be, and almost no one complains. Trade is not so fortunate.

Once again, let's ask *why*.

One reason is that international competition—by definition—comes from foreigners. If efficient new plants in Chino, California, destroy jobs in Detroit, Michiganders won't be happy. But they won't petition the federal government to stop technical progress in California. Nor would they succeed if they tried. Let those competitors be Chinese, however, and both attitudes and political prospects change. The job losses in Detroit may be identical regardless of whether the new competition comes from China or from Chino. But the politics are starkly different. And it's not just the jobs. The *profits* from domestic technological change are apt to remain in the United States. But when Chinese manufacturers outcompete American companies, the profits go abroad.

Another plausible explanation is that trade-related job losses often can be traced *directly* to government decisions, such as trade agreements. They appear to be "made in Washington." By contrast, job losses that stem from anonymous technological advance "just happen." There are no obvious acts of Congress, no clear villains. When domestic winners face off against domestic losers in the political arena, the lobbying battle is a fair fight, at least in principle. (*You bring your lobbyists; I'll bring mine.*) But when a domestic loser is pitted against a foreign winner, the politics are remarkably one-sided.

Third, recall the educational failure cited earlier. People accept technological improvement as part of the natural order of things. They know it enhances efficiency and raises living standards, and they are apparently willing to accept the hard facts that the buggy whip and candle-making industries were doomed. But few people understand the principle of comparative advantage, which demonstrates that more open trade has precisely the same sorts of effects: efficiency and overall living standards rise, even though some people and some businesses lose.

Toward a Soft-Hearted Trade Policy

The hard-headed attitude toward trade policy just summarized emphasizes *efficiency*. But what about *equity*? Is it fair to ask the losers from trade agreements to take the pain so the winners can reap the gains?

Remember that trade's winners and losers are not selected randomly. In a country as wealthy as the United States, there is a strong tendency for owners of capital and highly educated workers to win from trade, and from globalization more generally, while poorly educated workers lose. One unhappy consequence is that the income redistribution from trade goes mostly up the income ladder. Such redistributions are all the more painful when the proverbial economic pie is not growing very fast anyway, and when the slices are already quite unequal—two facts that characterize the contemporary United States.

Could we do a better job of sharing the gains? Of course we could; we just don't try very hard. Let's go back to trade basics. As I've said, trade always creates both winners and losers, but the winners win more than the losers lose—leaving the nation as a whole better off. That little bit of arithmetic opens the way for mutually beneficial deals whereby the winners share *some* of their largesse with the losers—perhaps enough to turn the losers into winners, on net. We know from Ricardo that the arithmetic works in principle. But it's not easy to design ways to achieve it in practice. Making the politics work is even harder.

One piece of the puzzle is easy. America's tax-and-transfer system automatically taxes some of the income gains away from the winners and transfers them to the losers via familiar mechanisms such as unemployment insurance, food stamps, and the progressive income tax. Those programs are even more helpful when, as seems to be the case these days, the losers from trade are, on average, poorer than the winners. But they don't come close to turning trade's losers into net winners.

Some of the losers from trade collect additional aid from something called *Trade Adjustment Assistance*. TAA began in this country with the Trade Expansion Act of 1962. President John F. Kennedy stated the basic argument clearly at the time: "Those injured by trade competition should not be required to bear the full brunt of the impact. Rather, the burden of economic adjustment should be borne in part by the federal government." "Borne by the federal government," of course, meant borne by taxpayers—which, in turn, meant borne at least partially by the winners.

Kennedy saw TAA as paving the way to more open trade by cushioning the blow to the losers. (The Democrats were the pro-trade party then.) Notice that his basic argument is precisely the same as the one commonly used to rationalize unemployment insurance, Medicaid, and other social safety net programs. In all these cases and others, the government collects taxes from "winners" to pay benefits to "losers." For that matter, *private* insurance—whether it be life insurance, fire insurance on your home, or property and casualty insurance on your business—does the same thing. In all these cases, insurance socializes the risks rather than letting them fall on the unfortunate few.

TAA benefits originally came with a stern eligibility test: job losses had to be shown to be *direct consequences* of US trade concessions. That's hard to prove. Furthermore, the Kennedy-Johnson boom kept unemployment low for years. In consequence, not a single worker received TAA benefits during the 1960s! We had an umbrella, but it didn't rain.

Things began to change with the Trade Act of 1974, a landmark statute that, among other things, liberalized TAA benefits and eased eligibility requirements. For example, injured parties needed to prove only that imports *contributed importantly* to their job loss—a much lower bar (which still holds). And payments to eligible workers were set at a fairly generous level: half the average weekly earnings in manufacturing. Soft-hearted economists applauded these changes.

On top of these legislative changes, the nation had a severe recession in 1974. So Trade Adjustment Assistance more than tripled, albeit from a very low base, between 1975 and 1979, in terms of both beneficiaries and dollars. It then exploded in 1980 as a result of a surge of displaced autoworkers. The 1980 election, however, saw allegations that the Carter administration was doling out TAA benefits to gain political advantage. So the new Reagan administration, on the prowl for budget cuts, proposed ending TAA entirely but settled on reducing benefit levels and making eligibility tougher. Much tougher. Between 1980 and 1981, the number of recipients certified for TAA benefits fell by 93 percent. TAA almost died.

As time went by, support for both trade agreements (especially among Democrats) and TAA (especially among Republicans) waned. Importantly, labor leaders lost whatever enthusiasm they ever had for TAA. They wanted to retain the jobs, not cushion the blow. If TAA helped get further trade liberalizations through Congress—which is precisely what JFK had intended—organized labor counted that as a negative, not a positive. The TAA program has been changed by Congress many times over the years, most recently in June 2015, and now exists in four different variants, called the 2002, 2009, 2011, and 2015 programs. Complicated enough for you?

It is fair to say that Trade Adjustment Assistance has not lived up to President Kennedy's expectations, either politically or economically. Politically, it has failed to take the edge off the hostility to free trade. Economically, it has operated on too small a scale and has emphasized assistance more than adjustment. In 2016, for example, only about a hundred thousand workers were covered, and funds for job training were capped at $450 million. Adjustment? The average participant remains on TAA for almost two years, suggesting pretty slow adjustment.

There are at least two related reasons for TAA's small scale. One is the meager resources the US government puts behind the program. All TAA programs for workers spent only about $850 million in FY 2017, a comparative pittance.

The other reason is that TAA benefits such as job training, assistance with job searches, relocation allowances, help with health care premiums, and other income support are hard to access. A group of displaced workers must petition the Labor Department, showing that their job losses were due importantly to foreign trade. Then the petition must be certified by the Department of Labor, which happened in 72 percent of cases in 2015. Finally, benefits are received only while displaced workers remain unemployed and are in training. The consequence of all these requirements is that a mere 57,631 workers were certified to receive TAA benefits during fiscal 2015.

Some of these shortcomings could be mitigated by a more generous TAA budget and by making it easier for trade's victims to access the program, both of which Congress can and should do. But there are deeper problems, not so easily fixed. Most prominently, displaced American workers want a hand *up*, not a hand*out*. They want a job, not a glorified form of unemployment insurance. Some labor leaders have derided TAA and other palliatives as "burial insurance." They'd rather block the trade agreements and skip the funeral. As Robert Shiller, one of the few economists who pays attention to psychology, put it, "people desire a sense of vocational accomplishment, rather than simply money to live on. . . . Redistribution feels demeaning. It feels like being labeled a failure."

Regardless of the underlying reasons, when a program designed to help labor gets so little support from organized labor, its political prospects are bleak. The lack of support for TAA actually points to a broader and deeper problem—one that may lie at the heart of many Democrats' disdain for free trade. It is one thing to proclaim that every worker is entitled to a job. The landmark Employment Act of 1946 did precisely that more than seventy years ago. But it's quite another thing to proclaim, even if tacitly, that every worker is entitled to *his or her present job*—a promise that is impossible to keep in an ever-changing economy.

No one ever wants to be fired. But policies that lock specific workers into specific jobs in specific places are a recipe for stasis and stagnation, as several European countries have demonstrated over the years. Remember, about five million Americans gain or lose jobs every month. Five million! If that huge volume of job churn were severely reduced, the dynamism and productivity of the US economy would be diminished accordingly. Indeed, some observers fear this loss of dynamism is already happening. Trade is one of several market mechanisms that move capital and labor to where they are most needed. The process can be painful, but it is highly functional—indeed, essential.

Soft-hearted but hard-headed economists and politicians should want to make it less painful.

Bogus Arguments Against Free Trade

You hear many antitrade arguments in the political arena, but few in academia. Some of these arguments have elements of validity; I'll come back to these. But let's start with the ones that generally don't.

First, no one—well, *almost* no one—opposes fairness. But when you hear someone express support for *fair* trade but not *free* trade, watch out. More often than not, it's a smokescreen for protectionism. Just think about how often President Trump bemoans how *unfair* it is that Mexican companies can sell goods to American consumers without paying any tariff.

A rough translation of the fair trade argument is this: because Country X engages in restrictive trade practices, we should, too. Taken literally, the assertion is false. If Country X deprives its citizens of (some of) the gains from trade, it does not follow that we should follow suit by hurting our own citizens as an act of spite. That's what Henry George had in mind when he wrote 130 years ago: "What protection teaches us, is to do to ourselves in time of peace what enemies seek to do to us in time of war." George understood that Americans lose out if our trading partners erect barriers to our exports, but we also lose out if we retaliate by barring imports.

A much older case for trade protection, often attributed to Alexander Hamilton, is the so-called infant industry argument. It holds that fledgling industries with the potential to grow into mighty behemoths may need temporary shelter to allow them to mature—sort of like shielding a fragile flower from the harsh elements. Premature exposure of these promising infants to tough foreign competition, the argument goes, could kill them before they get a chance to blossom. Sounds plausible, superficially. Very superficially.

Remember, Hamilton developed this argument for the brand-new United States of America, where almost every industry was an infant.

Applying it to an advanced economy like the contemporary United States is a bit weird. If the "infant" industry really has glowing prospects, why doesn't private capital rush in to seize the profit opportunities—as it did for railroads in the nineteenth century, automobiles in the early 1900s, the personal computer industry in the 1970s and 1980s, the Internet in the 1990s, and social media today? Every one of these industries eventually flourished, even though many of the earliest companies went bust. That's the nature of entrepreneurship, which is not for the faint-hearted. Hamilton's America was no doubt short on venture capital and private equity; modern America is not. So the argument was a lot stronger in 1790 than it is now.

Furthermore, once an infant industry grows accustomed to being sheltered from competition, whether foreign or domestic, it may be difficult to find the right moment to take the diapers off. Industry executives will explain to attentive local politicians that their marvelous businesses—which employ *so many* constituents—would be devastated if trade protection were lifted. And they might be right; competition does kill off inefficient firms. However, it also yields huge benefits to the general public. Besides, it's the American way.

A third bogus argument alleges that American workers, with their high wages and generous benefits, cannot compete successfully with cheap foreign labor. That belief, for example, led Donald Trump to let slip in a November 2015 presidential primary debate that "wages are too high" here—an impolitic remark. And do you remember Ross Perot's "giant sucking sound" in 1992? That was supposed to be the sound of American jobs going to low-wage Mexico.

But the assertion that cheap foreign labor will decimate employment in the richer country flies in the face of the principle of comparative advantage. Trade leads to job *changes*, maybe lots of them, but not to mass *unemployment*—as David Ricardo explained two hundred years ago. Moreover, as American labor moves into industries in which we have a comparative advantage—which, you'll recall, typically pay higher-than-average wages—average American earnings should rise, not fall.

FIGURE 8.3 Import Share and Unemployment, United States, 1984–2015

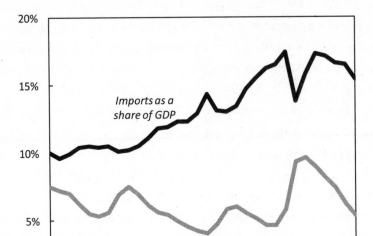

Source: US Bureau of Labor Statistics; US Bureau of Economic Analysis.

These are not just abstract arguments from economics textbooks. If import competition really kills jobs, we should have seen unemployment in the United States rising as import penetration rose. But Figure 8.3 shows no such correlation. Chronic trade deficits arrived in the United States in the early 1980s, and since then the share of GDP imported (upper line) has risen almost steadily, moving up from about 10 percent in 1984 to nearly 18 percent before the Great Recession hit. But the unemployment rate (lower line) displays only ups and downs, reflecting cycles of boom and bust, with no trend whatsoever. Unemployment is actually lower today than it was in the late 1980s. Yes, just as Ricardo foresaw, American workers exposed to import competition found employment elsewhere.

How did they manage that? The essence of the answer is that a nation's real wages depend fundamentally on the productivity of its workforce, not on foreign trade. The main determinants of labor productivity are the skills and education of the nation's workers, the amount and quality of capital each has to work with, and the state of the nation's technology. American workers score highly on all these criteria. So productivity and wages are high here and will remain so whether we trade or not. Many poor countries, by contrast, score poorly on these same criteria. That's why they're poor.

Modern incarnations of the "cheap foreign labor" argument go beyond wages, pointing out that labor standards (child labor, workers' rights, and so forth) and environmental standards are far laxer in poor countries than in the United States. This is, allegedly, another aspect of unfair competition. Okay, suppose we feel aggrieved that Chinese workers can't unionize and are choking on filthy air. For these reasons, modern trade agreements virtually always include chapters on environmental and labor standards. But the basic argument for trading with poor nations stands more or less where Ricardo left it. It is true that poorer countries have lower wages, lower labor standards, and fewer environmental controls. They also have fewer iPhones and cable TV channels, and they pay their soccer players less. They're poor! But if we refuse to trade with such countries, their workers will become even more impoverished. Besides, in order to sign a trade agreement with us, their governments will almost certainly have to upgrade their labor and environmental standards.

Politicians and others who oppose trade agreement often lean heavily on faulty reasoning. Here are four examples.

"Trade agreements" are not "trade." The biggest trade issue of the 2016 campaign was the Trans-Pacific Partnership. US participation in it died the day Donald Trump was elected. To call the fuss over TPP "much ado about nothing" would be an exaggeration. But "much ado about little" is about right for the United States, where the estimated effects of TPP on the economy were projected to be small. According to a massive study by the US International Trade Commission, the TPP would have raised real GDP in the United States by 0.15 percent and employment by 0.07 percent after fifteen years. No, that's not

0.07 percent per year, but 0.07 percent in total. In a word, TPP would have created too few jobs to notice. Sure, it would have been better to have those jobs than not, but no one can call this a big deal.

Second, the agreement was to be among eleven nations in addition to the United States. That sounds like a lot, but we already had free trade agreements with six of them. The remaining five were Brunei, Japan, Malaysia, New Zealand, and Vietnam. Apart from Japan, I don't see any giants there. And we have had a variety of trade agreements with Japan over the decades. So to a first approximation, TPP was about further liberalizing trade with Japan, which is neither a poor nor a low-wage country.

Third, you may have noticed that China, the bête noire of protectionists these days, was not on the list. Which brings me to my main point: "trade agreement" is not synonymous with "trade." Trade across national borders is a natural economic phenomenon; it takes place unless the power of the state is used to prevent it. In particular, trade does *not* require trade agreements, which makes it easy to exaggerate how much trade agreements really matter. Our volume of trade with China at present is huge. Yet apart from the fact that both the United States and China belong to the World Trade Organization (along with 162 other countries), we have no trade agreements with the People's Republic of China.

As a matter of fact, most trade agreements are no longer mainly about tariffs and quotas. They concentrate instead on nontariff barriers, impediments to trade that derive, for example, from different regulations in different countries. For example, the European Union bans a number of genetically modified American agricultural products from its markets. The ban is based on health worries that the US government believes are unfounded. Another important example was the preservation of patent rights of US pharmaceutical companies in the TPP negotiations, which elicited howls of protest from a number of poor countries that could ill afford the high prices that US drug manufacturers charge.

Trade restrictions may not save jobs. It seems obvious that, say, protecting the US automobile industry from foreign competition will save the jobs of some American autoworkers. Doesn't it? Yes, that *is* obvious. But think a little harder, and you'll see the wisdom of Ronald Reagan's warning about looking over your shoulder.

Suppose trade restrictions force Americans to buy fewer Japanese cars, thereby saving some auto jobs here—as happened in the 1980s (under Reagan, ironically!). One side effect is that American banks, acting on their customers' behalf, will offer fewer dollars for sale on the world market to buy yen. The reduced supply of dollars will pull up the value of the dollar relative to other currencies. That, in turn, will make US goods and services more expensive to potential foreign buyers, who will react by buying fewer American products—thereby costing some other Americans their jobs. The job losses will probably be just a few here and a few there, sprinkled all over the economy. But they add up. The cheaper yen will also make Japanese goods—say, electronics—less costly to American buyers. As we buy more (non-auto) items from Japan, still more American jobs will be lost.

That's presumably what President Reagan had in mind when he observed, "No one ever looks over their shoulder to see who lost their job because of protectionism." Unfortunately, the chain of logic leading to this conclusion is a bit long for politics. Try turning the preceding paragraph into a sound bite.

Protectionism is a clumsy way to redistribute income. Trade protection is often advocated as a way to save American workers from job loss, wage compression, or both. The claim has surface validity. As just noted, protecting American autoworkers from Japanese competition will preserve some particular jobs and may also allow some particular wages to be somewhat higher.

But as we have just seen, other American workers will lose their jobs or suffer wage losses as a result. Consumers will also pay higher prices for imported goods. So, in a real sense, protectionism robs Peter to pay Paul. If you are concerned with the distribution of income, you should wonder about who is richer, Peter or Paul? Often it's Paul.

Start with jobs and wages. For decades, some of the strongest trade protection went to the US steel and automobile industries, which happened to pay about the highest wages in American manufacturing. Thus low-wage Peters were being asked to sacrifice for high-wage Pauls.

But don't stop there. Protected industries also get their profits protected, and this aspect of the redistribution from trade is clearly regressive. If more money flows to capital, and less to labor, income inequality is almost certain to rise.

Finally, let's remember all those Walmart shoppers—that is, most of the citizenry. The rich can easily afford to pay a bit more for the goods and services they buy. The poor cannot. The evidence shows that poor people, both in the United States and elsewhere, gain more from easing trade restrictions than rich people do. Why? Because they buy more cheap foreign products. One study of forty countries found that the wealthiest consumers would lose 28 percent of their purchasing power if trade was cut off, while those in the bottom tenth would lose 63 percent. Here's an amusing US example: imported stainless steel spoons, which are cheap, presently face a 14 percent tariff, while expensive imported silver spoons pay just 3 percent.

Bilateral trade deficits are not important. President Trump singled out Mexico and China for special disapprobation because the United States runs large bilateral trade deficits with each. He has argued that we are "losers" because Mexico and China sell more to us than we sell to them. Does that make sense?

No. Just like domestic trade, international trade is inherently multilateral, that is, many-sided. Your iPhone or iPad or Mac has components made by companies in China, Taiwan, the Philippines, South Korea, and elsewhere—and, of course, by other American companies. Apple presumably runs large bilateral trade deficits with its suppliers. So what? The company's multilateral trade surplus looks pretty good.

Closer to home, you undoubtedly run a sizable and persistent bilateral trade deficit with your local grocery or supermarket: you buy lots of stuff from them; they probably buy nothing from you. Does that make you a "loser"? Of course not, and you probably never go to bed worrying about it. After all, you run a huge bilateral trade surplus with your employer, who buys your labor and probably sells you nothing. If, however, the dollar value of everything you buy starts to exceed the dollar value of everything you sell, you may have cause for concern.

Thus, in a nutshell, while multilateral trade deficits and surpluses may matter, bilateral trade deficits and surpluses do not. You may now be thinking, "But doesn't the United States have a sizable and persistent multilateral trade deficit?" Yes, it does, and I turn to that now.

The fact that the United States has been running large multilateral trade deficits for years means, as a matter of arithmetic, that our indebtedness to foreigners has been rising—pretty dramatically, as Figure 8.4 shows. Since it first turned negative in 1989, the share of GDP represented by foreign debt has gone from about zero to about 40 percent. That's quite a lot.

Does this burgeoning debt threaten America's prosperity? Well, you may worry less about the deterioration in our net investment position once I tell you that the United States earns a much higher rate of return on our investments abroad than foreigners earn on their investments here. In terms of income flows, we are still running in the black.

But a far more fundamental reason not to worry—at least for the foreseeable future—is that the world *wants* those dollar assets; they are not being shoved down recalcitrant throats. The US dollar occupies center stage in both the world financial system and the world trading system. When Japan sells goods to Switzerland, for example, both sides may settle their accounts in US dollars, not in yen or in Swiss francs. So an ever-growing world economy needs an ever-growing supply of US dollars just to conduct its daily business. And where do those new dollars come

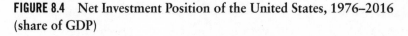

FIGURE 8.4   Net Investment Position of the United States, 1976–2016 (share of GDP)

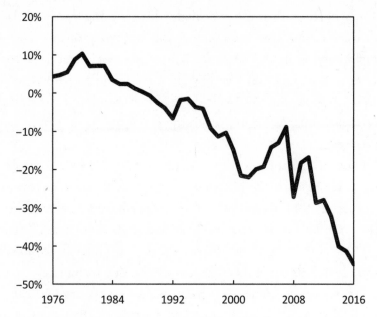

Source: US Bureau of Economic Analysis.

from? From the US trade deficit. If we were suddenly to balance our trade, the net flow of new dollars into the world economy would cease, and businesses the world over would have to find alternative currencies. That's not as easy as it sounds.

Looking at this same phenomenon from the US perspective, the central position of the dollar gives us what has been called an "exorbitant privilege." Because the world needs and wants more US dollar assets year after year, we can run trade deficits year after year, thereby acquiring more goods and services from the rest of the world than they get from us—and giving our trading partners paper assets in return. Yes, there is presumably some limit to this privilege. But that limit is nowhere in sight.

How do we know that? Because if the world was starting to get satiated with dollars, the international value of the dollar would be sinking and US interest rates would be rising. And as Figure 8.5

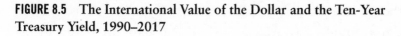

FIGURE 8.5   The International Value of the Dollar and the Ten-Year Treasury Yield, 1990–2017

The international value of the dollars is the trade-weighted US dollar index for major currencies, indexed to March 1973 = 100. Source: Federal Reserve Board, Release H.10 and H.15.

shows, they are not. In fact, the dollar exchange rate (the dark line, measured against major currencies) is about where it was in 1990—and has risen notably since 2013. Long-term Treasury interest rates (the light line) have, of course, been falling almost throughout this period.

Some Valid Arguments for Trade Protection

All that said, any honest economist will admit that free trade is not *always* the best solution. So let's consider some valid reasons why a country might want to restrict trade to protect some industries. I emphasize *might*.

I begin with the so-called national defense argument. Imagine that the United States lacks comparative advantage in manufacturing aircraft (say, France is better), in nuclear weapons (say, Russia is better), and in tanks (say, China is better). None of this is true, by the way. Should we then allow our aircraft, nuclear power, and arms industries to be decimated by foreign competition, leaving the United States relying exclusively on imports? Certainly not, for in time of international peril Russia and China might be on the other side, and France might be cut off. So even if the United States lacks comparative advantage in industries vital to our national defense, there are sound arguments for keeping those domestic industries alive, whether via trade protection, subsidies, or something else.

Okay. But it's easy to get carried away with the national defense argument for protection. After all, armies also need clothes, shoes, food, can openers—pretty much everything. For example, the US watch industry received trade protection for years on the grounds that soldiers in battle would need to tell time! (In case you're wondering, the US Army is apparently less worried nowadays. It imports most of its watches from Canada and Japan.) And as I mentioned in an earlier chapter, the US maritime industry argued for more American-flagged ships than even the Pentagon wanted.

Noneconomic goals—whether conservationist, humanitarian, or diplomatic—are a second possibly valid reason to cut off trade in particular products or with particular countries. The bans on trade in ivory and whaling products are two prominent examples. The United States is not trying to protect our domestic elephant-hunting or whaling industries. We are trying to protect elephants and whales. There may also be valid geopolitical reasons, from time to time, to ban or interfere with trade with bad actors—as we have done, in recent years, with Iran and Russia. In such cases, we *know* we are hurting American consumers, but we judge the harm to be worth it.

This thought leads naturally to what may be the toughest anti-trade argument for economists to deal with. Imagine that the US body politic was totally convinced that unfettered free trade is the best system. (That's not true, of course.) But imagine also that some other country, say, China, erects trade barriers against US goods. Now someone suggests that we threaten China with trade barriers of our own, not because we want to stop Chinese goods from getting into our country but because we want the Chinese to tear down barriers against our exports. The goal, you will note, is more open trade in both directions. The danger is that both nations wind up with high trade barriers and less trade.

Do such strategic threats make sense? It's hard to know. There is a clear analogy here to decades of disarmament negotiations with the old Soviet Union. We would threaten to build or deploy more intercontinental ballistic missiles as a goad to get the Soviets to reduce their own stockpiles. Eventually, it all worked out, and the world became a safer place. But for decades, it produced a frightening arms race. Analogously, it's possible that threatening to interfere with trade could actually lead to more open trade. But the strategy can also backfire.

So Why Can't Economists Sell Their Case?

If you have read this far, you have no doubt noticed that we economists find the case for open international trade compelling. Politicians and the body politic, on the other hand, do not—as the 2016 election amply demonstrated. Yes, economists have failed to sell the case for free trade despite two hundred years of trying. Why?

One reason was enunciated already by Adam Smith in 1776. In his words, the case for free trade "is so very manifest, that it . . . could [never] have been called into question had not the interested sophistry of merchants and manufacturers confounded the common sense of mankind." Such interested sophistry continues to this day. Those who would benefit from restricting trade continue to press their case and flex their political muscles, always cloaking their self-interest in some alleged higher national purpose. This is where, one would hope, better understanding of economics would help the electorate spot a con. But it apparently hasn't—yet.

Why not? One important reason, I believe, is that economists and other people hold starkly different visions of the basic purpose of an economy.

In the economist's vision, an economy is a mechanism for maximizing benefits to consumers. It should therefore be designed and managed to provide more and better goods and services at the lowest possible prices (relative to the wages people earn). Free and open trade helps accomplish this, just as free and open domestic competition does. We teach this lesson diligently to our youth. If you ever studied economics, you've probably heard it.

But people are also producers. A minority of them—Smith's "merchants and manufacturers"—actually run or own businesses. The vast majority works for these businesses, earning their livelihoods by producing the things consumers buy. In fact, virtually every working-age person wears two hats: we are both consumers and producers.

Economists are, of course, aware of this dual role; we are not *that* obtuse. But we emphasize the consumer part: that people live to consume. And that's where we lose touch with much of the population, which seems to place more weight on their role as employees—that is, on their jobs. As an example, a May 2015 poll by *Consumer Reports* found that nearly 80 percent of American consumers would prefer buying a product made in America (and thus made by American labor) rather than an import (made by foreign labor). More than 60 percent say they'd even pay a 10 percent premium to do so. But actions speak louder than words, and we know that Americans buy tons of foreign-made consumer goods. Still, if the well-being of producers—including businesses and their workers—takes precedence over the well-being of consumers, much of the case for free trade evaporates.*

In fact, this intellectual divide may be the biggest barrier separating economists from the public at large. In trade negotiations, gaining access to another country's market is generally scored as a "win" by politicians and the public, while granting that country's businesses

---

*But not all of it. Protecting Company A may cause harm to Companies B, C, D, and so on.

access to our own market is counted as a "concession"—meaning a sacrifice we make reluctantly to seal the deal. To economists, that's topsy-turvy. How's that again? We treasure the opportunity *to work for others* but shun the opportunity *to get them to work for us*? From the consumer's perspective, that prevailing view seems nutty. Don't we want more and cheaper goods and services, not more work? From the producers' perspective, however, it's not nutty at all: we value our jobs and want to keep them. If most people think of themselves as workers first and consumers second, we economists have been barking up quite a few wrong trees for two hundred years. Maybe it's we who need some illumination.

The disjuncture between consumer and producer interests also infects—and sometimes poisons—the politics of trade negotiations. Businesses, especially large businesses, have more political clout than consumers. While the latter are far more numerous, they are unorganized and therefore constitute a nearly negligible political force. Advocates of trade agreements understand that. So when the political battles over trade are joined, free traders typically seek help from the industries that stand to benefit from trade openings. They do not expect (or get) much help from consumer groups, even though consumers would benefit.

When corporations, seeing themselves as potential winners, step up to the plate to help push trade agreements through Congress, economists typically count that a good thing. Without such corporate support, free traders would march into battle mostly unarmed. But corporations are out to make money, not to do good deeds. Their support comes at a price, and, in consequence, the nation's trade agenda winds up looking more like a corporate agenda than a people's agenda. That corporate slant, in turn, does not endear trade agreements to the political left.

In this respect, at least, Bernie Sanders and other critics had a point: freer trade is good for (much of) corporate America. But a little illumination would help here, too. Someone should explain to critics on the left what Adam Smith explained to the world in 1776:

the fact that more trade is good for some American corporations does not imply that it's bad for most American citizens. If that point was better understood, America's trade agenda might start looking less corporate and more populist.

Finally, let's not forget the important point that globalization creates losers as well as winners. It would be one thing if the losers from more open international markets were a random sample of the population. But as pointed out earlier, they are not. Rather, they tend to be disproportionately blue-collar workers without a college education who see their jobs being "shipped abroad" either literally (when their company moves the plant) or figuratively (when their company suffers from import competition). These workers imagine, mostly incorrectly, that their jobs could have been saved by tougher trade agreements—or by no agreements at all. And they blame the government for making "bad trade deals."

Worse than that, they see correctly that the so-called elites—the owners of capital and many college-educated workers—are doing very well from globalization, the very force that is clobbering them. Which makes them angry, very angry. This anger was harnessed effectively by Bernie Sanders in the 2016 Democratic primaries, where he gave Hillary Clinton an unexpectedly strong run for her money. Then Donald Trump took the anger to an entirely new level—and to the general electorate. Despite his evident inexperience and ignorance, despite his vulgarity, misogyny, and trail of falsified claims, Trump came out on top. Globalization lost.

If anyone thought taking better care of the losers from trade was a secondary issue of minor importance before the 2016 election, they should not think that now. In the realm of economics, it may be our most urgent policy priority today.

Chapter 9

With Liberty and Inequality for All?

The white man knows how to make everything,
but he does not know how to distribute it.
—Sitting Bull

Like Sitting Bull in the nineteenth century, some people think of the rise in income inequality in the United States, which has proceeded for thirty to forty years now, as an urgent socioeconomic problem that needs to be addressed. Some people don't. Like it or not, one's views on inequality hinge sensitively on value judgments—making this an inherently *political* question, not one on which technocrats hold any advantages over politicians. That said, sound economics still can shed light on important questions like *why* inequality has risen so much (for example: Is it the "natural" working of markets, or has public policy contributed?) and *what* we as a society can do about it, if we choose to. That's what this chapter is about.

President Barack Obama clearly *did* think inequality had become a serious problem by Inauguration Day 2009, and he *did* want to do something to mitigate it. To that end, he subsequently pushed a recalcitrant Congress to make the tax code considerably more progressive, with several increases in top-bracket rates. And he created, again over stiff congressional resistance, what we now know as Obamacare, whose benefits—not to mention the taxes that finance them—are decidedly progressive. Add them together, and it amounted to a substantial redistribution of posttax income.

Eight years later, Donald Trump was elected president after campaigning as, among other things, the tribune of the working class. You may recall that he declared "I am your voice" in his acceptance speech at the Republican National Convention in 2016. Yet once in office, his policies turned mainstream Republican: his health care proposals sought to strip tens of millions of Americans of their insurance coverage, his budget proposals sought to shred the social safety net, and his tax "reform" was perhaps the most regressive tax cut in history. Democrats objected vociferously to all these things.

Yes, the two parties disagree vehemently on redistributive policy, and have for years. But what are the facts?

The Age of Inequality

The years since around 1980 are sometimes referred to as the Age of Inequality. The label fits because virtually every measure of income or wealth inequality has risen substantially since then. Three basic facts sum up the phenomenon of rising inequality in the United States: it's been *large*; it's been *long-lasting*; and inequality here is *higher* than in other advanced countries.

Start with "large." There are many ways to measure inequality. Some are simple, such as the share of income received by the top 10 percent, 5 percent, or 1 percent of the population. Others are rather complicated, such as the so-called Gini coefficient, which is computed using a mathematical formula I'll use but not torture you with.* In consequence, there is no single, crisp answer to the seemingly straightforward question, How much has inequality risen since 1980? Check that. If you don't insist on a number, there *is* a simple answer: *quite a lot.*

_____

*If you want the torture, you can find it on Wikipedia: en.wikipedia.org/wiki
/Gini_coefficient.

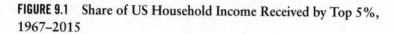

FIGURE 9.1   **Share of US Household Income Received by Top 5%, 1967–2015**

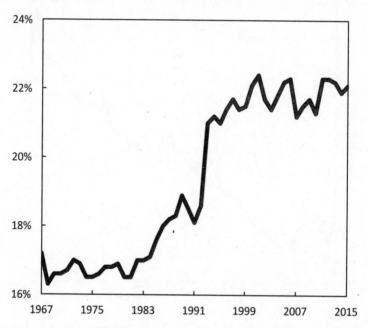

Source: US Census Bureau, Current Population Survey, Annual Social and Economic Supplement, Table H-2.

Here are three possible *numerical* answers, all based on the *same* underlying data from the Bureau of the Census. But each measures a different aspect of inequality and so gives a different quantitative answer. Had I taken data from multiple sources, the differences would have been greater still. But the picture they paint would have been consistent.

Figure 9.1 displays the share of household income received by the top 5 percent of households, ranked by income, from 1967 to 2015. This measure of the share of "the rich" was trendless (at around 16.5 percent) until 1981 and then began a steep climb up to 22.3 percent by 2006. It has been pretty stable since then.

Figure 9.2 shows an alternative measure derived by comparing the incomes of the "rich" with those of the "poor." Specifically, it's the ratio of income at the ninetieth percentile (meaning the income level

FIGURE 9.2   The 90/10 US Household Income Ratio, 1967–2015

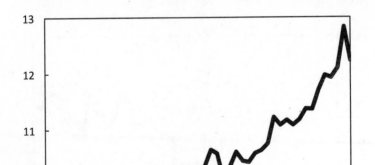

The figure shows the ratio of income at the ninetieth percentile to income at
the tenth percentile. Source: US Census Bureau, Current Population Survey,
Annual Social and Economic Supplement.

exceeded by only 10 percent of households) to income at the tenth percentile (which 90 percent of households exceed). This indicator starts
at 8.7 times in 1977 and rises to a peak of 12.8 in 2014. That last number means that a rich family in 2014 (income of about $157,700) had
almost thirteen times the income of a poor family (about $12,300).

Finally, Figure 9.3 depicts the behavior of the aforementioned Gini
coefficient, a complicated measure that pays attention to the entire
income distribution, not just the extremes. The Gini measure ranges
between zero (when every household has the same income) and 1.00
(when one household has all the income). Typical real-world numbers
run around 0.4. The Gini coefficient for the United States rose from
0.398 in 1976 to 0.477 in 2011, and then roughly leveled off. As Gini
coefficients go, a rise of 0.08 is a big deal. It's roughly the difference,

FIGURE 9.3   Gini Coefficient for US Household Income, 1967–2015

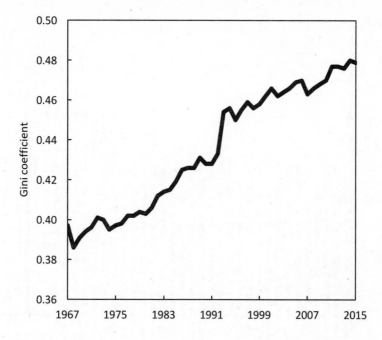

The Gini coefficient ranges from 0 (perfect equality) to 1 (perfect inequality).
Source: US Census Bureau, Current Population Survey, Annual Social and
Economic Supplement.

for example, between inequality in the unequal United States versus
in egalitarian Ireland (based on data from the Organization for Economic Cooperation and Development [OECD]).

Thus across just these three measures, and there are many others,
the rise in inequality ranged between 21 percent and 47 percent, and
the increase took place over the years 1976–2011 or 1977–2014 or
1981–2006. Take your pick. Fortunately, statistical quibbles like these
need not detain us here. The basic fact is clear: income inequality
has risen quite a lot since the late 1970s. (So, by the way, has wealth
inequality, which I won't deal with here.)

We need no additional data to demonstrate the second important
fact: that the rise in inequality has persisted for decades. Just glance
back at the three previous figures. The lines move steadily upward

FIGURE 9.4   Gini Coefficients for Household Income, 2013–2014

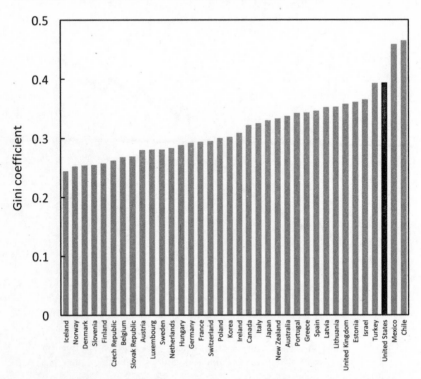

The Gini coefficient ranges from 0 (perfect equality) to 1 (perfect inequality). Data are from 2013 or 2014, whichever is the most recent year available. Source: OECD database.

with few interruptions. Yes, there is a good reason why this period of US history has been dubbed the *Age* of Inequality. It has lasted a long time—and it may not be over yet.

The final basic fact, that inequality is higher in the United States than in other advanced countries, is much harder to establish because different countries measure both income and inequality differently. Indeed, it takes a somewhat Herculean effort to create consistent data that enable scholars and policymakers to make apples-to-apples comparisons across nations. Fortunately, several teams of researchers have done exactly that over the years, and they all find that inequality in the United States is at or close to the highest among all the world's advanced industrial nations. Figure 9.4 is an example. It displays

2013–2014 data for thirty-six OECD countries. Only Mexico and Chile, which are hardly advanced industrial nations, had Gini coefficients higher than the United States.

Having looked first at *income* inequality, I now turn to *wage* inequality, which is where I want to concentrate. Why? Because for all but the richest Americans, income from work is almost the whole story. For most people, the income derived from owning capital or running businesses doesn't amount to much. The Congressional Budget Office (CBO) estimates that 80–86 percent of market income in the four lower quintiles of the income distribution derives from labor. Only in the top 1 percent is labor income a minority of total market income (36 percent). So if your concern is either envy or how vast fortunes are amassed, then by all means dote on income from capital. Neither Bill Gates nor Jeff Bezos got rich by earning high paychecks. (But LeBron James and Tom Cruise did.) If, however, you're more concerned with what's happened to the lower 99 percent of American families, you should concentrate on income from work, as I will.

Figure 9.5 is a stunner. It displays the *cumulative* increases in real hourly wage rates between 1980 and 2015 at various points in the wage distribution. The shape of the graph is disturbing. The lower 60 percent of the working population (the first six bars) garnered only meager real wage gains—in all cases, less than 9 percent over thirty-five years. Even at the 90 percent percentile, real wage gains averaged only about 1 percent per annum. But workers at the ninety-ninth percentile (the rightmost bar) did fabulously well.* Numbers like these depict a national tragedy. The Age of Inequality has left almost all working people behind.

---

*A wonkish but important note: Unlike the other percentile bars, the ninety-ninth percentile is based on annual earnings, not hourly wage rates. The former depends, in addition to wages, on hours of work per year. The annual data can be found at Lawrence Mishel and Teresa Kroeger, "Strong Across-the-Board Wage Growth in 2015 for Both Bottom 90 Percent and Top 1.0 Percent," Economic Policy Institute Working Economics Blog, October 27, 2016, epi.org/blog/strong-across-the -board-wage-growth-in-2015-for-both-bottom-90-percent-and-top-1-0-percent.

FIGURE 9.5   Real Wage Growth by Income Percentile, 1980–2015

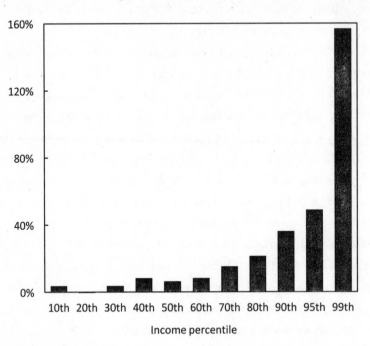

Source: Economic Policy Institute (epi.org/data/#?preset=wage-percentiles).

Why? Harsher Labor Markets

Enough data; you get the point. Why in the world did this happen? Economists have written tons of research papers—literally, I think, if you put them all on a scale—on the causes of rising inequality in the United States. An extremely short summary of all that research is that changes in the labor market—who gets paid how much for doing what—did it.

Specifically, almost all researchers agree that the most important factor by far has been what is sometimes called the race between education and technology. Many people forget about the first contestant in that important race (education) and concentrate on the second. They note that skills in the middle and bottom rungs of the US labor force have failed to keep pace with rapidly advancing technology. If technological change favors highly educated workers over poorly educated ones, as it surely has in recent decades, then we expect wages near the top to rise faster than wages near the bottom, thereby opening up wider and wider wage gaps. Which is exactly what happened.

But let's not forget the other contestant in the race: education. Many people are surprised to learn that what was once a huge American advantage in international competition—our highly educated workforce—is no longer an advantage. Rather, we've dropped back into the middle of the pack and are in danger of slipping even further behind the leaders. There are many ways to look at this phenomenon, none of which paints a pretty picture. If we compare US adults with those of other countries, we find that our college completion rates, once the envy of the world, now rank us behind such countries as Spain, Slovenia, and Russia. If we look at what students actually *learn* in school, as measured by the latest Program for International Student Assessment (PISA) tests of high school students, the United States ranked fortieth in the world in math literacy, twenty-fifth in science literacy, and twenty-fourth in reading literacy. I could go on.

Now apply some rudimentary economic analysis to the two-contestant race. Suppose rapidly improving technology boosts the *demand* for highly educated labor, relative to that for poorly educated labor. And suppose further that the school system fails to keep pace, so the *supply* of highly educated labor doesn't keep pace. Highly educated labor then becomes *relatively* scarcer, and markets naturally bid up its price. We would then expect wages near the top of the educational ladder to race ahead of wages near the bottom, which is exactly what US data so vividly show.* In 1983, the average college graduate earned 49 percent more than the average high school graduate—a hefty pay gap, to be sure, but not quite like living on different planets. By 2013, that margin had soared to a mind-blowing 83 percent.

---

*More educated workers also experience fewer, shorter spells of unemployment. So not only do they earn more per hour, over the years they work more hours.

So education lost the race to technology. But that's not the whole story. Some additional inequality can be laid at the doorstep of the dramatic decline in unionization, which fell from 20 percent of all employed workers in 1983 (and was once much higher) to just 11 percent in 2015. Muscular unions once extracted higher wages from employers. But *muscular* unions are hard to find these days. Indeed, outside the government sector, it's getting increasingly hard to find unions at all. Across the entire private sector, unionization is down to a paltry 6.7 percent of workers—just one worker in sixteen.

Another piece of the inequality puzzle stems from international competition, which we discussed at length in the previous chapter. Here's an astounding fact. Taken together, the rise of China, the awakening of India, and the collapse of the Soviet Union essentially doubled the world economy's effective labor force over a period of a decade or two while bringing in little usable capital. You don't have to be an economist to understand that a huge increase in the world's supply of labor thrust American and Western European workers, especially less skilled workers, into a much tougher competitive environment. Capital, on the other hand, benefited from its relative scarcity. No wonder profits fared better than wages and high wages fared better than low wages.

A third factor leading to increased inequality, especially at and near the bottom of the US wage ladder, is the sagging minimum wage. Figure 9.6 shows that the federal minimum wage fell from 50 percent of the average wage in 1978 to barely over 30 percent by 2015. (Many states have minimum wages above the federal minimum wage.) Had the national minimum wage remained at half the average wage, it would be over $11 per hour today.

Finally, let me mention a possible factor that economists hesitate to talk about because we can neither measure it nor even define it precisely: the breakdown of the previous social contract between labor and capital. Virtually every profitable business generates a little surplus here and there—company revenue that exceeds what the firm must pay to attract the labor, capital, and other factors of production it

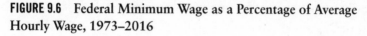

FIGURE 9.6   Federal Minimum Wage as a Percentage of Average Hourly Wage, 1973–2016

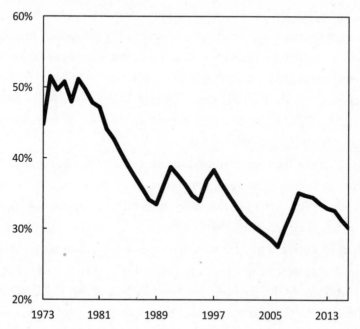

Source: US Department of Labor; Economic Policy Institute.

needs. In the "good old days" of the 1950s and 1960s, management used to share some of this largesse with its workers, perhaps by paying wages above what the market demanded or by granting employees generous fringe benefits. A bit of corporate paternalism was the norm then. Today, it's closer to devil take the hindmost.

What happened? One major development was the shareholder value revolution, which glorified the idea that every dollar of surplus belongs to the shareholders. The one and only proper goal of the corporation, according to many academic economists and practitioners, is to maximize the company's stock market value. Giving any of the surplus to workers interferes with achieving that goal. Thus did kinder, gentler capitalism give way to meaner, tougher capitalism—to the detriment of American workers. The latest manifestation of this phenomenon is the so-called gig economy, in which workers receive virtually no fringe benefits and corporate paternalism is pretty much unknown.

I believe that story, as do some other economists. The problem is that we believers cannot prove our case either theoretically or, more important, statistically. And in economics, what cannot be measured and demonstrated with data might as well not exist. (That's not so in politics. Remember, they are two different civilizations.) The social contract theory of rising inequality may or may not be true, but we have no way to put a number on it.

Or do we? One highly imperfect measure of the dominance of shareholder value over corporate paternalism is the ratio of CEO pay to average wages. After all, those sky-high CEO compensation packages are dominated by bountiful stock options and the like, not by high hourly wages. The idea was that paying top executives in stock options would align their interests with those of the shareholders. Data compiled by the Economic Policy Institute show that CEO pay at America's 350 largest firms rose from 30 times the compensation of their average workers in 1978 to 276 times in 2015. Do we really believe that CEOs became almost ten times more valuable, relative to ordinary workers, over those years?

Then Tax Policy Piled On

So markets turned ferociously against labor, especially against low-skilled and manufacturing labor, during the Age of Inequality. That's most of the story. But perhaps the saddest part is what came next, when the US government, unlike most other governments around the world, decided to pile on with regressive tax policies that cut taxes for the richest Americans, rather than try to limit inequality's rise. In a football game, such nasty behavior would be flagged as unnecessary roughness and penalized fifteen yards.

The tax part of the story starts with Ronald Reagan. In fairness, no one in 1981 knew that market-based income inequality would rise for the next thirty-five years or so. So don't blame Reagan for gratuitous cruelty to labor. Nonetheless, the income tax cuts he pushed through Congress were decidedly regressive. Some of this regressivity was reversed under Bill Clinton, who, for example, raised the top income tax rate and increased the Earned Income Tax Credit drastically. But Clinton was followed by George W. Bush, and another huge round of tax cuts tilted strongly toward the rich. Once again, Barack Obama took a lot of this back with tax hikes on the rich and other equalizing measures like Obamacare. But he was followed by Donald Trump, who failed to undo Obamacare but pushed through one of the most regressive tax cuts in American history in 2017.

Add all this up, and you are forced to conclude that the tax policies of the US government joined hands with the anonymous but powerful forces of the market to push income inequality higher.

But wait. Taxes are only one of two pieces of the tax-and-transfer system that transforms *market-based incomes* that people earn into the *net disposable incomes* they live on. Taxes are taken out, but transfers get added back in. Needy Americans receive payments from such programs as Social Security, unemployment insurance, food stamps, Medicaid, housing subsidies, and more. Presidents Reagan, Bush, and Trump all railed against what is colloquially called "the welfare state." Perhaps because of congressional resistance, their barks were far worse than their bites. Nonetheless, there were some bites.

You have no doubt noticed that each of these attacks on the social safety net was mounted by a Republican administration. Democrats have been cast as the party either defending the safety net or seeking to expand it. This is not a selective reading of history.* Not only is it accurate to portray Democrats as friendlier to the poor and near-poor than Republicans, but the difference goes beyond attitudes: the data clearly show that income inequality rises under Republican presidents and falls under Democrats.

---

*It is true that the 1996 welfare reform passed under a Democratic president, Bill Clinton. But Republicans then held majorities in both houses of Congress.

Now add up all the federal government action on taxes *and* transfers over periods of both Democratic and Republican control, and stir the pot. What do you get? According to a comprehensive CBO study, the tax-and-transfer policies of the federal government reduced income inequality by almost exactly the same amount in 2013 (the final year of their study) as in 1979. Thus over the Age of Inequality, the free market turned ferociously against low- and moderate-income Americans, and the federal government basically sat back and let it happen.

The Tradeoff Between Equality and Efficiency Revisited

Could the US government have helped more? Could it have battled back against the powerful market forces that were pushing inequality up? Certainly, though at some cost. And it might not have won the battle.

I mentioned several chapters ago that economists generally believe there is a tradeoff between equality and efficiency. Society can deploy such tools as progressive taxation, more generous transfer programs, and higher minimum wages to reduce inequality. But each takes a toll—even if a small one—on economic efficiency by dulling incentives. That annoying side effect is pretty much inherent in the idea of using taxes and transfers to redistribute income. The market dishes out highly unequal rewards, based on each person's success or failure in the economic game. If the government increases taxes on the rich, it diminishes the rewards for success. If it provides more generous benefits to the poor, the jobless, or the homeless, it diminishes the penalty for failure. So, as in the well-worn metaphor, as you cut the pie more equally, you probably also shrink it.

For those who live near the bottom of the income distribution, a larger slice of a smaller pie is a good deal. But if you live near the top, a smaller slice of a smaller pie holds far less appeal. For this obvious reason, political wars over redistribution often pit rich versus poor, with the rich, or rather their lobbyists and sympathetic politicians, not mounting the Gordon Gekko defense ("greed is good"), but rather arguing that higher taxes and more generous transfer payments damage economic efficiency.

Do they? Almost certainly yes, though the damages are frequently exaggerated. Neither the advent of the progressive income tax in 1913 nor the New Deal in the 1930s ended capitalism as we know it—despite the jeremiads of the times. The US economy also did very nicely, thank you, during the Eisenhower and Kennedy years, despite top marginal tax rates above 90 percent. Indeed, statistical evidence that the US economy grows faster when income tax rates are lower is sorely lacking—despite the confident claims of Presidents Ronald Reagan, George W. Bush, and Donald Trump. (More on this in the next chapter.)

That said, no economist argues that incentives don't matter, and having a social safety net certainly dulls them. Workers covered by unemployment insurance are a bit fussier about taking the first job that comes along. Businesses invest less when the returns on investment are taxed more heavily. Taxpayers bend themselves into proverbial pretzels to take advantage of tax loopholes. Each of these actions takes a toll on efficiency.

So what do you do if you find current levels of inequality intolerable—or at least undesirable? (Remember, not everyone does.) The tradeoff teaches us three main lessons.

First, if society decides to deploy the power of the state to reduce inequality, it should concentrate on redistributive policies that do the *least* harm to economic efficiency. If there was any bipartisanship left in America, this lesson would command broad bipartisan support. It's one place where more economic illumination could do a lot of good.

Second, redistributive tools should generally be used in moderation. There is a reason why socialist economies like Cuba's and North Korea's look economically lifeless; incentives have been dulled to the point where they barely exist. These are extreme examples, to be sure. Closer to home, the 90 percent income tax rates of the 1950s and 1960s were probably too high, even though Americans of the day adapted to them. So is a $15 *national* minimum wage. (In Mississippi, the *average* wage is just $18. Think about it.) Besides, this is America, not France or Denmark. Compared to Europe, the political appetite for redistribution here is limited. Republicans understand this better than Democrats.

Third, the US government probably doesn't have enough firepower to beat back powerful market forces pushing toward greater inequality. So it's unlikely that even determined government action could have turned the Age of Inequality into an Age of Equality. But liberals think it would have been nice to have tried; we could at least have made a bad situation somewhat less devastating. Democrats understand this better than Republicans.

With these three broad lessons in mind, let's get more specific. Where might more *illumination* about redistribution actually take us? And would American politics go there?

For openers, consider the following important principle of taxation: it is harder to raise taxes on mobile factors of production than on immobile factors—whether "mobility" refers to geography, industry, or type of economic activity. Thus, for example, high geographical mobility makes it hard for city governments in liberal bastions like San Francisco and New York City to redistribute income too much. Rich people facing high tax rates can (and will) move out, eroding the city's tax base. Poor people offered generous benefits can (and will) move in, ballooning the cost of the city's generosity. It is therefore more sensible to assign the job of redistribution to the federal government because people are far less likely to change countries than to change cities.

A second doleful application of the same mobility principle is to the relative taxation of labor versus capital. The rich own almost all the capital; that's why we call them rich. So egalitarians often favor higher taxes on interest, dividends, and capital gains. It makes sense. But watch out; here's where illumination can help. The distressing reality is that capital is far more mobile than labor. So if a country—not to mention a state or a city—tries to tax capital more heavily, money may simply flee to a kinder jurisdiction. Moving is harder for labor. So while concern for equality calls for higher taxes on capital, recognition of efficiency costs may call for lower ones. There is indeed a tradeoff.

What Policy Can Do: The Social Safety Net

That said, every Western democracy tempers raw, free-market capitalism with some sort of safety net that employs progressive taxes and transfer payments, among other tools, to mitigate inequality. Not all safety nets are created equal, however. And too few Americans, it seems, realize that ours is thin by international standards.

How thin? To make comparisons across countries, I turn to data compiled by the OECD, focusing on the United States and eight other advanced nations—our peer group, so to speak. Using the Gini coefficient to measure inequality, the top line of Table 9.1 shows that all taxes and transfer payments, taken together, reduced income inequality by 22 percent in the United States. Is that a lot or a little? Well, judge for yourself, but every other nation in this table did more redistribution. By this metric, the US government stands out as providing the *weakest* safety net.

Whether that's something to be proud of or ashamed of is a matter of opinion. To soft-hearted believers in the principle of equity, it's a source of shame. America looks mean-spirited toward its poor. To hard-headed believers in noninterventionist government and the principle of efficiency, it's a source of pride. It means we interfere less with market outcomes. Judging by the battles that frequently roil American politics, Americans seem pretty divided on whether more redistribution would be a good thing or a bad thing. For example, since 1998 the Gallup poll has been asking Americans intermittently whether taxes on the rich should be increased for the purpose of redistribution. The country is almost evenly divided on this question. Many of us prize equality of opportunity—even if it's a myth—over equality of outcomes.

TABLE 9.1   Government Redistribution in Nine Countries

Country	Gini Coefficient Before Taxes and Transfers	Gini Coefficient After Taxes and Transfers	Percent Change
United States	.508	.394	−22%
Canada	.440	.322	−27%
Australia	.483	.337	−30%
Japan	.488	.330	−32%
United Kingdom	.527	.358	−32%
Sweden	.443	.281	−37%
France	.504	.294	−42%
Denmark	.442	.254	−43%
Germany	.508	.292	−43%

Source: Author's calculations based on OECD data.

What, concretely, does a thinner safety net look like? After all, no country practices social Darwinism. While the orderings are not identical, as you move down the list of nations in Table 9.1, you generally find countries with more progressive tax systems, higher taxes in general, and more generous social welfare programs to support the poor and near-poor.

The United States and Germany offer a convenient case study because, by sheer coincidence, the two countries displayed exactly the same amount of inequality in market incomes that year. The level of inequality generated by a country's markets depends on myriad factors, and the US and German economies differ in numerous ways. Yet somehow, when all the dust settled, markets in the two countries dished out precisely the same degree of inequality—to three decimal places! (As Table 9.1 shows, the Gini coefficient in each country was 0.508.)

But that's before the two governments got into the act with redistributive taxes and transfer programs. Once taxes were taken out and transfers added in, Germany's after-tax (and transfers) Gini coefficient dropped all the way to 0.292, but ours fell only to 0.394. That huge difference stemmed from different government policies, not from different market outcomes. Like most Western European democracies, Germany has a thick social safety net for its workers, unlike anything we have ever seriously considered in the United States. Germans, for example, take universal health insurance for granted and, should they need it, receive unemployment benefits for up to two years. In a word, the United States is kinder to its rich—the government lets them keep more of their money—and Germany is kinder to its poor.

At this point, readers with an egalitarian bent may start jumping to a premature conclusion: the US should emulate Germany by thickening its social safety net and making its tax system more progressive. After all, other rich European countries have lived that way for years and seem to have prospered.

Hmm. But first let's remember that average market incomes are higher in the United States than in Germany—and *after-tax* disposable incomes are higher yet because the tax burden is smaller here. Yes, Americans are richer than Germans on average, and part of the reason is that we allow free markets a freer hand.

Second, American attitudes toward redistribution by government fiat differ from the attitudes that characterize most other Western democracies. The Declaration of Independence may have declared that "all men are created equal," but its main author kept slaves and believed "that government is best which governs least."* Forget the eighteenth century, and jump to the twenty-first. Modern Americans appear not to be a very equality-loving people by first-world standards. I guess it's part of American exceptionalism. The amount of inequality a country gets depends critically on its citizens' value judgments, as voiced through their political representatives. Let's face it. The United States is a high-inequality country partly because we're content to be a high-inequality country.

---

*The famous quotation "That government is best which governs least" is often attributed to Thomas Jefferson, but historians have never unearthed evidence that he said it.

But wait. Suppose our politicians paid closer attention to the principles of equity and efficiency and accepted a bit more illumination from economics. Maybe then the American government would design more efficient redistributive mechanisms. According to Table 9.1, we now use the tax-transfer system to reduce inequality by 22 percent. Suppose doing so costs us X percent of GDP in terms of lost efficiency. What if sounder policy choices could reduce that cost to, say, half that amount? Would we then "buy" more equality? No one can know for sure, but I'd like to think the answer is yes.

What Policy Can Do: Market Wages

When it comes to income inequality, however, markets are far more important than government redistributive policies. If natural developments in labor markets increase wage disparities by large amounts, as has happened in recent decades, governments will almost certainly be unable to reverse the trend toward greater inequality by using progressive taxes and transfers. In Germany, for example, inequality in market-based incomes rose (by the Gini measure) from 0.429 in 1990 to 0.508 in 2013.

Furthermore, the "losers" may not welcome the types of governmental assistance that economists typically recommend. Nobel Prize–winning economist Robert Shiller put it this way, in explaining Donald Trump's appeal to the working class:

> Those on the downside of rising economic inequality generally do not want government policies that look like handouts. They typically do not want the government to make the tax system more progressive, to impose punishing taxes on the rich, in order to give the money to them. Redistribution feels demeaning. It feels like being labeled a failure. . . .
>
> The desperately poor may accept handouts, because they feel they have to. For those who consider themselves at least middle

class, however, anything that smacks of a handout is not desired. Instead, they want their economic power back. They want to be in control of their economic lives.

Perhaps. But there may also be an important asymmetry. Potential recipients of public benefits such as Trade Adjustment Assistance, unemployment insurance, or food stamps may be less than eager to acquire them, seeing receipt as stigmatizing. But once actual recipients are collecting such benefits, they may feel sorely aggrieved if the monies are taken away. They will certainly be poorer.

That said, Shiller's claim that people greatly prefer dignity and a job to dependency and the dole is probably both true and important. Unfortunately, applying this notion to policies that would mitigate inequality is no mean trick. It involves, among other things, changing labor market outcomes—something the US government has traditionally been loath to do.

Yes, we have a minimum wage that sets a wage floor that businesses may not breach. That's not a handout; it's something earned by working. But the federal minimum wage now stands at a meager $7.25 per hour, so few firms would want to breach it anyway. (Many states and a few cities set higher minimums.) Similarly, the Fair Labor Standards Act currently decrees that employees earning under about $24,000 a year must be paid extra for overtime work. Again, that additional income is earned, not given. But such a low-income cutoff covers only about 7 percent of full-time salaried workers—compared to 62 percent when it was set in 1975.* Once a worker gets above such low thresholds, the US government basically leaves wage setting to the market.

---

*Late in President Obama's second term, the Department of Labor issued a rule that would have roughly doubled the overtime ceiling. President Trump cancelled it. US Department of Labor, "Overtime for White Collar Workers: Overview and Summary of Final Rule," May 18, 2016, dol.gov/sites/default/files/overtime -overview.pdf.

Sadly, in recent decades market forces have pushed toward greater inequality. As mentioned earlier, the rise of China, the awakening of India, and the fall of the Soviet Union—three powerful disequalizing forces—tilted the playing field strongly against labor and in favor of capital. Those same forces also produced greater inequality *within* the distribution of wages by hurting low-skilled workers while helping (at least some) highly skilled workers.

The upward march of technology—a force vastly stronger than international trade—has had similar effects. The Luddites have been proven wrong time and time again: automation did not make jobs disappear. But they might have been right if they had concentrated on relative wages instead. Certainly in recent decades, technological advances have improved the job market prospects of highly skilled workers, especially college-educated workers, while creating a hostile environment for low-skilled workers. Like globalization, technology has been a force for greater inequality.

As noted, the US government has barely even tried to counteract these powerful market trends. Could it have done more? I think so.

For openers, strong evidence supports the unsurprising hypothesis that tight labor markets reduce wage inequality while slack labor markets exacerbate it. Look at the two scatter plots in Figures 9.7 and 9.8. The upper panel shows that real wages grow faster when unemployment is low and slower when unemployment is high. You might have guessed that! The lower panel shows that wage *inequality* (measured, again, by the Gini coefficient) is lower when the unemployment rate is lower and higher when the unemployment rate is higher. Put those two findings together, and you have this conclusion: tight labor markets benefit labor as a whole and especially low-wage labor. Tight labor markets are medicine against inequality.

How have we been doing on this score? Quite well, if you look only at very recent years, but not so well if you look back a bit further. Over the period from January 2015 through June 2017, the national unemployment rate averaged 5 percent. You can call that "full employment," or at least a reasonable facsimile

FIGURE 9.7 Real Wage Growth and Unemployment, 1948–2013

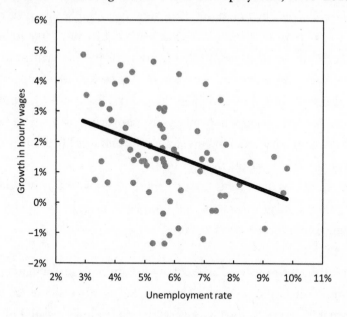

FIGURE 9.8 Wage Inequality and Unemployment, 1968–2012

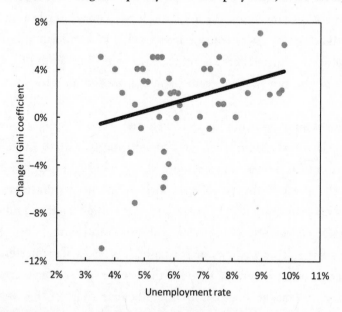

Figure 9.7 shows changes in inflation-adjusted compensation per hour and the unemployment rate between 1948 and 2013. Figure 9.8 shows changes in the Gini coefficient and the unemployment rate between 1968 and 2012. Source: Alan S. Blinder, "Petrified Paychecks," *Washington Monthly* (November/December 2014): 29–34.

thereof. But now consider the years during and after the Great Recession, 2009–2014. The unemployment rate averaged 8.2 percent over that six-year period, a high rate that both held back wage growth and exacerbated inequality. While inequality is not uppermost in the minds of Federal Reserve officials when they make monetary policy, nor of members of Congress when they make fiscal policy, running a high-pressure economy is probably the government's single most powerful weapon for reducing inequality. Recessions breed inequality like stagnant water breeds mosquitos.

But there is also a long list of other, albeit weaker or slower-acting policies the government could pursue if it really wanted to reduce wage inequality. Here are a few:

A higher minimum wage. Raising the minimum wage obviously puts more money into the pockets of the lowest-paid workers—as long as they don't lose their jobs. Conservatives have long resisted higher minimum wages both because they intrude on the prerogatives of business and because they allegedly kill jobs. The scholarly evidence refutes the claim of large-scale job loss—at least for modest minimum wage increases. But all bets are off for the more-than-doubling of the federal minimum wage that some people proposed in 2016.

More profit sharing. Though it's largely an unknown story, many US companies pay a share of their profits—normally a small share—to their workers as a wage supplement. Many others do not, however. Should the government encourage more companies to share profits, perhaps by providing tax incentives for so doing? That would certainly interfere with free markets; as things stand today, every firm decides for itself. But perhaps surprisingly, this particular interference with market outcomes might not violate the principle of efficiency—or at least not violate it much. Why not? Because research shows that profit-sharing firms get better performance from their workers in return. So firms reap a productivity dividend that offsets part or all of their higher labor costs.

The upshot is that a little nudge from the government might lead to more efficiency, not less. Such a nudge would not be difficult to provide. Here's one simple idea: amend the tax law so that corporations may deduct the high-powered incentive pay they offer to top executives only if they offer incentive plans to all their workers. (If you must know, it's Section 162[m] of the tax code.) I guarantee you that will get the CEO's attention.

Strengthening unions. Declining unionization has been one factor holding down wages. And intermittent hostility from government has been one reason behind that decline since President Reagan broke the back of the air traffic controllers' union in 1981. George W. Bush's appointees to the National Labor Relations Board (NLRB) were decidedly less friendly toward organized labor than Bill Clinton's or Barack Obama's, and Republican intransigence left two NLRB seats open when Donald Trump moved into the White House. He quickly named Philip Miscimarra, a lawyer with extensive experience representing management against labor, as the new NLRB chair. If the US government wanted to take a stand against rising inequality, rather than piling on, it could switch sides and start helping unions win wage gains, rather than undermining them. Good luck with that in this administration.

Vocational training and apprenticeships. Our comparatively free labor markets place the United States near the bottom of the league tables in both apprenticeships and vocational training. Here's one set of shocking statistics: the United States has just 0.2 percent of its labor force in formal apprenticeship programs, compared to 2.2 percent in Canada, and 3.7 percent in Australia. Canadians and Aussies seem a lot like Americans. Why can't we do as many apprenticeships as they do? In 2017, President Trump proposed that we up our game here. Americans are also light-years behind such world leaders as Germany in providing vocational education to students who are not bound for college, even though the prospective income gains for people trained to be, say, plumbers, electricians, or carpenters are quite high. (Have you tried to get one to your house lately?)

The United States can and should provide much more apprenticeships and vocational training, each of which can open the door to well-paid jobs for non–college-educated workers. Instead, we seem bent on ignoring the experience of other nations and leaving ourselves trapped in a situation in which the government thinks businesses should do it and businesses think the government should. It would be better if both would.

Occupational licensure. You probably wouldn't want to be treated by a doctor who is not licensed to practice medicine. You may also prefer a licensed electrician when you need work done in your house. But what about the locksmith who makes new keys, the stylist who does your hair, and the truck driver who delivers packages? Must they be licensed too? Here's a stunning fact that few people know: in the early 1950s, fewer than 5 percent of US workers were required to have a license; by 2008, that share had risen to almost 29 percent. Was that sixfold increase really warranted by mounting health and safety concerns, the considerations typically used to rationalize licensing requirements? Or might it echo the medieval guild system—erecting barriers to keep people out of certain lines of work? Many economists think it has strong elements of the latter, and that less licensure would open up more opportunities, especially for non–college-educated labor.

K-12 education. Taking a longer and broader view, the now-creaky American education system was once the envy of the world—and one of the main nonsecrets of our fabulous economic success. In the nineteenth century, the United States created "universal" primary education—a revolutionary idea at the time. Then we started graduating record numbers of teenagers from high school and eventually sending unheard-of numbers to college. No other major country came close. Today, however, the education levels of America's workforce no longer give us a leg up on the competition. We're mediocre at best.

This is not the place for a lengthy disquisition on what's wrong with K-12 education in the United States, nor am I the right person to offer it. Suffice it to say that the agenda is lengthy and goes way beyond just spending more money. But one important point is vital in the present context: for the K-12 education system to help us reduce inequality, we must focus a disproportionate share of any incremental resources on the poor and middle classes. The private market doesn't do this so well. Government has to take the lead.

Pre-K education. I have saved what may be the most important education policy for last, mainly because society must wait almost a generation to see it bear fruit. Many kids from lower-income backgrounds do not receive high-quality pre-K education—and that puts them at a distinct disadvantage relative to richer kids, who do. While not entirely unequivocal, the weight of the evidence suggests that this disadvantage is large and long-lasting. For example, several studies have found that poor children put through high-quality educational programs at age three or four subsequently perform better in school and drop out less. As adults, they commit fewer crimes and earn higher incomes.

A comprehensive report by the President's Council of Economic Advisers in 2014 estimated that each dollar invested in early learning programs eventually returns about $8.60 to society, roughly half of which comes from higher earnings as adults. Some think that estimate is too high. But even if the benefits are only half as large, pre-K is still an outstanding investment. How many for-profit businesses return four times the original investment? But here's the rub. While investment in pre-K education pays rich dividends, most poor people cannot afford to make it—which is why government should step in. The question for Congress and state legislators needs to change from "How can we afford it?" to "How can we afford not to do it?" And it's not very expensive. Pre-K teachers do not cost much.

Why Doesn't Policy Do More?

So while there is no magic bullet, there is a long list of ways in which public policy could chip away at the inequality problem. And some of them would hold broad, bipartisan appeal if there was any bipartisanship left in America. Why, then, hasn't the US government tried harder to reduce inequality? Here, I think, the economic reasons are relatively unimportant, while the political reasons are crucial.

But let's start with the economics—in particular, with the nagging tradeoff between equality and efficiency, a lesson we may have learned too well. Since most policies that reduce inequality also reduce efficiency, many people seem to have concluded that the game is not worth the candle. "Let's not try to redistribute income," the reasoning goes, "for it might hurt our fragile market economy." But the right lesson is that we should pursue greater equality in the most efficient ways. The tradeoff creates a speed bump, not a wall.

Furthermore, recent evidence suggests that it's a mistake to apply the tradeoff idea to economic *growth* (how fast does the pie grow?) as opposed to economic *efficiency* (how big is the pie today?). While scholarly debate continues, the preponderance of evidence to date— and there's a lot of it—suggests that higher inequality may actually retard, rather than promote, growth.

Figure 9.9, which comes from an International Monetary Fund study, is just one example among many I could show. It displays a modest *negative* statistical association between a country's inequality of net income (after taxes and transfers) and its GDP growth over the following decade, using all available data from 153 countries over the period 1960–2010. No, don't jump to the conclusion that greater equality is a sure path to faster growth. The correlation is weak, as you can see. My point is simply that it's not possible to find a *positive* relationship in these data. Higher inequality does not lead to faster growth.

How can this be, in view of standard incentive arguments? In extreme cases, the answer is obvious: workers so poor that they're

FIGURE 9.9   The Correlation Between Inequality and Growth

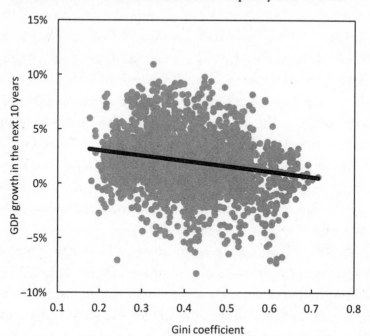

Growth rates are from the Penn World Tables, and Gini coefficients are from Frederick Solt's Standardized World Income Inequality Database. Source: Jonathan Ostry, Andrew Berg, and Charalambos Tsangarides, "Redistribution, Inequality, and Growth," Staff Discussion Note, International Monetary Fund, February 2014, 16.

undernourished aren't productive. But that observation can't be terribly relevant to the contemporary United States or other rich countries. Yes, low-income Americans are poor by first-world standards, but few of them are starving. Rather, the main problem in the rich countries seems to be that low-income families cannot avail themselves of the educational opportunities that would make their children more productive as workers. So the poor and near-poor build less human capital, and in consequence both they and the economy suffer.

If inadequate education within, say, the bottom 40 percent of the income distribution is the essence of the problem, the remedies are clear. Economics, having pointed the *way*, can step aside and let the political system find the *will*. Sadly, there are good reasons to think it won't do so. If you've read this far, you know most of them, so I'll be brief.

First, political decision making in America is highly partisan, and the currently dominant party systematically opposes virtually every policy that would reduce inequality, whether it's Medicaid, food stamps, "welfare," or whatever. In fact, Republican proposals from health care to budgets to tax reform actively seek to *widen* inequalities. Remember Speaker Paul Ryan's concern that our tattered social safety net might provide an alluring "hammock" for the lazy and indolent. Or perhaps you recall *Wall Street Journal* editorials some years ago that labeled people too poor to pay federal income taxes the "lucky duckies." How lucky to be so poor!

Those political attitudes were not changed by Donald Trump's "working man" rhetoric in the 2016 campaign. On the contrary, the new administration embraced congressional Republicans' regressive health care bills, offered an amazingly regressive set of budget cuts that would have eviscerated the social safety net, and proposed an even more amazingly regressive tax plan that feathered the richest nests. Fortunately for America's working class, only a little of this agenda made it through Congress.

Second, money talks in American politics—loudly. And money does not normally speak out in favor of redistribution. That the rich have a disproportionate influence on political decisions is obvious to everyone and extends well beyond the realm of redistribution to almost all facets of American political life. Political scientist Martin Gilens has found, for example, that the opinions of people in the middle of the income distribution count for naught in terms of whether or not a particular policy becomes law. The opinions of those at the ninetieth percentile, by contrast, have a strong influence. Shocked? I didn't think so.

Third, redistribution in America has long labored under the burden of racial attitudes. Experts are fond of pointing out that more poor people are white than black. It's true. In 2015, for example, poor whites outnumbered poor blacks by almost three to one. But that's mainly because whites outnumbered blacks by about six to one in the general population. Poverty *rates* tell a different, and racially tinged, story: the share of blacks living below the poverty line in 2015 was 24.1 percent, more than double the share of whites (11.6 percent). In consequence, white people who harbor racial resentments can, with some statistical validity, view antipoverty programs as "for those people." In our society, sadly, attitudes like that undermine political support for antipoverty measures.

So the short answer to the question "Why doesn't the government do more?" is: politics. Economics provides a modestly long list of policies that could ameliorate, though certainly not eliminate, inequality. But the American political system won't adopt them. Attitudes toward redistribution are laden with value judgments, and, to put it bluntly, we Americans are not very egalitarian compared to, say, Western Europeans.

A Role for Illumination?

Could we do better? Economics certainly doesn't offer all the answers—not even close. Even if economists ran the world—a fanciful, or perhaps horrifying, thought—we would not know how to abolish poverty or inequality. Maybe we could only make a dent. But American politics has set the bar really low, making it child's play to improve on the status quo. That's the basis for my claim that our nation's policies toward income inequality could be more effective if politicians would accept more economic illumination instead of just insisting on political support for preconceived notions.

The Lamppost Theory of redistribution plays out quite differently for Democrats and Republicans. For Democrats, most of whom are disposed to tackle the inequality problem, the main need is to concentrate more on evidence-based policy rather than what's been called policy-based evidence. In many cases, redistributive policies *will* shrink the pie. Let's not deny that. Supply-side economics may be a comic exaggeration, but incentives do matter. So let's seek out redistributive policies that shrink the pie just a little, or maybe even expand it. And let's not get swept up by romantic ideas like a $15 national minimum wage. (A local minimum wage of $15 per hour in San Francisco is another matter entirely.) Nor that cutting the United States off from international trade will help reduce poverty. (It won't.)

For Republicans, let's recognize that those "lucky duckies" who are too poor to pay income taxes are not reveling in their good fortune, that the unemployed would prefer a hand up rather than a handout, and that sheer luck plays a larger role in economic success than the economically successful care to admit. And let's recognize, first, that the United States really doesn't do much for society's underdogs, and second, that we could do a lot more in ways that could be (but aren't now) bipartisan. I am thinking, especially, about education broadly conceived, ranging from pre-K for three-year-olds all the way to vocational training and apprenticeships for young adults who don't go to college. Remember that Horatio Alger was born into the New England aristocracy and attended Harvard—advantages not shared by many.

Here, as elsewhere, it's not a matter of finding a magic bullet that will return inequality to 1980 levels, nor even a boxful of such bullets. Rather, it's a matter of moving the needle a bit. We don't know how to solve the inequality problem, but we could manage it much better than we do. More hard-headed but soft-hearted thinking based on evidence—more illumination, if you will—and less partisan ranting would help.

Chapter 10

The Political Quicksand
of Tax Reform

This might mark the historic moment when Washington
decided that it no longer will bother to blush.

—George F. Will (December 2017)

Is there any hope for bipartisanship in today's Congress? The 2017
"debate" over tax reform suggested not. You might have thought that
reforming our mess of a tax code offers intriguing possibilities. After
all, here's what a column in the *New York Times* reported two influential members of Congress, one a Republican and one a Democrat,
as saying about taxes just four days before the 2016 election:

- Representative Kevin Brady (R-TX), the chairman of the
  House Ways and Means Committee: "Americans are sick of
  this broken tax code. . . . They're ready for someone to lead on
  tax reform and make it simpler and fairer."
- Senator Ron Wyden (D-OR), the ranking Democrat on the
  Senate Finance Committee: "I think we can all agree the tax
  code is a dysfunctional mess."

Pretty similar attitudes. And both correct. But when it came down to
cases, partisanship trumped everything.

Here's the problem. At the fifty-thousand-foot level, everyone—from taxpayers to economists to politicians of both parties—agrees that our income tax system is a hideously complex and unfair mess, crying out for reform. Everyone, it seems, hates the tax code—except the accountants and tax lawyers who earn nice livings from it. The paradox is that, even though seemingly everyone agrees that today's tax code is unfair, inefficient, and mind-numbingly complex, we don't fix it. Why not?

The answer is disarmingly simple. As the proverbial airplane descends through the clouds, and the passengers start to get glimpses of the ground, the superficial agreement falls apart. Yes, the tax code is a national disgrace. Yes, it needs fixing. At that level of generality, everyone is on board. But look a little closer and it's: No, don't take away *that* exemption or limit *that* deduction or take away the privileged treatment of *that* type of income. Get the money somewhere else—and from someone else.

This rampant disagreement played out dramatically in the congressional debate over the tax code in 2017. First, no Democrats were invited to the party; Republicans decided to push legislation through on a strictly partisan basis, without seeking opinions from the minority party. Second, even that proved difficult as different Republican senators and representatives had different ideas about what should—and should not—be in the tax bill.

The hard political truth is that the tax code wasn't created by a bunch of mischievous gremlins acting randomly. Every special interest provision got in there because some politicians, probably adhering to exquisite political (not economic) logic, wanted it there. Perhaps more important, the politicians, vested interests, and lobbyists still value those loopholes. Decades ago, the late Senator Russell Long (D-LA), who chaired the Senate Finance Committee for fifteen years, famously enunciated the first principle of tax reform as "Don't tax you. Don't tax me. Tax that fella behind the tree." Long's insight remains true today. *My* special tax preference, of course, is in there for good reasons—and is very much in the national interest. It's *his* loophole that should go.

Most economists—admirably brave because we never have to face the voters—oppose most of the special tax breaks that hide behind Long's proverbial trees. "Gimmicks" or "loopholes" we call them, and it's not meant as a compliment. If I tell you that Congress should end the carried interest loophole, the scandalous provision that taxes most earnings of private equity billionaires lightly, you'll probably agree—unless you're in the business or are a hired gun for those who are. Ditto for the numerous egregious loopholes for real estate developers that likely helped Donald Trump avoid federal income taxes for years. (More on real estate shortly.) Same with various and sundry preferences for oil and gas extraction, most of which are too complicated to explain and too painful to behold. The list goes on and on. In these obscure corners of the tax code, public opinion would probably align squarely with the critical views of economists—if the public had any idea what's going on.

But let economists continue their list of things they'd like to do away with under the banner of "tax reform," and you'll soon be in for a few surprises that won't bring smiles. Like abolishing the mortgage interest deduction. Like treating employer-provided health insurance as taxable income to workers. Whoa! At this point, virtually everyone except the economists will be jumping ship. (*You call those loopholes?*) Politicians will be leading the pack in defense of these (and other) subsidies to middle-class families. None of them wish to follow the economic logic of tax reform into political oblivion. Yes, Russell Long was right: one person's unjustifiable tax gimmick is another's mother's milk.

A Thought Experiment: Tax Reform Without Politics

No, this is not one of those three-guys-in-a-rowboat jokes. But it's close. Imagine that, instead of what happened in 2017, we could lock six people in a room: three economists who specialize in taxation (one Democrat, one Republican, and an independent) and three tax lawyers (ditto), none of them very political people, none of them ideologues, and none of them beholden to lobbyists. They're not allowed out until they agree on a plan for comprehensive tax reform—not every detail, of course (that could take weeks or months), but agreement on all major issues. Could they do it? How long would it take? My guess is that they could get it done in less than half a day.

Left to their own devices in an imaginary politics-free zone, the technocrats would almost certainly and quickly agree on four key principles for tax reform. First, the tax code should raise enough revenue to pay the government's bills. How large those bills should be is a matter for others to decide, but true tax *reform* would not lose revenue. Second, the tax code should be far simpler than it is today. Third, the code should promote fairness ("equity"), rather than redistribute income capriciously or along political lines. To those who lean left, equity is often identified with progressivity, but those who lean right don't always agree. Fourth, the tax code should promote efficiency, which often (but not always) means interfering less with market-based decisions. (Economists often speak of "minimizing tax distortions.")*

Then, if they were truly technocrats, our hypothetical sextet would follow these principles to their logical conclusions, which would lead them to vast areas of agreement and only a few major disagreements. Those could be ironed out in the spirit of compromise. Remember, the door is locked until the deal is done!

Now change the thought experiment by adding, say, twelve elected politicians to the mix—six from each party. In this second, and far more realistic, thought experiment, the politicians outnumber the technocrats two to one. Could this group of eighteen people get the job done in a day? Don't be silly. A week? Hardly. A generation? Maybe a slim chance, but don't bet on it.

---

*There are instances in which economists favor "distortions" because they correct some flaw in the market mechanism. The most prominent example is emission taxes to reduce pollution.

More likely, the politicians would start the process by undoing some of the handiwork of the technocrats as being political nonstarters. Then, adapting the memorable words that the late Senator Daniel Patrick Moynihan (D-NY) once used to describe the near-death of tax reform in 1986, "We commenced to overhaul the tax code . . . and with the best of intentions made things steadily worse. On the day we voted the depreciation life of an oil refinery to be five years, something told us our immortal souls were in danger." Yes, their souls, but probably not their political careers. Therein lies the problem.

The politicians would not think first about efficiency, maybe not even equity. They would think first about self-preservation. They would not want to do anything that endangers their reelection prospects—such as ending the home mortgage deduction. Next, if there was any next, they would start doling out political favors to constituents who can help their reelections—Moynihan's five-year refineries being one prime example. Since different politicians get their bread buttered in different places, the likely result would be intense partisan squabbling, presumably ending either in stalemate or in a bazaar of unprincipled political horse trades that make things "steadily worse."

Recent history offers a clear parallel to the stalemate scenario. Back in 2010, the issue was not tax reform but rather how to reduce the federal government's large budget deficit—something both parties professed to want. Looking for a bipartisan deal, President Obama and congressional leaders appointed eighteen members to the National Commission on Fiscal Responsibility and Reform, often called the Simpson-Bowles Commission after its two cochairs: Alan Simpson, a former Republican senator, and Erskine Bowles, a former Democratic White House chief of staff. The commission consisted of twelve members of Congress, six from each party, plus six distinguished public members appointed by the president. Its mandate was to devise a comprehensive budget plan "to improve the fiscal situation in the medium term and to achieve fiscal sustainability over the long run"—a plan that both parties could accept. The idea was that the plan would be sent to Congress for consideration, and—it was hoped—for a vote, if fourteen of the eighteen members agreed.

That didn't happen. In December 2010, the plan endorsed by the two chairmen—and lauded by many editorialists and budget experts—"won" by an underwhelming 11–7 vote, well short of the required supermajority. More interesting for present purposes is the way the vote broke down. Among the twelve sitting members of Congress, the vote was 6–6. Deadlock. Among the six public members (including Simpson, a former politician), it was 5–1 in favor. As would likely happen in any bipartisan commission on tax reform, the nonpoliticians were nearly unanimous while the politicians were hopelessly divided along partisan lines. *C'est la vie.* We live in a democracy, not a technocracy. Which, in a nutshell, is why tax reform is so hard.

Always a Bridesmaid?

There are few issues in which the clash between political and economic civilizations is more pronounced than on taxes. There are therefore few issues on which the illumination economists can offer is welcomed less by politicians. (*Please go home, and take your nutty ideas on the mortgage interest deduction with you.*) One result is that tax reforms always seem to be on the national agenda, as was true in the 2016 election and after, but rarely get enacted. (Remember, the last major tax reform that clearly closed loopholes came in 1986! The 2017 tax bill actually created several new ones.) Always a bridesmaid, never a bride. Why?

Rampant dissatisfaction with the tax code is apparent. Who in America thinks the code adheres to either the principle of equity or the principle of efficiency? Pretty much no one. Who in America thinks our tax code is no more complicated than it needs to be? Probably no one. So you might think that fixing the tax system presents members of Congress with a potential political gold mine. (*Anything is better than this!*) Since voters hate the tax code, improving it should bring smiles to many faces. *Should*. Yet those prospecting for political gold don't dig here. Why not?

One reason mentioned already is that Democrats and Republicans are nowhere close to agreement on the key ingredients of tax reform. The latest effort, which passed Congress in late 2017, held a lot of appeal for Republicans but little for Democrats. Here are a few components that were highlights from the Republican perspective but lowlights to most Democrats:

- The corporate tax rate, which was 35 percent at the time but ridden with loopholes, was cut dramatically to 21 percent.
- The top marginal tax rate for individuals was reduced to 37 percent.
- If your income comes from partnerships, sole proprietorships, or limited liability corporations—sort of like Donald Trump's—your tax rate is reduced more. But exactly how much requires complex calculations.
- The estate tax exemption, which then limited the tax to about 0.2 percent of all decedents (only the very wealthy), was doubled.
- The federal income tax deduction for state and local taxes—a key benefit to residents of high-tax blue states—was reduced drastically.

There's more, but you probably get the idea. Regardless of your party affiliation or opinions on tax reform, the Republican proposals were clearly not designed to attract bipartisan support. And they didn't.

In fact, when it comes to reforming the tax code, I think politicians in both parties agree on only one thing: that the (mainly unsolicited) advice they receive from economists is something between useless and counterproductive. The reasons are not mysterious.

One is that economists obsess over efficiency. They disdain most special interest provisions because such provisions enable congressional tax writers to override the market judgments of consumers and businesses, sometimes even turning investments that lose money on a pretax basis into profit makers after taxes. Economists call such overrides "tax distortions," and typically don't applaud them.

Politicians see the world entirely differently. Efficiency doesn't much engage them when it comes to the tax code, even if they pay ardent lip service to markets in other contexts. Nor does economic efficiency capture the minds of citizen-voters, who find it either obtuse or boring—probably both. The following is a major case in point.

Most economists agree that, with perhaps some minor exceptions, the share of GDP devoted to owner-occupied houses should be determined by market interactions between consumers deciding how to spend their money and builders and developers seeking profit. American politicians, however, have never accepted this market solution. They've decided to subsidize homeownership in some of the least efficient ways.

Start with the buyers. Mortgage interest payments have been tax-deductible on personal income tax returns since the income tax began—presumably based on a false analogy to *business* interest payments, which *are* deductible expenses. But the analogy doesn't hold. Businesses pay taxes, or at least should pay taxes, on the incomes they earn from their factories, offices, stores, and whatever else they finance with debt. Their interest payments are a cost of doing business, just like electricity; so they are tax-deductible, just like other business expenses. Homeowners, by contrast, *do not* pay taxes on the "imputed income" they "earn" by not paying rent to a landlord. So why should they be allowed to deduct their interest expenses, economists ask?

Yes, economists ask that question, *but almost no one else does.* Most American homeowners would be appalled by the idea of losing their mortgage interest deduction. It's only fair, isn't it? Actually, it isn't—and many other countries, like Canada, don't let taxpayers deduct mortgage interest. If Tweedledee, a homeowner, pays $2,000 a month in mortgage interest while Tweedledum pays $2,000 a month to rent an identical house, and if their incomes are the same, is it fair that Dee pays less income tax than Dum? Most economists say no. But virtually all politicians defend the mortgage interest deduction as if their political lives depend on it—which they well might. After all, about 64 percent of American households own homes. Politically, that's case closed, and President Trump knew that. (*Will someone rid me of these troublesome economists?*)

Actually, the politicians have a better *economic* point than they realize—or care about. When you go to the market to buy a house, its price will be *higher* because the mortgage interest deduction makes homeownership cheaper on an after-tax basis. That means that, in a real sense, *you pay for the loophole up front.* Well, sort of—and that's why the unfairness does not end with comparing owners and renters. You have to consider, among other things, people's incomes.

Why? Because the main tax benefits for homeowners are structured as tax deductions, which are worth more in higher income tax brackets, not as tax credits, which would be worth the same to every taxpayer. That $2,000 mortgage interest deduction is worth only $200 in tax savings to someone in the 10 percent bracket, but $740 to someone in the 37 percent bracket. Furthermore, many middle-class taxpayers claim the standard deduction (which was $12,600 for joint returns in 2016) rather than itemize their deductions. According to the latest IRS data, almost 90 percent of tax filers with adjusted gross income below $50,000 took the standard deduction, a number that will rise because of the new tax bill. For them, the mortgage interest deduction was worth exactly *zero*, while a mortgage interest credit would have been of value. Above the $200,000 income mark, 90 percent of taxpayers itemized their deductions and therefore benefited from the mortgage interest deduction. Does that sound fair?

Nor is it efficient. Making homeownership cheaper after taxes induces people in higher tax brackets to own rather than to rent. It also encourages such households to purchase bigger, more expensive properties with correspondingly bigger mortgages. In consequence, we Americans devote too much of our GDP to housing and shoulder too much mortgage debt.

The bucks don't stop there, though. There are more tax gimmicks on the sell side of the real estate market, where the builders, real estate developers, and others live. Thanks to revelations over Donald Trump's unreleased tax returns in 2016, more Americans than ever now realize that real estate is notoriously favored by the tax code. One particularly egregious example (out of many) is called "like-kind" exchanges, and you can bet that Mr. Trump has taken advantage of it numerous times. Here's how it works.

A developer, let us say, bought an apartment complex for $10 million some years ago and is about to sell it for $30 million. In principle, he should owe taxes on his $20 million capital gain—just as he would if he was selling an appreciated block of common stock. But since he's selling real estate, he can defer the capital gains tax by pairing the sale with what's called a "like-kind" purchase of another property. The rules for what constitutes "like-kind" are astonishingly lenient. The IRS describes them thus: "Like-kind property is property of the same nature, character or class. . . . Most real estate will be like-kind to other real estate." *Any* other real estate? A gambling casino and a condominium complex, perhaps?

A tax deferred is a tax reduced. But that's just the beginning. The deferral game can be played over and over again. Worse yet, when the developer eventually dies and passes his remaining properties on to his heirs, all capital gains taxes are forgiven, not just deferred. Are you outraged to learn this? You should be. But this egregious loophole is not in the tax code by accident. Someone put it there purposefully—to serve a particular interest group. The reasons were political, not economic. And the loophole survived the 2017 "reform."

The mortgage interest deduction and like-kind exchanges are emblematic of an entire class of tax loopholes that economists hate but politicians love. Economists hate them because they violate both the principle of equity and the principle of efficiency. Politicians love them because they buy votes. Sadly, both are right.

Here's the essence of the problem: as loopholes and gimmicks proliferate, the whole tax code becomes worse than the sum of its parts. Maybe it makes sense to favor homeownership. After all, homeowners take care of their properties better than renters do and have greater stakes in their communities. That's worth something to society, though we might wonder how Canada manages to be so civilized without it. We might also ask why we should shower these benefits disproportionately on upper-income groups.

But what about the huge tax breaks for private equity? Or for oil and gas extraction? Or for multinational corporations that stash their profits abroad? Maybe each tax break has a valid economic or social rationale, though I doubt it. But when you enact hundreds of such gimmicks, you wind up with an unholy mess that distorts economic decision making, consumes inordinate amounts of taxpayer time and money, disgusts the citizenry, and undermines faith in our democracy. That's our tax code, and the 2017 tax overhaul opened as many loopholes as it closed.

How did we let this garden get so badly overrun with weeds? The main answer is simple, and we have encountered it before. It inheres in the stark difference between economic calculus, which would never countenance such weeds, and political calculus, which revels in them.

Special tax gimmicks—especially complicated ones that hardly anyone understands—enable political entrepreneurs to bestow large favors on powerful constituencies, who will not only notice but be duly grateful. The costs of these gimmicks get spread across millions of taxpayers, who don't even know they're being victimized. That's an alluring combination to an enterprising politician: the winners love you, and the losers don't notice. But it's anathema to economists: a small number of sharp-eyed winners get to take advantage of a huge number of unknowing losers—and to damage the efficiency of the economy to boot.

Now turn that logic around, and you'll see why tax reform so often fails. Reformers are always trying to close loopholes, whether it's to raise revenue or to pave the way for lower tax rates. But terminating any particular tax preference would impose sizable costs on a small but identifiable minority in order to secure tiny per capita gains for the large but amorphous majority, most of whom won't even know it's happening. Under the naive calculus of economics, these are good deals. But when evaluated under political calculus, they are potential disasters. Naturally, politics trumps economics. The result is that privileged minorities rule.

This does *not* mean, I hasten to add, that no tax preferences are *ever* justified. For example, there may be good social reasons to provide tax breaks for charitable giving. (But why make them deductions rather than tax credits?) It *does* mean, however, that legislators should be more careful than they are about what gets labeled a "good cause" deserving of a tax break. One simple test is to ask "good for whom?" If the answer is the oil industry, real estate developers, or private equity moguls, maybe Congress should think twice. More generally, one person's good cause may be someone else's outrageous gimmick, as Russell Long understood. Maybe everyone agrees that tax preferences A, B, and C, which top the list, are well justified. But by the time we move down to tax preferences X, Y, and Z, our immortal souls may be in danger.

Even if the ethics of tax gimmicks doesn't concern you, a tax code that resembles a Swiss cheese undermines economic efficiency and forces overall tax rates to be higher because the tax base has been so severely eroded. Here, as everywhere, there is no such thing as a free lunch. A narrower tax base means higher tax rates.

Common Misunderstanding 1: The Flat Tax

When it comes to taxes, confusions, misunderstandings, and outrageously false claims abound. I'll deal with only a few, starting with a simple one: the oft-repeated claim that the so-called flat tax would be a vast simplification over what we have now. That's dead wrong, and here's why.

The computation of your annual income tax bill comes in two steps. Step 1, the calculation of taxable income, constitutes 99.99 percent of the work—and it's devilishly complicated. That's where you—or, more likely, your accountants—encounter the crazy quilt of exemptions, exclusions, deductions, puzzling preferences, and maddening rules that make the tax code such a nightmare. Unless your tax life is very simple—maybe you have only wages and a bank account—computing your taxable income can be a nightmare of complexity. If your tax life is at all complicated, it can try your sanity. Step 1 is where we need simplification—desperately. All serious tax reformers know that. But the 2017 tax "reform" was not about simplification.

Once you've calculated your taxable income, step 2, which is computing your tax bill, is a piece of cake. It takes about five seconds on a calculator. Yet that's where the political flat taxers claim to achieve major tax simplification. Can they be serious? No.

Flat tax proposals generally call for a single bracket rate on all taxable income above a certain threshold. For example, during the 2016 Republican primaries, Senator Ted Cruz (R-TX) proposed a ludicrously low 10 percent tax rate on all income above $36,000 for a family of four. (Ludicrously low because a 10 percent rate would bring in far too little revenue; more serious flat-tax plans have a rate more like 17 percent or 20 percent.) Under his plan, there would be just one tax bracket instead of the current seven. Does that constitute significant tax simplification? You be the judge after reading the next paragraph.

Under the 2016 tax code, if your taxable income fell below $99,000, which was true for about three-quarters of all taxpayers, you simply looked up your tax bill in a table. There was nothing to calculate. If your income was higher, you encountered a calculation such as the following, which applied to joint filers with taxable income between $152,000 and $231,000 in 2016: "Multiply your taxable income above $152,000 by 0.28, then add $29,518." Now, that's not too hard, is it? Under Cruz's flat tax, the corresponding instructions would read: "Multiply your taxable income above $36,000 by 0.10." That's a lot simpler?

To provide meaningful simplification, a flat tax must go back to step 1 and prune dozens, if not hundreds, of loopholes and gimmicks from the calculation of taxable income. That's not easy, as all genuine tax reformers know. In fairness, serious advocates of flat taxes generally do propose eliminating many tax preferences and gimmicks. That's where the simplification actually comes from—not from the flatness of the rate structure. Yet Cruz's plan explicitly retained the deductions for mortgage interest and charitable contributions, and one wonders what other preferences would have remained had his proposal ever made it to the halls of Congress.

If flattening the income tax bracket structure would not simplify tax compliance, what would it accomplish? And why do some politicians and economists plump for it? Simple. A flat tax would vastly reduce the tax bills of the very rich. Take the Cruz plan as an example. If your taxable income is $1,000,000, your federal income tax bill under the Cruz plan would be $96,400—instead of $341,666 under the actual 2016 bracket structure. Nice. Move up to a lofty $10,000,000, and a 10 percent flat tax would cut your tax bill from $3,905,666 to just $996,400. Even nicer. These are pretty sweet deals for the rich and super-rich, even though they would not make life much easier for their accountants.

Flat tax advocates do not, of course, brag about how regressive their plans are—except at the dog whistle level. (The rich hear the message.) Rather, they boast that a low, flat rate would give economic growth a big boost—the kind of growth miracle that radical tax cutters have been promising, but not delivering, since Ronald Reagan was a candidate.

Let's take a quick look at the evidence on the growth question, starting with a simple scatter diagram (see Figure 10.1). Here I have plotted the top bracket rate in the personal income tax, for each year from 1929 through 2012, on the horizontal axis, and the average real

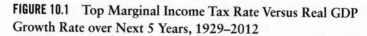

FIGURE 10.1 Top Marginal Income Tax Rate Versus Real GDP Growth Rate over Next 5 Years, 1929–2012

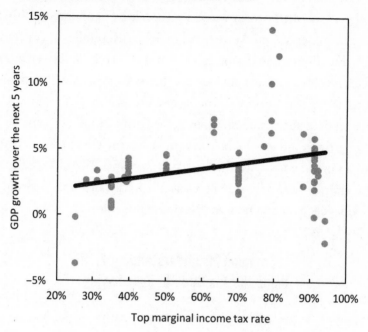

Sources: US Bureau of Economic Analysis; Tax Foundation.

GDP growth rate over the following five years on the vertical axis. The five-year period allows time for low taxes to have effects on growth. If low top rates were indeed an elixir, you would see slower growth, on average, when tax rates were higher. What you see instead is slightly faster growth when tax rates are higher, though the relationship is weak. Yes, some major events like wars and the Great Depression are buried in these data,* and I would never argue that raising tax rates is a sure route to faster growth. But this simple graph certainly makes it hard to argue the opposite case.

---

*That said, the positive correlation gets a bit stronger if I remove the data points for 1929 through 1950 from the scatter, thereby getting rid of the Great Depression and World War II.

While this picture may be worth a thousand words, literally thousands of pages of research bolster its message. A comprehensive recent review of that voluminous research by economists William Gale, a Democrat, and Andrew Samwick, a Republican, concluded that "while there is no doubt that tax policy can influence economic choices, it is by no means obvious . . . that tax rate cuts will ultimately lead to a larger economy in the long run." As they observe, "U.S. historical data show huge shifts in taxes with virtually no observable shift in growth rates"—including comparing the United States before it had an income tax with the United States since World War II.

In short, the supply-side boast is a leap of faith unsupported by any evidence. You might as well sprinkle pixie dust.

Common Misunderstanding 2:
Using the Tax Code to Spur Saving

One place where support and illumination from economics collide in more complex ways is the tax treatment of income from capital: interest, dividends, and capital gains. Many conservative economists and politicians argue, with some validity, that taxing the returns on saving distorts decisions by favoring spending now over saving for the future. A more efficient tax structure, they argue, would tax spending, not earning. Specifically, a consumption tax would be better than an income tax because, by not penalizing saving, it would induce more.

Many liberal economists and politicians line up on the other side in this debate, however, because they care more about equity. Compared to an income tax, a consumption tax is regressive for a simple and obvious reason: the poor and middle classes earn hardly any income from interest payments, dividends, or capital gains. Specifically, the CBO estimated that these three sources of income account for only 3–4 percent of total income in the lower two quintiles of the income distribution. The corresponding figure in the top 1 percent is about 30 percent.

So it appears we have a conflict between the hardheaded principle of efficiency, which may favor a consumption tax, and the softhearted principle of equity, which clearly favors a progressive income tax. Or do we?

Let's begin with an indisputable fact: American households don't save much. In the year 2017, they stashed away only about 4 percent of their disposable incomes—a saving rate far lower than in many other countries. The Aussies, for example, saved about 10 percent of their income; the Swedes saved about 15 percent.

The next step in the argument is the assertion that Americans *should* save more. This assertion sounds right but is not indisputable. After all, what gives politicians, economists, or anyone else the right to tell consumers how much they should spend now and how much they should save for the future?

But let's accept the claim so we can move on to the weakest link in the argument: that the way to solve this problem is to use the tax code to provide greater financial incentives to save—incentives that sometimes go as far as eliminating all taxes on interest, dividends, and capital gains, to wit, to replacing the income tax with a consumption tax. This policy conclusion does not follow, even if you think Americans save too little, for at least two reasons.

One was mentioned already: income inequality. Most of the interest payments, dividends, and especially the capital gains accrue pretty high up the income ladder. The poor, after all, don't own stock and have little money in the bank. Taxing income from capital more lightly than income from labor would seriously blunt the progressivity of the income tax. Liberals care about that.

The second problem goes deeper: surprisingly, most tax incentives for saving simply don't work. It is easy to dream up tax incentives that favor saving over spending. Just think of such well-known tax preferences as IRAs and 401(k) accounts, for example. Common sense tells us that reducing the tax burden on the returns to saving should encourage people to save more, and many people believe that. But the empirical evidence offers precious little support for this commonsense belief. With only rare exceptions, study after study has concluded that tax incentives for saving don't get people to save more.

Wait. Let me clarify that. What the research actually shows is that raising the after-tax rate of return, which is what Congress does when it reduces taxes on saving, does not induce people to save more. Why not? There are two leading hypotheses. One is that most people already live in a world where saving is free of tax; their IRAs, 401(k)s, and other retirement plans more than exhaust their ability to save. The other is that higher after-tax returns make it easier to reach your saving goal while socking away less each year. Both may have elements of truth, but the reason is less important than the fact. While it is easy to make saving more attractive financially, the evidence says that doing so does not increase household saving.

Other sorts of inducements do work, however. The most prominent and useful of these is changing the default option on a 401(k) plan. Under most such plans, an employee starts *out* of the plan—and therefore doesn't get the employer match—unless he or she takes action to opt *in*. But some employers, encouraged in recent years by the US government, have changed the default option to "in" rather than "out." In such plans, workers are enrolled automatically but can opt out if they wish. That requires taking some action, though the action may be as little as making a phone call, filling out a simple form, or going to a website.

Perhaps surprisingly, research has shown that the default option—which seems trivial—makes an enormous difference to the choices real people actually make. One of the earliest studies of this phenomenon documented a stunning 48-percentage-point increase in 401(k) participation among newly hired employees who had to opt out rather than in. Another found an 85 percent enrollment rate after six months of employment when the default option was "in" versus only 26–43 percent when the default was "out." These are huge differences in behavior. We humans seem to be highly inertial creatures.

Notice that changing the default option does *not* increase the after-tax return on saving. It's not an "incentive" as economists normally use that term. Instead, changing the default works by overcoming inertia—or, more accurately, by transforming inertia from an anti-saving force into a pro-saving force. Notice also that changing the default option does not add any complexity to the tax code. The 401(k) provision is already there.

Sounds good, right? Yet shortly after assuming office, President Trump nixed an Obama-era rule that would have enabled cities to help small businesses start pension plans with automatic enrollment—something many employees of large firms already have but small firms find hard to do. Go figure.

Common Misunderstanding 3:
The Corporate Tax Was High

Actually, it wasn't. There was lots of talk in recent years about the fact that the US statutory tax rate on corporate income, at 35 percent, was among the highest in the world. That much was true. But it's also highly misleading because America's high statutory rate was married to a bewildering profusion of exceptions, exemptions, exclusions, deductions, and other assorted gimmicks—most of which remain. If you look instead at the taxes that American corporations actually paid, you find that our corporate taxes were actually a smaller percentage of GDP than the OECD average.

Table 10.1 demonstrates this fact by comparing the United States to six other high-income countries that might be considered our peer group. We see that the US statutory rate in 2016 was indeed the highest on the list, but the US tax yield was not. Contrary to popular myth, we didn't actually tax corporations more heavily than most other countries. What *is* true is that we were, and remain, heaven for tax lawyers, who whittle our high statutory rate down to an effective rate that's below average.

TABLE 10.1   Statutory Corporate Tax Rates and Corporate Taxes as a Share of GDP, Selected Countries

Country	Statutory Corporate Rate, All Levels of Government (Percent)	Corporate Tax Receipts as a Share of GDP (Percent)
United States	38.9	2.2
Germany	30.2	1.7
Japan	30.0	4.3
Canada	26.7	3.1
Switzerland	21.2	3.1
United Kingdom	20.0	2.5
Ireland	12.5	2.7

Source: OECD. Statutory rates are for 2016. Tax receipts are for 2014 or 2015, depending on which is the most recent year available.

Don't get me wrong. I am not praising America's unseemly combination of high statutory rates and egregious tax loopholes. In fact, that homely combination constituted a stern indictment of our corporate tax law. We should be ashamed of it. Huge amounts of socially unproductive effort went into turning our high statutory rate into a middle-of-the-road effective rate. Companies that are truly skilled at this game, like General Electric, or are blessed with bountiful loopholes, like Apple, have been known to reduce their tax bills all the way to zero. So we had the worst of both worlds: the high 35 percent rate energized business lobbyists and propagandists, while the zero tax paid by some large corporations enraged ordinary citizens.

Clearly, our corporate tax code prior to 2018 flunked on both equity and efficiency criteria. It was also a nightmare of complexity. It cried out for change—badly. Let me take up just a few hot button issues.

Pass-through entities. Subchapter S corporations, like partnerships, don't pay taxes as corporations. Instead, their profits are passed through to their owners, who pay personal income taxes on their business profits at their own bracket rates. That's a really simple tax treatment, one I have long thought should be applied to ordinary corporations, too. (See below.) But there is one big issue which, if not handled properly, can create a loophole large enough to drive a good-sized company through.

Many modest-sized firms, and some big ones, can choose between being organized as a partnership (or an S-corp) and as an ordinary corporation (called a C-corp). If the top personal income tax rate and the corporate tax rate are reasonably close, as they were when Donald Trump was elected (39.6 percent versus 35 percent), this choice may not be momentous from a tax perspective. But if we tax all pass-through business income at a substantially lower rate, we create two big problems for the tax man. First, people who earn their incomes in pass-through businesses—a broad category that includes hedge funds, law firms, real estate partnerships, and the like—will get large tax cuts. Second, lawyers and accountants will have powerful incentives to create millions of new pass-through entities solely for the purpose of reducing taxes. It's easy. Just turn a company's cook, driver, or accountant into an independent contractor (a pass-through) rather than an employee. Same work; lower taxes.

After considering opening a more drastic gap between the tax rate on earnings and the tax rate on pass-through income, Congress settled on exempting 20 percent of the latter from taxation—with a number of exceptions (don't ask!).

Tax inversions. A few years ago, many large US corporations discovered the joys of what are commonly called "tax inversions." In brief—please don't check this with a tax lawyer—an American company can vastly reduce its tax bill by changing its legal domicile to some tax haven like Ireland or Bermuda without changing the actual location of its business operations much, if at all.

A wave of tax inversions in the years 2014–2016 garnered huge press attention because several were accomplished by merging a larger American company into a smaller foreign company based in a low-tax country. Voilà! The magic potion—plus some heavy lawyering—created a new company, based abroad, that paid far less tax than its corporate ancestors. It also deprived the US Treasury of tax revenue, which did not make inversions popular with the Obama administration.

Seeing little prospect for bipartisan legislation to close this loophole, the Obama Treasury issued new rules that made inversions less attractive financially and more difficult to engineer (don't ask!) in 2014, 2015, and 2016. The 2016 rules had at least one dramatic effect, persuading Pfizer (headquartered in New York City) to call off its proposed $152 billion merger with Allergan (headquartered in Dublin). In 2017, Donald Trump and congressional Republicans argued that lowering the corporate tax rate would reduce the incentive to invert.

Nonrepatriated profits. The biggest corporate tax issue, however, may be the nontaxation of profits parked abroad. Many large US corporations generate profits in multiple countries; that's why we call them multinationals. The tax law gives these companies enormous discretion over where they book those profits—and therefore where they pay taxes. Naturally, the more profits a company books in tax havens like Ireland, Luxembourg, and the Cayman Islands, the lower its total tax bill.

There are many ways for a multinational to distribute its profits across the globe—on paper. But one method merits special attention because it showers huge benefits on, for example, drug companies and tech companies. In today's economy, a great deal of corporate profit derives from intellectual property. Just ask the tax departments at Apple, Google, Merck, and Bristol-Myers Squibb—to name a few. These companies have enormous discretion over how much of their profits to ascribe to their intellectual property and, most germane to the current discussion, to what locale. Of course, it is tempting to assign your intellectual property to low-tax jurisdictions and therefore to book most of your profits there. Multinational tech companies, drug companies, and others naturally succumb to that temptation. You'd be amazed at how many inventions get used in Ireland!

Then these companies face a problem. If their profits are "earned" in Ireland, how does the corporate treasurer repatriate the money back to the United States? The answer, in many cases, is that he or she doesn't. Instead, the money stays abroad to avoid US taxes. While no one knows for sure, some estimates put this hoard at around $3 trillion. The big problem is that the US Treasury loses a lot of revenue. A secondary problem is that the American companies find it harder to use the money for, say, more investment or hiring at home; it's stuck abroad. Or is it? One well-known dodge is to leave the funds in Ireland, say, and borrow money in the United States to fund whatever investments you want to make.

What can be done about this? Over the years, many people, including President Barack Obama in 2015, suggested variations on the following theme: allow multinational companies to repatriate profits at a sharply reduced corporate tax rate, provided they comply with certain conditions, such as spending the repatriated funds on investment or hiring, or perhaps investing in approved infrastructure projects. The 2017 tax bill incorporated just one part of this suggestion: the lower tax rate on repatriated profits (again, with several complications). Many companies quickly announced repatriations.

Territoriality. None of these remedies gets at the root of the problem, however. The United States is one of the few countries to tax its corporations on their worldwide profits—*if* they bring their foreign-earned profits home. Most countries rely instead on a territorial system, under which profits generated in the United Kingdom are taxed by the UK government, taxes generated in Germany are taxed by the German government, and so on.

This territorial system seems "fair" in that it recognizes that multinational companies are truly multinational. Apple, for example, sells the majority of its wares abroad. Is Apple an American company? (In 2016, the EU tax authorities decided it is not and asked the company to fork over $14 billion in back taxes.) Or think about the fact that most Toyotas sold in the United States are assembled here by Toyota

Motor North America. Is Toyota Motor North America a Japanese company?

It may seem natural to tax corporate activity where it takes place. At least two gigantic problems arise, however. First, less and less business activity is physical, and more and more is conceptual, making it increasingly difficult to decide where corporate activity actually takes place. Is it at headquarters, in the research lab, in the factory, at the location of sale? Second, because different nations tax corporate income so differently, corporate treasurers have ample possibilities to game the system by booking profits in low-tax jurisdictions.

Which tax treatment, worldwide or territorial, is right? There is no clear answer. It would certainly be both fairer and more efficient if every nation in the world defined corporate income in the same way and taxed it at the same rate. Good luck with that. There is no world government, and a few countries have adopted tax sheltering as their business model. For example, profits on the foreign operations of US-controlled corporations amounted to 38 percent of GDP in Ireland, 103 percent in Luxembourg, and an astounding 1,578 percent in Bermuda in 2010.

A second approach would be to give up on taxing corporate income entirely, treat all corporations as pass-throughs (as we do with S-corps), impute the company's earnings to its shareholders, and then tax *people* where they live. After all, it is far easier to determine the domicile of a person than the domicile of a multinational corporation.

There is just one big problem with this elegant plan: it would lose 0–100 in the Senate and 0–435 in the House. I know. I've advocated it for years. As soon as you suggest abolishing the corporate income tax, you lose every Democrat in Congress. And as soon as you tell Republicans that the income would become taxable on *personal* returns, you lose every Republican. (*Keep your illumination to yourself, thank you!*)

The 2017 tax overhaul claimed to move the US to a territorial corporate tax system. Well, not quite. The legislation also applied a "minimum tax" on *some* profits that multinationals shift to jurisdictions where the tax rate is very low. Yes, more complexity.

But It All Worked Out in 1986

The prospects for comprehensive tax reform are always bleak. To economists seeking to enhance the public good, our tax code looks like an ugly duckling that could be turned into a beautiful swan. There is so much room for improvement! But to politicians, tax reform is fraught with perils and offers only paltry rewards for success. The same things could have been said (and were) in the 1980s, however. Yet the miraculous Tax Reform Act of 1986—an economist's dream—passed. Might we do it again?

Well, Congress did make dramatic changes in the tax system in 2017, calling it tax "reform." But the new tax code is no simpler and, in many people's eyes, is less fair than it was before. The tax changes also lost a lot of revenue, thereby boosting future budget deficits. That's not what we normally mean by *reform*—which is always a long shot. Why?

For openers, look at the date: 1986 was more than thirty years ago. Since then, the tax code has acquired more barnacles than an abandoned ship, and every one of them has political defenders. Numerous tax reform plans have started the arduous journey through Congress over these three decades, the latest in 2017. But true reform has been elusive. It's no accident.

Second, tax reform came pretty close to failing back then, even though it was promoted by a wildly popular president (Ronald Reagan). It took a political miracle—which I'll describe in the next chapter—to bring reform back from the dead. Miracles don't happen frequently.

Third, much of the low-hanging fruit was picked in 1986 and can't be picked again. The essence of tax reform is trading fewer loopholes for lower tax rates. "Broaden the base; lower the rates" is the standard rallying cry. The former provides revenue to "spend" on the latter, which is the politically attractive part. But if you can broaden the base only a little, there is not much new revenue to spread around. Economists can rail against tax expenditures—the use of special tax provisions to favor particular activities. And we do. But when the four largest tax expenditures in the personal income tax code are (1) the exclusion of employer-paid health care benefits from workers' taxable income, (2) tax-free saving in retirement accounts, (3) the mortgage interest deduction, and (4) the preferentially low tax rate on capital gains (which Republicans always want to reduce further), you're stuck in a pretty tough political cul-de-sac. I know. In 2000, I brought a similar list to then presidential candidate Al Gore, who didn't know whether to laugh or cry. (He was far too polite to just kick me out of his office.)

Yet a pretty wonderful tax reform did pass in 1986. How? What was the secret sauce? We'll examine that in the next chapter.

Chapter 11

Toward Remedies:
Moving the Needle

Cross the river by feeling for the stones.
—Deng Xiaoping

In February 2017, a star-studded group of Republicans headed by two former secretaries of both the Treasury and State, James Baker and George Schultz, introduced an imaginative idea for combatting global climate change: impose a sizable tax on carbon emissions, as economists have long recommended, but rebate the proceeds to Americans as a "dividend," leaving no *net* tax increase. Clever? Maybe. It at least gets around the taxaphobic reactions that stop most carbon-tax plans in their tracks—or so Baker and Schultz hoped. My immediate reaction on hearing about the plan was this: that's a terrific idea, but it will get nowhere politically. Regrettably, I was right. Can't we do better?

Can We Amend Murphy's Law?

This book could have been written even if Donald Trump had never been elected president of the United States, for he is far from the first politician to look to economics for support rather than for illumination. Mr. Trump's shunning of any kind of expert opinion, even to the point of denying basic facts, merely took a familiar phenomenon and drove it to previously unheard-of heights, making it hard for even a president to enlist the support of any economists. (Have you noticed the dearth of "validators" for Trump's proposals?)

He claimed he could fix everything wrong with Obamacare at lower cost and with greater insurance coverage by replacing it with "something great." (He couldn't.) He called for "the biggest tax cut in history," arguing that it would pay for itself with growth. (It won't.) He called NAFTA the worst trade deal in history. (It wasn't.) As a candidate, he claimed that unemployment was vastly higher than the official data said, but once elected, he reveled in the published low unemployment numbers of 2017. He even promised to reopen coal mines that newer technology and competition from other energy sources had firmly shut. (Really?) The list could go on and on.

But long before Trump declared his candidacy for the highest office in the land, politicians of both parties had been spouting misleading slogans about international trade, enacting tax changes that flouted the principles of both equity and efficiency, and making only flimsy efforts—if that—to mitigate the long trend toward greater inequality. Most politicians also refused even to consider such policies as the above-mentioned tax on carbon emissions, using congestion charges to alleviate traffic problems, or eliminating the tax deduction for interest on home mortgages—all of which are mother's milk to economists.

Because the Lamppost Theory did not begin with the Trump administration, the end of his presidency will not signal any sort of solution. Even a complete return to the status quo before Trump would leave the interaction between economics and politics in a very bad place—and economic policy the worse for it. So I ask in this chapter and the next what we can do to push back against the Lamppost Theory. Not to make economic policy perfect, mind you, or even good. Just better than it is.

Let's be clear. I don't have a handy list of wondrous remedies, and certainly no panaceas. I don't believe there are any. As I said at the outset of this book, there are some problems you solve and others you just manage. The Lamppost Theory falls squarely in the latter category. So I am only looking for palliatives—changes that might take the hard edge off the Lamppost Theory, not invalidate it. Changes that might get more sound economic advice met by less political dissent. Such improvements come in two main variants; I call them Moving the Needle and Moving the Line.

This chapter is a search for ways to move the needle a bit—away from economics as an exercise in partisan support and toward economics as useful illumination for serious policymakers. Amendments to Murphy's Law of Economic Policy, you might call them—a few practical steps that might get the political system accepting a bit less nonsense and a bit more horse sense. Some of these steps came up in earlier chapters, as partial solutions to specific problems. Others are new here, and broader in scope.

The next chapter then turns to possibilities for moving the line between political and technocratic decision making in the technocratic direction—again just a bit, for I would not advocate more. Every society must decide which policy decisions should be left to experts (examples: how best to shoot a rocket to Mars, what cancer research holds the most promise) and which should be placed in political hands (example: how much public money should be spent on Mars exploration versus cancer research). At least where economic policy is concerned, I believe the United States has drawn the line in the wrong place. We could get better economic policy, I believe, if a few more decisions—not all, just a few—were made by technocratic experts rather than by politicians.

Before we proceed, it is important to understand that Americans need not choose one of these two strategies over the other. The nation can and should try to move both the needle and the line. After all, the Lamppost Theory now has a firm choke hold on our politico-economic system. Loosening its grip is a goal worth pursuing.

Wanted: A Better-Educated Electorate

Let's start with something that would work well if only we could do it, but that may be out of reach. The abysmal economic illiteracy of the US electorate poses a severe challenge to any policymaker looking to advance the commonweal. Imagine that a politician proposed an irrigation project predicated on the notion that he could make water flow uphill without pumps. A flood of objections would follow—not only from wonkish engineers expert in hydraulics, but also from competing politicians, the media, and any citizens who were paying attention. People do, after all, understand enough physics to know that water won't flow uphill without a lot of help.

Amazingly, however, the average American seems not to understand even that much economics. So nostrums that are the economic equivalent of water flowing uphill sell readily in the political marketplace, often aided and abetted by well-paid lobbyists. Supply-side economics is a prime example encountered several times in this book already. It's a nonsense notion that the Trump administration nonetheless revived in its 2017 budget and tax proposals, when the Treasury secretary, among others, advanced the preposterous theory that tax cuts would prompt so much additional growth that they would more than pay for themselves. A second example is the idea that we can solve the climate change problem without putting a price on carbon. A third is the notion, successfully sold by Trump as a candidate in 2016, that we can reverse the historical (and worldwide) trend toward a shrinking share of workers engaged in manufacturing. Too few citizens understand—much less accept—the obvious and noncontroversial (among economists) reasons why each of these ideas is deeply flawed.

Here's a poignant example of the low level of economic illiteracy we are dealing with. Economists Annamaria Lusardi and Olivia Mitchell, sometimes with co-authors, have asked various groups the following trio of very easy questions about financial matters:

1. *Interest*: If you invested $100 for five years at 2 percent annual interest, at the end of the five years would you have more than $102, exactly $102, or less than $102? (Notice that the "break-even" amount here is $102, not $110; they were not testing whether people understand compound interest.)

2. *Purchasing power*: If your savings account pays 1 percent annual interest and the annual inflation rate is 2 percent, after one year would you be able to buy more than, exactly the same as, or less than you can buy today with the money in the account?

3. *Diversification*: Does buying a single company stock or a stock mutual fund usually provide a safer return?

Yes, I told you they were easy. But only about 30 percent of Americans got them all right. (In case you're wondering, Germans did a lot better, and Russians did a lot worse.) In view of such embarrassing results, how would you like to let polling results decide how to restore seventy-five-year actuarial balance to Social Security, or how to reform the corporate income tax code?

A more economically literate public would be a blessing. Such a citizenry would find it easier to distinguish between support and illumination, and would likely demand more of the latter. That makes it a fine Holy Grail to pursue. By all means, we should support efforts to teach basic economic principles to kids. But pursuits of Holy Grails have a way of taking a long time—and coming up empty. What can we accomplish in the shorter term?

Putting the Gain Before the Pain

Perhaps the easiest way to find a loophole in Murphy's Law was exemplified by the success of the Greenspan Commission on Social Security in 1983, which I mentioned earlier. The essential idea amounted to performing an act of political jujitsu: turning a weakness into strength. We all know that politicians have super-short time horizons. So why not take advantage of that failing by legislating *now* something that is politically unpalatable, but postponing its effective date until much later? If there's some upfront gain, myopic politicians might find such a deferral of pain irresistible.

Here's how it worked back in 1983. Much prospective political pain inhered in raising the normal retirement age for Social Security benefits from sixty-five to sixty-seven. It was a pretty sensible way to reduce benefits, and it avoided the unappealing phrase "cut benefits." But few members of Congress wanted to cut Social Security benefits, no matter what you call it. They knew then, as they know now, that old people vote. So a proposal to increase the normal retirement age from sixty-five to sixty-seven *immediately* would have been both terrible economics and suicidal politics. Terrible economics because people need time to adjust their retirement plans. Suicidal politics because it stepped firmly on what was then called the "third rail" of American politics.

Fortunately, the pure economics of the matter implied no need to rush. It was better to give prospective retirees plenty of advance notice anyway. Postponing the higher retirement age until well into the future—we are still in the adjustment phase—also obviated the political pain. After all, what politician looks decades ahead? Members of Congress in 1983 discovered that the third rail was thereby de-electrified, and the legislation sailed through both chambers by huge margins.

You may now be thinking: Okay, but isn't Social Security unique? Unlike other government programs, the natural time unit for planning changes in the Social Security system is the generation. So the Greenspan Commission's trick cannot be repeated, right? Wrong.

First, and most obviously, Social Security's long-run finances are out of balance again. The system needs a fix, but not right away. If Congress were to enact today some combination of small payroll tax increases and minor trims in benefits that start, say, ten or twenty years from now, it could put Social Security back on firm financial footing without much political pain—just as it did in 1983. Please explain that to your senators.

The same timing jujitsu can be applied elsewhere. Medicare, for example, operates under a similar generational clock. According to the most recent trustees' report, the Health Insurance Trust Fund will shrink from about two-thirds of a year's expenditures today to about zero in 2029. So, yes, a "crisis" in Medicare funding is coming, but the day of reckoning is more than a decade away. That doesn't mean we should mark time for the next ten years; the problem will only fester and get worse. But it does mean that we can legislate *today* some combination of revenue increases and/or cost reductions that begin, say, a decade from now. The political pain would thereby be diminished severely.

Similar logic applies to economists' favorite remedy for climate change: an emissions tax. If human life as we know it is to continue on our planet, we earthlings must reduce carbon emissions. There is little doubt about that. But it's fine to start out slowly—say, with a very small carbon tax—and build from there. In fact, it's better policy. If Congress were to enact a scaled-down version of the Baker-Schultz plan today—starting, say, with a $5 per ton tax that rises by $5 per ton each year for the next nineteen years—hardly anyone would notice its effects at first. They'd be too small—roughly 5 cents per gallon of gas. But the legislation would eventually push the carbon tax up to $100 per ton, through nineteen increments, each too small to notice. (The exact numbers are not important; the idea of a phase-in is.) Such a time path, if set forth in law well in advance, would offer businesses and households attractive opportunities to save money by refitting their offices, factories, stores, and homes with carbon-efficient technologies before higher carbon taxes kicked in. The predictable result would be a boom in green investment.

As one final example, think about the federal budget deficit. According to the Congressional Budget Office's latest long-range forecast, federal government debt held by the public is slated to grow from about 77 percent of GDP in 2016 to a frightening 150 percent of GDP by 2047 under present policies. Such projections make some people fear financial Armageddon and recommend drastic, disruptive budgetary changes right away. But hold on. The projected rise in the debt-to-GDP ratio is extremely gradual. By 2020, for example, that 77 percent figure is up to only 79 percent. So we have time to legislate higher taxes and/or cutbacks in expenditures soon but have them take effect well in the future, and yet in plenty of time to avoid any pending catastrophe. By exploiting that simple calendar trick, we can create the modern version of Russell Long's aphorism: don't tax you; don't tax me; tax that fellow in 2033.

The idea of pocketing (some of) the gains up front while deferring the pain until later cannot work everywhere. Some policy issues demand more immediate attention. But the potential scope of this approach is not trivial. Think about the list I just ran through: Social Security, Medicare, climate change, and the budget deficit. Those are among the nation's biggest long-run economic problems, and each can be addressed by policy changes that defer the pain.

The Greenspan Commission's success came so long ago that most contemporary politicians seem to have forgotten it. And yes, mimicking that success might be harder today, with fewer people willing to listen to expert advice and with bipartisanship a flickering ember. But it's worth a try, maybe multiple tries. After all, putting the gain before the pain looks like the low-hanging fruit of improving economic policy. And there's not much low-hanging fruit around.

About Those Time Horizons

I have emphasized that one main reason why economists and politicians often talk past one another is that the time horizons of politicians are too short and the time horizons of economists are too long. That seems a tough gap to bridge. But I also suggested that the four-year presidential term might offer a goldilocks solution: not too short for the economists and not too long for the politicians. Given the preeminent role of presidential campaigns in American politics, politicians and their handlers should find it attractive—even natural—to focus attention on years divisible by four. So that's my second "easy" palliative. Notice that, to make it work, politicians need not become high-minded. Crassly political will do just fine.

Such farsighted behavior, however, stands in marked contrast to the way politicos act today—which is to focus, say, on the next tweet. Can we change political time frames that radically? It may sound impossible, but I think there's a chance because it's in their vested interest. Everyone in politics knows that presidential elections are the main events and that the state of the economy just prior to a presidential election has profound effects on the vote. So making voters happy about the economy by the next presidential election should be a natural focal point for any newly elected president (and for Congress). Ronald Reagan understood this intuitively. ("Are you better off than you were four years ago?") Modern political operatives seem to have forgotten it. They need reminding.

Of course, once the country is a year into a president's term, that "natural" political time horizon will have shrunk to three years—which is still fine for economic policy. After two years, the time horizon will have shrunk to just two more years—which is getting a little short for some economic policy purposes. But remember, there is scant hope for enacting any sensible economic policy beyond the midpoint of a presidency anyway. The political silly season will be in full swing.

Getting politicians to exercise enough self-control to maintain two- to four-year time horizons during the first half of each presidential term would constitute a major step forward. The quality of tax policy, trade policy, and regulatory policy—to name a few—could take a quantum leap upward. Getting from here to there won't be easy, however. Elected politicians would have to ignore much "sage advice" offered by their media consultants and spinmeisters. But neither would it be the first time that human behavior was changed by pointing out that something is in someone's self-interest. And politicians are marvelously adaptable folks.

Enough with the low-hanging fruit. Let's now move on to the hard stuff, much of which derives from the partisan misuse of economics in political combat, that is, from the Lamppost Theory.

Can We Reduce Extreme Partisanship?

Upon reading the title of this section, you may be tempted to answer a contemptuous no and skip to the next section. Feel free. I'd be the first to admit that reducing partisanship in the contemporary dis-United States is like climbing an icy slope without the aid of grappling hooks. Intrepid climbers who attempt such an ascent are likely to slip and fall, injuring both their egos and their political prospects. The best guess is that the hyper-partisanship we have suffered with since Barack Obama's first day in office (or even before) will be intact at the end of Donald Trump's presidency—probably worse. As President Trump would say: sad! But before we give up, let me try out a few ideas for reducing partisanship just a bit. (Yes, my goal is modest.)

I mention this perhaps-impossible dream because it might help move the needle toward more illumination and less support. As things stand today, politicians seek the assistance of economists mainly to garner highly partisan support for policies they have already embraced. They want economists to demonstrate political fealty, not to offer hard data or cool-headed logic. In fact, American society in the Age of Trump looks to be in danger of losing even Senator Daniel Patrick Moynihan's wise dictum, "Everyone is entitled to his own opinion, but not to his own facts." You may recall that the first week of the Trump administration saw the invention of a new euphemism for lies: "alternative facts."

That's a shame because many of the hard-headed, soft-hearted policies that I advocate in this book are not inherently partisan. Typically, they marry the hard-headed, market-oriented attitudes of conservatives to the soft-hearted, underdog-favoring attitudes of liberals. Or rather, they would do so if there was any bipartisanship left in America.

Obamacare, which had its origins as Romneycare in Massachusetts, could have been a great case in point. It tackles a big and widely recognized social problem—too many Americans without health insurance—mainly by market means. Unlike the single-payer systems of most advanced countries, Obamacare did not install the government as the provider of health care, nor even as the monopoly insurer. Instead, it sent the millions of people without health insurance to the marketplace, where private insurance companies would offer them plans on the so-called exchanges. None of these plans were to be run by the government, though there were and are regulations. Everyone had to buy from a private company.

In the abstract, you might expect Republicans to be attracted to a private-sector approach like that—as opposed to, say, a single-payer system. Massachusetts Republicans in 2006 certainly were. In a world that drew limits around partisanship, the congressional GOP might have offered modifications to the Democrats' plan in 2010, some of which would have been adopted in the interest of enacting a bipartisan bill.* Instead, however, rank partisanship ruled the day. As the outline of what eventually became Obamacare took shape, the loyal opposition subjected it to fusillades of criticism with barely a hint of what they'd like done differently.

Obamacare was vilified as a "government takeover" of the health care system. Really? Republicans conveniently forgot that the essence of the plan was forcing people into the private insurance market as buyers. That is, by the way, probably the main reason why insurance companies supported the ACA in 2010.

Is Obamacare "too regulatory," as many Republicans have charged for years? Well, maybe. Its design certainly was not perfect. Had Republicans participated in crafting the legislation—which they mostly refused to do—the ACA might have come out a bit less

---

*One such modification that *was* adopted was to drop the idea of including a government-run plan among the private plans. When a number of private insurers dropped out of Obamacare in 2016 and 2017, leaving either one or no insurers in some markets, some observers questioned this decision.

regulatory. But remember, *some* regulation follows ineluctably from the goal of universal insurance. For openers, if Congress didn't compel participation, that is, if it dropped the hated mandate, younger and healthier people would opt out of the system, leaving an older and sicker insured pool that is more costly to cover. One consequence would be higher insurance premiums. And as those higher premiums induced more healthy people to opt out, the cycle would repeat, and the system would start to unravel.

Which brings me to the second major reason for regulation. If universal coverage is the goal, and markets—not government—are to set insurance premiums, someone needs to worry about how the sick, the poor, the near-poor, and even the not-so-near-poor will pay the freight. Private, for-profit companies don't worry much about things like that: if you can't afford what they offer for sale, you don't get it. But that attitude won't get you to universal health insurance. So like Romneycare before it, Obamacare included an elaborate system of subsidies. Those subsidies, in turn, required some new revenue (aka taxes) to fund them.

At this point, partisan Republicans were virtually jumping out of their skins: *Both* new regulations *and* new taxes?! It was more than they could bear. On the eve of a critical vote in the House in March 2010, then Speaker John Boehner declared that the nation was nearing "Armageddon" because the Democrats' bill will "ruin our country." History records that it did not.

But what was the alternative? The details could surely have differed—and would have if Republicans had shown interest in participating in the design of the new system. White House Chief of Staff Rahm Emanuel angered many on the left when he told his staff early in the process, "The only nonnegotiable principle here is success. Everything else is negotiable." Sounds pretty pliable.

But the plain fact is that any bill that relies on private insurance to provide universal coverage must mandate participation and provide subsidies for those who cannot afford it. To wit, it must resemble Obamacare. It is no accident that, from the time the health care bill was debated in Congress in 2009 right up to Donald Trump's inauguration in 2017, Republicans never offered a single coherent alternative to Obamacare. They just fulminated against it and voted for repeal scores of times. Such scorched-earth nihilism was nothing new. As Boehner reflected at a health care conference in February 2017, "In the 25 years that I served in the United States Congress, Republicans never, ever one time agreed on what a healthcare proposal should look like. Not once."

Once Trump became president, the Republicans found themselves in the awkward position of the proverbial dog that caught the fire truck. Now what? House Republicans' first attempt was criticized by the right as "Obamacare Lite" because it (sort of) maintained the three key elements: a very weak version of a mandate to purchase insurance, much smaller and less progressive subsidies, and slightly more market-oriented (hence less regulatory) provisions. It was criticized from the left as being regressive, heartless, and likely leaving tens of millions of Americans uncovered. And it died in the House without ever coming up for a vote.

Their second attempt moved the bill further to the right by loosening requirements such as the benefits package, the mandate, and coverage for people with preexisting conditions. It picked up a few right-wing votes and passed the House—barely. The Senate's first attempt at a bill leaned a bit more left than right, even maintaining some of the taxes Democrats had passed in 2010 to fund Obamacare. But despite strenuous efforts by Majority Leader Mitch McConnell to find 50 votes, it never even reached the Senate floor. A few subsequent attempts by McConnell did reach the floor, but failed. One came very close—losing on a dramatic no vote from Senator John McCain (R-AZ), who was fighting cancer.

A little bipartisan cooperation to fix Obamacare, rather than to "repeal and replace" it, might have worked in 2017—or even in 2016. After all, the 21st Century Cures Act, which a lame-duck President Obama signed into law in his waning days in office (December 13, 2016), was a health care bill. Designed to streamline FDA procedures in approving cures for several fatal diseases, it was fashioned in a bipartisan way and passed both the House and Senate by overwhelming margins: 392–25 and 94–5, respectively.

But bipartisanship was never even tried in the case of the ACA. Republicans, after all, scored enormous political success between the elections of 2008 and 2016 just by saying no to everything Democrats proposed. The GOP cast itself as the antigovernment party and then demonstrated just how dysfunctional the federal government could be by keeping it hamstrung after 2010. When the 2016 elections brought Republicans control of the White House, the Senate, and the House, they "owned" the government. But it turned out to be hard for them to switch from opposing to governing—and Donald Trump's antics didn't help.

One of the silliest aspects of the long-running partisan battle over economic policy is the debate—if you want to grace it by that name—over "big government" versus "small government." Democrats tend to look to government to solve social problems. Republicans tend to wish government away. That sounds like a major philosophical divide, but the debate is actually sterile for many reasons.

The simplest is that it's no contest; the small-government side almost always wins in the United States, at least if you grade us on the international curve. As pointed out earlier, we have a smaller government than most advanced countries, whether measured by public expenditures or by taxes. Yes, it's true that both Roosevelt's New Deal and Johnson's Great Society increased the size and scope of the federal government; some Republicans would like to repeal both. But those two expansions of federal power mainly got the United States doing what other rich countries had been doing for years. Neither made us a "big government" nation.

Besides, the 1930s and the 1960s are ancient history by now, and it is pretty hard to make a case that the federal government has grown larger since the 1960s. In fact, by most measures it has been shrinking, relative to the economy, for decades. For example, federal civilian employment is now down to less than 1.4 million. (Walmart's workforce is

FIGURE 11.1   Federal Civilian Employment as a Percentage of
Total Civilian Employment, 1981–2016

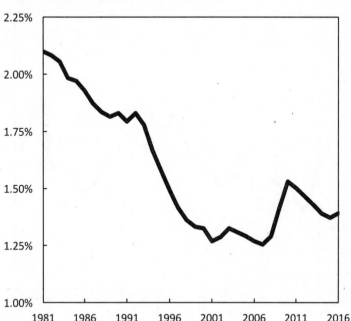

Federal employment includes all full-time-equivalent civilian executive
branch employees, including civilian personnel at the Department of
Defense and excluding Postal Service employees. Source: US Bureau of
Labor Statistics; Budget of the US Government, Table 16.1.

about 50 percent larger!) If that still sounds like "big government" to
you, remember that this is a huge country. With total civilian employment topping 150 million, federal employees are the chump change of
our workforce. Furthermore, the number of federal civilian employees
has barely changed since the 1980s, even though the country grew. As
a share of the total, it has declined. (See Figure 11.1.)

Employment may not be the best measure of the size and scope of
government because it doesn't take many people to push a lot of money
around. Total federal outlays—which include transfer payments and
monies granted to states and localities—may be a better indicator.
As Figure 11.2 shows, federal outlays as a share of GDP are about

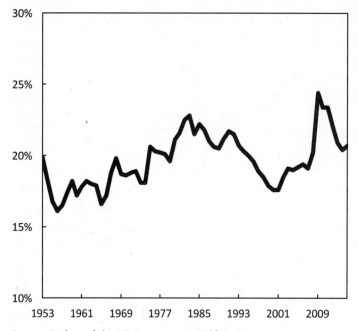

FIGURE 11.2   Federal Outlays as a Percentage of GDP, 1953–2015

Source: Budget of the US Government, Table 1.2.

where they were in 1953—roughly 20 percent. Dwight D. Eisenhower presided over a government of this size.

Enough numbers. The broader and more important point is that Americans should worry less about whether their government is "big" or "small" in some abstract sense and more about whether it is doing the right things and doing them well. Here are three illustrative cases:

- The Department of Homeland Security (DHS) was thrown together hastily from a hodgepodge of existing agencies amid the George W. Bush administration's mad dash to react to the horrors of 9/11. The annual DHS budget is about $41 billion, and it employs nearly a quarter of a million people. Big government for sure. But does anyone question that its mission is a vitally important federal function? No. The structure of the

DHS, however, remains a bureaucratic nightmare practically crying out for reform. As just one simple—but stunning—indicator, the department is subject to oversight by over ninety congressional committees and subcommittees.

- The Social Security Administration runs one of the nation's largest federal programs—another clear case of "big government." These days, the system takes in over $825 billion in taxes annually, collects interest from its trust fund, and disburses over $900 billion in annual retirement and disability benefits to more than sixty million beneficiaries. All huge numbers. But Social Security is wildly popular with the electorate, and the Social Security Administration does its job cheaply—with an annual administrative budget of only about $6 billion, under 0.7 percent of its outlays. Private life insurance and retirement companies cost far more than that to run.

- No one doubts that many aspects of the nation's food supply, ranging from safety inspections to what we used to call food stamps, are vitally important. And some very smart and dedicated people work at the Department of Agriculture. Nonetheless, the USDA is a sprawling colossus employing nearly a hundred thousand people and spending over $150 billion per year. In case you're wondering, roughly a million Americans work on farms, so the USDA has about one employee for every ten farmers. In part, the department's huge size is a throwback to an earlier age when agriculture constituted a far larger share of our economy. There is an old joke about a man who walks into an agricultural extension service office somewhere only to find the agent crying at his desk. "What's wrong?" the visitor asks. "My farmer died," comes the tearful reply. Yes, the ag budget is ripe for cutting, but just try that politically.

In my judgment, the USDA is a case of a bloated government agency that is too big for the functions it performs, the Social Security Administration is right-sized and efficient, and the DHS is right-sized but bureaucratically inefficient. You may have different judgments. That's fine. In fact, it's my point. We should be arguing about specifics, not engaged in a sterile debate over "big" versus "small" government. Sadly, that looks like what we're in for in a politics dominated by spin.

At some point in your life, you have probably watched the "post-game show" that follows a major political event such as a State of the Union address or a presidential debate. These slightly absurd TV performances invariably feature a "spin room" to which the media are invited to hear partisans on both sides make claims that border on the comic. No one takes these displays of braggadocio seriously; we all know we are being spun. It's harmless fun—until spin turns into lies. That's a line we must guard more zealously than we have.

Unfortunately, it is unrealistic to expect a public afflicted by massive economic illiteracy to distinguish between exaggerated half truths (aka spin) and outright lies about economic policy. So it would be nice if politicians respected the line more. Sadly, Donald Trump set new lows for dishonesty during his 2016 campaign and has continued to shun the truth during his presidency. We know he admires winning more than anything as frivolous as, say, honesty. No one should expect him to change. The danger is that other politicians, mesmerized by his electoral miracle, might start emulating him. Can we prevent that?

I don't pretend to have the answers. But thank heaven for the wonkish Congressional Budget Office (CBO), whose objective analyses of policy options are widely respected, sometimes get huge press coverage, and occasionally keep politicians honest. The furor over health care reform in 2017 was an excellent case in point. The CBO's estimate that the original House proposal would have left twenty-four million more Americans uninsured was widely cited in the press and likely played an instrumental role in the proposal's defeat. When House leaders revised the bill, they rushed it through before the CBO had a chance to score it. But when that score belatedly came in, it estimated that twenty-three million more Americans would be left uninsured, which made the bill pretty much a dead letter in the Senate. When the CBO comes under attack, citizens should rise to defend it.

And I wish the fine work of the Bipartisan Policy Center, a Washington think tank founded by four former senators to conduct and publish serious research on a range of policy issues, would get similar media attention. It really is bipartisan. Look it up at bipartisanpolicy.org.

Public broadcasting, a precious resource that we citizens should take pains to preserve, is also under siege from the Trump administration. So are nonpartisan websites like ProPublica. It would also be wonderful if the mass (and profit-driven) media would give greater prominence to fact-checking efforts like PolitiFact, FactCheck.org, and the *Washington Post*'s Fact Checker—with its colorful but insufficiently famous Pinocchio awards. Here's a wild idea: some media outlet could keep a scoreboard of the biggest political liars. Leading the pack might not bother President Trump, who likes to be first on any list. But how many other politicians would want to see their names on a list of the ten biggest liars? It would also help if social media giants like Google, Facebook, and Twitter would police themselves a bit more for obvious lies and fake news. They claim to be trying now—without becoming censors. It's a fine line to walk. Let's see.

Don't cringe. I'm not totally naive. None of these "reforms" will come close to curing the partisanship problem. But remember, I'm only looking for palliatives.

Politics as Unusual

Even if all this were somehow to happen, it would not be nearly enough. We need meaningful changes in our political system, changes that do not rely for their success on politicians behaving like saints.

Journalist Jonathan Rauch, among others, has argued that many of the cherished political reforms of recent decades have backfired in ways that both encourage extreme partisanship and elevate narrow parochial interests over the broad public interest—the exact opposite of what reformers intended. What we need, according to Rauch and others, is a partial return to the bad old days when politicians chomped cigars and cut deals. (Well, we could probably leave out the cigars.)

Rauch may exaggerate the case, and not even he wants to re-create Tammany Hall writ large. But consider:

- We made nominating procedures more open and democratic—by, for example, replacing backroom deals by primaries and caucuses. It sounded like the right thing to do. But it turns out that most people don't want to participate in the nomination processes. So hyper-partisan minorities dominate—often with threats of primarying more moderate candidates in grotesquely gerrymandered (and hence one-party) congressional districts. It's an odd form of democracy. And it extends even to presidential campaigns, where Donald Trump upended a long list of establishment Republicans in 2016, and Bernie Sanders, a self-proclaimed socialist, almost did the same to Hillary Clinton. Turnout in the 2016 primaries was considered high. Do you know what that meant? Under 29 percent of eligible voters. Maybe backroom deals among party apparatchiks would give us better candidates. Or how about open primaries, of the sort they have in California, with both Democrats and Republicans on the same ballot? That should make it harder for extremists to prevail.

- We "reformed" the sources of money in politics only to discover that we had not reduced the oceans of cash but merely shifted the balance of financial power from political parties (though they still handle plenty of cash) to wealthy individuals and interest groups making use (or perhaps abuse) of PACs, Super PACs, and the like. These independent private entities are harder to regulate—after all, what they do is all "free speech," and they often operate in the dark. Is that what the public wanted? Public financing of elections would be far better. But it's another one of those holy grails: something to wish for, but not to expect. In the meantime, maybe we can improve things by requiring more disclosure and providing incentives for small donations.

- We reformed Congress in a number of ways that pulled the rug out from under party leaders, especially in the House, thereby making it more difficult to cut deals across party lines. On the Republican side, the Tea Party's Freedom Caucus took this transfer of power from the top to the bottom further yet. Then we learned that, in former Speaker Boehner's memorable words, "a leader without followers is simply a man taking a walk."

- We moved more political negotiations out of proverbial smoke-filled rooms and into the sunshine—which often meant in full view of cameras. Now we realize that smoke-filled rooms are better suited to cutting deals and making compromises than are TV shows, which are for posturing. Yes, sunshine is the best disinfectant. But it's an indiscriminate disinfectant.

- An unholy alliance of Tea Partiers and good-government progressives got congressional earmarks banned in 2011. It seemed like a good idea at the time. After all, some of those pork-barrel projects were outrageous. But we later learned that earmarks helped hold the fractious political system together by, in Rauch's words, "giving members a kind of currency to trade." Or, I might add, to reward cooperation in passing legislation. Bringing back earmarks, with all their warts, might help get more deals done.

All these reforms added up to a destruction of the comparatively orderly, albeit unattractive, political system that America had decades ago—a system that frequently produced that rarest of all things today: compromise. Think of Ronald Reagan cooperating with Democrats in Congress or Bill Clinton with Republicans. Then, with the best of intentions, we removed the glue, and now what do we have? A disorderly, hyper-partisan, dysfunctional Congress—and Donald Trump as president. That's progress?

Going back to (some of) the old ways won't be easy. How many members of Congress will stand up to defend earmarks—or backroom deals, for that matter? How can America control political money after *Citizens United*, with the Supreme Court we now have? Can Speaker Ryan exert control over his unruly House Republican caucus, especially the Tea Party faction? It's hard to be optimistic about any of these things, and I'm not. But maybe, just maybe, American citizens will get so fed up with politics-as-usual that it will demand reform.

Or maybe the electorate will start demanding more of that recently dirty word *compromise*. Its banishment from contemporary political discourse in the United States is a mistake of epic proportions because the Founders bequeathed us a constitutional system that requires compromise—else all those checks and balances will freeze us in place.

Not every form of democratic governance is designed that way. The British parliamentary system, for example, does not rely on compromises. Rather, it's been referred to as a sequence of dictatorships punctuated by periodic elections. A British prime minister with a majority in the House of Commons can pass pretty much anything without consulting the opposition. If the voters grow unhappy with what the governing party is doing, they can throw the rascals out at the next election. That's the way their system works.

But America's constitutional system was designed quite differently. With its three branches of government and elaborate checks and balances, our Constitution is designed to produce next to nothing unless compromises are struck—between the parties in each chamber of Congress, between the House and the Senate, between Congress and the president, and so on. As I've mentioned before, Madison and Co. wanted it that way. In seeking a system of government that abjured tyranny, they created one with a strong status quo bias that makes it hard to change anything. And they succeeded brilliantly—we've had no dictators in over 230 years. But overcoming the inertia built into the US Constitution normally *requires* compromise.

How can we get more of it? One route was mentioned above: use a little pork-barrel spending to grease the wheels of Congress. Like many people, I used to denigrate earmarks. If you want to shock members of your book club, try defending them. But compared to what we have now, a little pork here and there doesn't look so bad. Think of it as a small toll we would pay to make our heavily checked and balanced system of government functional.

Now let's generalize, and perhaps ennoble, the thought. Pork-barrel spending is a small-scale example of something I call *linkage*, that is, putting together in a single bill bits and pieces that enable its sponsors to cobble together a majority in the House and 60 votes in the Senate—even though no one gets exactly what they want. Linkage can lead to some unwieldy, even downright ugly, legislative packages. But when it's done well, it can produce serious, even landmark, legislation. And even when it's done not so well, it at least moves us off square 1.

How so? At least up to some point, the more things you bring into a legislative package, the broader the coalition. And the broader the coalition, the more closely it comes to the whole Congress. Remember, parochial thinking fosters narrowly crafted bills that favor specific interest groups over the commonweal. What we want to create, as a counterweight, is an interest group that approximates a committee of the whole.

It *Did* Happen Here

Can it be done? Yes. The legislative history of the Tax Reform Act of 1986 is one of the finest examples ever. A capsule history of how that remarkable bill made its way through Congress is worth heeding, for it holds valuable lessons for the future.

President Ronald Reagan got the ball rolling in his 1984 State of the Union address with a brief call "to simplify the entire tax code so all taxpayers, big and small, are treated more fairly." Short, pretty vague, but right on the mark. Lesson 1: Presidential leadership helps—a lot. (You knew that.)

Remarkably, the president placed hardly any constraints on the technocrats in his Treasury Department, who went to work with gusto—guided by economic, not political, principles. It took them a while to get the job done, and then more time to iron out a number of political bumps in the package, for technocrats are not always politically astute. But the carefully crafted tax reform bill that Reagan's Treasury sent to the Democratically controlled House of Representatives in the summer of 1985 was in many ways an economist's dream.

Then it met up with, among others, the formidable Dan Rostenkowski (D-IL), then chairman of the Ways and Means Committee. "Rosty," as everyone called him, was a master of his craft—which was legislative and political deal making, not economics. So when his committee reported out a bill around Thanksgiving, it was based a lot more on political than economic principles. Rosty readily admitted that "we have not written a perfect law," and few were inclined to disagree.

But the loophole season began in earnest when Rostenkowski's turkey was sent for carving to the Senate Finance Committee—whose chairman, Bob Packwood (R-OR), had already declared himself an opponent of tax reform. At one point, the committee voted outrageously generous depreciation allowances to what it called "productivity property." What kind of property was that? Well, the list included dental equipment, musical instruments, and caskets, but excluded office furniture, communications satellites, and nuclear power plants. See a pattern there? I don't either—or rather no economically logical pattern. But you can bet that some senator's home state had a casket manufacturer.

The pundits who declared tax reform dead were soon proven wrong, however. Packwood, under political duress as he sought reelection, felt the need to burnish his image. So with important prodding from Senator Bill Bradley (D-NJ), who may have been the only senator devoted to tax reform on principle, he turned a complete 180 degrees in April 1986 by introducing a radical bill that swept away loopholes in order to lower tax rates dramatically. Quicker than you could say, "K Street lobbyist," Packwood formed a core group of six senators who shepherded the bill through the committee in record time, voting down dozens of special interest amendments along the way. Stunningly, the final vote on the bill was 20–0 in the committee and 97–3 on the Senate floor.

Lesson 2: Strike while the iron is hot. (Trump and the Republicans remembered that in 2017.) The Senate Finance Committee moved lightning fast after Packwood's Damascene conversion. Just nineteen days elapsed between Packwood's reversal and the committee's unanimous vote in favor of tax reform. A mere forty-eight days later, the full Senate passed the bill with almost no amendments. Lobbyists barely had enough time to shine their Gucci loafers, much less to mount a credible counterattack. As one shell-shocked lobbyist for the real estate industry noted at the time, "At least our people have nice, big buildings of their own to jump from."

My goodness. Had economics triumphed over politics? Not quite yet. The starkly different bill passed by the House, laden with loopholes and gimmicks for individual taxpayers, was still in the congressional hopper. Since the two bills had little in common, a major House-Senate conference would be necessary to reconcile them. Lobbyists girded for battle, expecting to win on this round.

But Rostenkowski surprised them. Impressed by both the lopsided votes in the Senate and the symbolic power of super-low tax rates, he had become an unlikely convert to the cause of tax reform. The two chairmen dominated the conference and prevailed. One astonished Republican staffer put it this way in a limerick:

Here's to the tax-reform conference,
Home of low rates and high drama
Where Rosty speaks only to Packwood
And Packwood speaks only on camera.

Together, the two chairs—one a Republican, the other a Democrat—produced the landmark Tax Reform Act of 1986, which President Reagan signed with delight in October. Many economists, including me, consider it the best tax bill ever to emerge from Congress.

Lesson 3: It helps (and it's rare) when some congressional leader or leaders (in this case, Packwood and Rostenkowski) decide to act like statesmen. You knew that, too. But notice that statesmanship can be made operational only if leaders can lead, rather than just go out for a walk. Back in 1986, the two committee chairs had enough clout to bulldoze a radical tax bill through their committees and onto the floors of both chambers. That may be impossible today. In any case, no leaders devoted to real tax reform emerged to shepherd a bill through Congress in 2017.

I mentioned the power of a symbol in Rosty's conversion to tax reform: the promised 27 percent top bracket rate (which ultimately became 28 percent). Offering an eye-catching top rate that low—the top rate at the time was 50 percent—got wealthy hearts beating faster. But to make the arithmetic work, senators had to take a meat ax to a long list of tax shelters and other preferences, which is exactly what they did. Coupling the super-low top rate with an all-out assault on tax loopholes married good economics to good politics in a way that is rarely seen. And it worked. Lesson 4: Often, you gotta have a gimmick to make the sale politically.

A fifth essential ingredient in the success of tax reform was the proverbial smoke-filled room, especially the secrecy that went with it. Listen to James Baker, who switched jobs from White House chief of staff to secretary of the Treasury while the tax bill was in the works: "We saw what happened in this committee when we tried to mark up a tax bill in public. If we hadn't gone into back-room sessions, you wouldn't have ever gotten a bill." Packwood agreed: "When we're in the sunshine, as soon as we vote, every trade association in the country gets out their mailgrams and their phone calls in twelve hours, and complains about the members' votes. But when we're in the back room, the senators can vote . . . for what they think is good for the country. Then they can go out to the lobbyists and say: 'God, I fought for you. I did everything I could. But Packwood just wouldn't give in, you know. It's so damn horrible.'" Note, by the way, that both Democrats and Republicans were sitting in Packwood's smoke-filled room.

Hence Lesson 5: As noted earlier, sunshine is an indiscriminate disinfectant. Sometimes politically risky compromises require backroom deals. Of course, not all backroom deals are attractive.

The final, and crucially important, ingredient in the secret sauce of 1986 brings us squarely back to linkage. Tax reform suffers from the classic political flaw that I've discussed several times: most loophole closings inflict noticeable pain on a small minority in order to reap tiny (and hence mostly unnoticed) gains for everyone else. That combination, as I've emphasized repeatedly, is a winner economically but a loser politically.

Something clever was needed to break the logjam in the Senate Finance Committee in 1986, and Bradley and Packwood found it in linkage: holding the whole reform package together rather than letting it be picked apart the way a bunch of hungry birds devour roadkill. Suppose you sweep away, say, twenty loopholes all at once, rather than one by one. Many taxpayers will be aggrieved by one or two of these twenty reforms, from which they benefit. But they will be pleased by the other eighteen or nineteen, each of which reduces their tax bills a bit. So on balance, their representatives in Congress may support the package as a whole *if they are forced to vote that way.* As Bradley put it at the time, "Our approach was to start out asserting the general interest—lower tax rates—and now you have fratricide when somebody tries to change it." Thus persuaded by Bradley, Packwood proposed a radical overhaul that closed loophole after loophole, and then he insisted on holding the package together rather than letting the committee consider provisions one at a time. The whole proved to be far stronger, politically, than the sum of its parts because it promised net benefits to almost everyone.

This rare transformation of good economics into good politics was helped along enormously by an ingenious change in the rules of the Finance Committee. In May 1986, Packwood's core supporters won an agreement that any revenue-losing amendment (e.g., the restoration of some loophole) had to be accompanied by a revenue-gaining amendment of equal dollar value. Several years later, this idea would come to be called "pay as you go" (or "pay-go" for short) and would help reduce the budget deficit (see just below). But in the spring of 1986, it was a new—and politically brilliant—idea.*

Pairing amendments in this way—linking them—transformed the political calculus fundamentally. The contest was no longer between my favorite loophole and some abstract principle of sound taxation. It was between my favorite loophole and your favorite loophole. So specific pieces of the tax reform no longer presented the politically distasteful combination of diffuse, hidden benefits and concentrated, visible costs. Instead, senators found they could gain clemency for one ox only by goring another—which is not nearly as attractive. With the fights thus made fairer, virtually every antireform amendment lost. The public interest won. Amazing.

Lesson 6: Linkage can move political calculus closer to economic calculus by making the "interest group" closer to the whole population. Whether this happened in 2017 is debatable.

Can We Do It Again?

Well, we did—though it was a while ago and in a different context. The pay-as-you-go rule adopted by President George H. W. Bush and the Democratic Congress as part of the 1990 budget agreement required that any proposed tax cut or increase in entitlement spending be accompanied by what came to be called, in an awkward English construction, "pay-fors," meaning tax increases or spending cuts of

---

*The idea apparently originated with Representative George Miller (D-CA) and other House members in 1982 but was not adopted then. Congressional Budget Office, "Pay-As-You-Go Budgeting," CBO staff memorandum prepared by Roy T. Meyers, March 1990, 1, cbo.gov/sites/default/files/101st-congress-1989-1990/reports/90-cbo-019.pdf.

equal magnitude. Pay-go was the sleeper in the much-maligned 1990 budget deal, dwarfed in political salience (at the time) by President Bush breaking his "no new taxes" pledge. But it worked splendidly, not just for the remainder of the Bush administration but also in the Clinton administration that followed.

Pay-go was, in fact, one of the main reasons why Congress was able, first, to balance the budget and, then, to produce a surplus during Bill Clinton's second term. Sadly, it was abandoned under President George W. Bush so that Republicans could pass budget-busting tax cuts in 2001 and 2003. With the pesky pay-as-you-go obstacle out of the way, the budget deficit soared again. Thus the nation's politicians ran something close to a controlled experiment: pay-go was turned on in 1990, and the budget deficit shrank. It was turned off in 2001, and the budget deficit exploded. Neither was a coincidence.

What about tax reform? Can we do a repeat of 1986? Well, President Trump claimed to "reform" the tax code in 2017. But did he? Most economists would say no. The truth is that tax reform is always an uphill political climb. Why?

On the positive side, bundling things together under a pay-go banner is now much less novel than it was in 1986. That part is definitely doable, but it's about where the good news ends. Yes, powerful symbols that move legislation are always possible; skilled politicians do that well. But such symbols seem to be used more often for ill than for good these days. Statesmanship is in short supply. Partisanship is more extreme than ever. Compromise is treated as treason to your party. Backroom deals are frowned upon. The political system is awash in special interest money, and the Supreme Court makes sure it stays that way. Party leaders are finding it tough to lead when there aren't enough followers. And Donald J. Trump is president of the United States.

That doesn't sound hopeful. And when it comes to true tax reform, I'm not. But remember that my broad goal for this chapter is modest: to find ways to move the needle in the direction of illumination *just a bit*. As Deng Xiaoping advised in the chapter's epigram, you should cross a wide river with small, carefully calibrated steps. And the river that divides good economics from good politics is wide indeed.

This chapter has offered no magic bullets. And some of my ideas for reducing partisanship may sound more like wishful thinking than practical advice. Maybe they are. But don't forget the two politically "easy" pieces with which I began the chapter: stretching the political time horizon to four years and searching for policy solutions that postpone the pain while reaping the gain. Neither of these ideas violates any laws of politics. Finally, don't forget about linkage, which is not only possible but actually sometimes happens—to good effect.

One potentially valuable form of linkage harkens back to an older meaning of the term *earmarking*. That word used to refer to tying specific taxes or other revenue sources to specific spending programs. Perhaps the best-known example at the federal level is earmarking receipts from the gasoline tax to funding road building and repairs.* The payroll tax for Social Security is another example, one that involves far more money. Most of what you pay in payroll taxes is assigned to the Social Security Trust Fund, where it is used to finance retirement and disability benefits. At the local level, governments typically earmark the lion's share of property tax payments to financing the public schools.

Economists have always found earmarking, by this definition, peculiar. Why, for example, should we expect the gasoline tax to bring in exactly the amount of money we wish to spend on highways? Or that payroll tax receipts will just cover what we need for Social Security benefits? To an economic purist's way of thinking, Congress shouldn't earmark tax revenues. Rather, it should decide how much it wants to spend on everything, and then design a fair and efficient tax system that raises the requisite amount of money in total. What sense does it make to tie Tax A to Spending Project B?

---

*Congress departed from this norm in the December 2015 budget agreement, which transferred some Federal Reserve assets to the highway trust fund.

Political sense, perhaps. Citizens may be more willing to pay taxes if they see a direct, tangible link between the taxes they pay and the benefits they receive. They will almost certainly find it fairer. On both counts, people may see earmarked taxes as less burdensome, and the spending programs they finance as more appealing. Looked at from the conservative perspective, an earmarked tax makes it clear that more government spending is not a free lunch. To get more, you must pay more. Either way, bad economics may be good politics.

One seemingly nutty example of such earmarking has been much discussed in recent years. As mentioned in the previous chapter, American multinational corporations park a large stash of profits abroad rather than bring the dollars home and pay taxes on them. A long list of politicians, both Democrats and Republicans and including both Presidents Obama and Trump, have suggested deals under which companies would pay a sharply reduced corporate tax rate on repatriated profits if they pledged to do X with it. Several choices of "X" have been bandied about over the years, investing the money in infrastructure being the recent favorite.

Most economists scoff at this idea. They ask a perfectly legitimate question: What in the world does the number of repatriated dollars have to do with the amount of infrastructure we need to build? Is the amount of money companies have squirreled away in Ireland somehow related to the number of bridges needing repair in Boston? As a matter of pure economics, there are no good answers to such questions. So most economists ridicule the idea of tying the tax receipts to the spending. But what if the promise to build more infrastructure paves the way for a sensible political deal that gives the US Treasury more revenue from repatriation—a deal that would not be made otherwise? In that case, tying repatriation and infrastructure together might make good political sense.

At the risk of losing my economist's union card, let me suggest that breaking a few logjams by earmarking specific funds to specific purposes might harness political logic to produce some good, if not ideal, economic policies. If so, such linkage would be a step in the right direction.

So maybe all is not lost. Maybe, if we set modest goals, there are realistic prospects for moving the needle a bit in the direction of greater economic illumination and less partisan support. Toward more good economic advice and less political dissent. Maybe. But perhaps there is even more mileage in moving the line between politics and technocracy. Let's see.

Chapter 12

Toward Remedies: Moving the Line

Insanity is doing the same thing over and over again and expecting different results.

—attributed (perhaps falsely) to Albert Einstein

Professor Alan Auerbach of the University of California, Berkeley, is a top-notch economist—one of our nation's leading experts on taxation. When I'm puzzled by a tax issue, I often call on him for help. Some years ago, Auerbach and co-authors began advocating a creative, though complicated, solution to the vexing problem of how to tax multinational corporations. With so many different tax systems around the world, there is no perfect solution, and Auerbach's plan doesn't solve every problem. But my guess is that 90 percent of economists, maybe 99 percent, would score it an improvement over the current mess that passes for a corporate income tax. (Yes, that's a low bar, but a highly relevant one.)

Under most tax systems, a multinational's tax bill depends inter alia on where the company is headquartered, where it produces its products, and where its profits get reported. Within limits, companies can manipulate all of these—sometimes with little more than paper transactions. As I mentioned earlier, an astounding amount of US corporate income somehow gets "earned" in tax havens like Bermuda, Ireland, and Luxembourg.

Auerbach's central idea was that it's harder to manipulate where a firm actually sells its products. So, he concluded, we could make the tax code simpler and less distortionary if we taxed corporate income based on where the output is sold, rather than on where it is (allegedly) produced. That means, for example, exempting US products made here but sold abroad (our exports) and taxing foreign-made products sold here, regardless of who makes them (our imports). This tax treatment is called "border adjustment," and so was born an awkward name: the destination-based cash-flow tax with border adjustment. (Try saying that fast.) A sensible idea? Well, mostly. For example, it would eliminate the incentive for American multinationals to move either factories or corporate headquarters abroad. Yes, there are some technical problems, but they won't detain us here because technocrats don't make US tax policy; politicians do.

In June 2016, Paul Ryan (R-WI), Kevin Brady (R-TX), and other House Republicans, realizing that US imports far exceed US exports, latched onto border adjustment as a politically attractive way to raise revenue. By taxing imports and exempting exports, you can raise a lot of money to use for other purposes—such as the large income tax cuts they wanted. Besides, border adjustment looks as if you're taxing foreigners. Who cares if a little economic illumination suggests otherwise?

So a version of Auerbach's idea became part of House Republicans' "Better Way" tax plan. And when a Republican-controlled government was elected in November 2016, it began to be discussed heavily in the media and the markets. At that point, it quickly became clear that the destination-based cash-flow tax with border adjustment held a lot more appeal for technocrats than for politicians. The latter had to confront, among other things, vehement opposition from big retailers like Walmart (and their millions of customers) who rely heavily on imported goods. Besides, it was hard to explain. Soon it was bye-bye border adjustment. So much for expert opinion.

And Now for Something Different

The previous chapter explored some ways in which society might move the needle in the direction of more illumination and less political support from economics—and thereby toward better economic policy. Here I explore a more radical approach: the idea of moving the line that divides political decision making from technocratic decision making—specifically, placing more authority in the hands of technically trained experts and less in the hands of politicians. We already do this in a few policy arenas. So in deference to Monty Python, doing it more would not constitute something completely different. Nonetheless, taking more economic decisions out of the realm of politics and moving them into the realm of technocracy would constitute a dramatic departure from current practice.

Some twenty years ago, I published an article in *Foreign Affairs* with a deliberately provocative title: "Is Government Too Political?" I did not mean, of course, that we should depoliticize government. That's oxymoronic. Nor did I mean that economists should be put in charge of running economic policy—a notion I rejected in the opening chapter of this book. What I meant to suggest twenty years ago, and even more so today, is that a few economic policy decisions might be made better by technocrats than by politicians—and with no substantial diminution of democracy. The tax code may be a prime example, and I'll return to that later.

When you stop and think about it, every society, indeed every level of government, makes some decisions politically and leaves others to lower-level experts and bureaucrats. Congress appropriates funds for major arms programs, but the precise functionality of the new rocket launchers and tanks is left to military experts. State legislatures decide how much to spend on highways—and probably also where to put them—on political grounds, but civil engineers generally decide on how to get the work done. City governments decide how many cops to hire, but typically let the (nonpolitical) authorities select the people for the jobs and decide where to deploy them. Each of you can probably think of cases where this prototypical division of decision-making labor broke down—usually because some politician crossed the line into what should have been technocratic territory. And usually to bad effect.

So suppose we moved the line of demarcation in the other direction. Suppose we took some economic decisions that are now being made politically and placed them in the hands of economists and other experts. Might we get better results? Of course, we can't transfer all economic policy decisions in this way and still preserve democracy. Nor would we want to. But maybe it would work for a few.

Actually, it already has. We do depoliticize some functions of government, even some economic functions. The most prominent and important example is monetary policy, which is run by the independent Federal Reserve.

Monetary Policy

Article I, Section 8, of the Constitution grants Congress the power "to coin money and regulate the value thereof." The latter role—regulating the value of money—leads directly to what we now call *monetary policy*. The framers, of course, knew neither the term nor the concept, so they didn't know they were assigning to Congress what would later become monetary policy. After more than a century and two false starts, Congress delegated that authority to an independent central bank, the Federal Reserve System, in 1913.

It is often said, erroneously, that the Fed doesn't take orders from Congress. On the contrary, it has to take orders—whenever Congress gives them. The Fed is, after all, a creature of Congress, created by an ordinary law (the Federal Reserve Act) with no special constitutional protections (the Constitution makes no mention of a central bank). Congress can therefore take back or modify the central bank's authority any day it wishes. Fortunately, Congress has resisted the urge to do so.

You might ask what persuaded Congress to hand such awesome power over to a bunch of unelected technocrats in 1913—and then to leave it there for more than a century (so far). There are probably several reasons.

First, Congress had no idea how awesome the power to set monetary policy would become. Neither did anyone else in 1913. In the language of the day, the Federal Reserve was established and empowered to provide "an elastic currency," which meant, for example, preventing violent contractions of money and credit during financial panics. (The frightening Panic of 1907 was the last straw.) This the Fed still does. But while there were precursors, what we now think of as monetary policy—moving short-term interest rates to influence the growth of aggregate demand—became the Fed's most prominent mission only after a historic 1951 "accord" with the US Treasury gave the Federal Reserve authority over interest rates.

Second, history is replete with examples of monarchs, presidents, and parliaments—all with short time horizons—causing ruinous inflation by printing too much money. So people around the world came to see an independent central bank as a bulwark against inflation—or more specifically, as a bulwark against giving politicians control over money. Because the United States has a relatively benign inflation history, controlling inflation was not seen as the Fed's central mission for decades. That only happened after the brief inflationary outburst following World War II. Since then, however, controlling inflation has been central to Federal Reserve policy, thereby bolstering the case for independence.

Third, monetary policy has always been a bit technical, and it has grown more so in recent decades. Few members of Congress profess to have the training and ability to make good monetary policy decisions themselves. They know that their comparative advantage lies in criticizing the Fed, not running it. So it is no accident that even recent—and in my view, misguided—attempts to limit the Fed's power have focused on things like pushing the central bank to follow mechanical rules, not on transferring monetary policy decisions to Congress.

Finally, an inflation-fighting monetary authority must sometimes inflict (one hopes short-term) pain on the citizenry by raising interest rates when that is not politically popular. (Is it ever?) As William McChesney Martin, the longest serving Federal Reserve chair in history, famously quipped, the Fed's job is to take away the punch bowl just as the party gets going. Inflicting pain on constituents is not a job many politicians relish. They'd rather join the party than end it.

Look back over that list. The first reason—not knowing what they were doing—is a poor basis for Congress to decide whether to delegate authority over any function of government and not one we want to replicate. But the other three make sense. When a task is highly technical, requires a long time horizon, and entails displeasing the voters now and then, it just might be something that Congress—or even the president—would willingly hand over to a bunch of nonpoliticians.

These same criteria, more or less, characterize other prominent examples of nonpolitical—or, more accurately, less political—decision making in American economic policy today.

Fast-Track Authority

Serious trade negotiations are incredibly complicated, multifaceted, and in places highly technical affairs, requiring the skills of dozens of economists, lawyers, and assorted other experts with specialized knowledge on particular matters. Just reading the text of a trade agreement is a monumental task demanding large doses of caffeine and copious amounts of time. For example, the full text of the ill-fated Trans-Pacific Partnership, which President Trump killed in a stroke in January 2017, ran to 7,318 pages—not including several hundred more pages of side agreements.

The agreements that emerge from such laborious negotiations are intended to last a long time. And the necessary economic adjustments— as some industries expand and others contract—can take decades. So the costs and benefits of trade agreements must be appraised over very long periods. In the case of the TPP, the background analytical work done by the US International Trade Commission traced the estimated effects of the agreement for thirty years.

Most important, every trade agreement creates long lists of winners and losers. If members of Congress conducted the negotiations themselves, we'd get either an unholy mess (perhaps resembling the tax code) or, more likely, nothing. In recognition of that reality, Congress periodically grants the president "fast-track" authority to negotiate trade agreements with other nations relatively free of congressional meddling. At the end, the final agreement is supposed to come back to Congress for a straight up-or-down vote. If Congress is unhappy with the agreement, it can vote it down, but it can't amend it.

Well, that's the idea, anyway. The reality is a good deal messier, involving sporadic congressional interference in the negotiations, amendments in Congress prior to the straight up-or-down vote, or even outright refusal to bring the agreement to the floor for a vote. Nonetheless, fast track still strengthens the hand of US trade negotiators in making binding (sort of) commitments, and hence getting better agreements. Members of Congress understand that and willingly relinquish some (but not all) of their ability to pick the agreement apart piece by piece. Thus fast track does not eliminate congressional interference but greatly reduces it. It's a technique, I think, that could be utilized elsewhere.

Fast track offers the same three ingredients that characterize monetary policy: heavy use of technical expertise, adopting a very long time horizon, and being willing to inflict pain where necessary. Congress seems to recognize the virtues of unloading such tasks on technocrats—at least occasionally, though the degree of independence granted to trade negotiators is nowhere near what the Federal Reserve has.

Military Base Closings

Closing down obsolete or redundant military installations is nothing new. General Grant presumably had to deal with that problem after the Civil War. But when a base designated for closure is located in one of the 435 congressional districts, as opposed to abroad, you can count on vocal opposition to the attendant loss of jobs and collateral damage to local businesses. If not constrained or bought off, the state's two senators and the local members of Congress will be up in arms, on the Pentagon's back, and making their displeasure known to the president.

This particular version of NIMBY (Not in My Backyard) became an acute problem when the Cold War ended. Our military was far too big for the post–Cold War world, and scores, if not hundreds, of installations had to be downsized or shut down. The Department of Defense knew it had to shrink. So did President George H. W. Bush. So even did Congress. But there was a big political problem: most of the redundant bases were located in somebody's backyard.

What to do? Drawing on some past precedents, Congress established the Defense Base Realignment and Closure Commission (BRAC) to evaluate the Pentagon's recommendations on objective, nonpolitical grounds. Yes, BRAC decisions are somewhat technical, so you want people on the commission with real expertise. Yes, deciding which bases to close demands a time horizon that extends well past the next election, so you want to minimize political influence. But the main problem in this case was dispensing economic pain. The BRAC's charge was to decide which bases to close, not where to open new ones. Thus, it was handing out only pain and no gain—hardly a recipe to induce congressional envy.

Perhaps surprisingly, the BRAC process has worked extremely well over several rounds. Bases have been closed all over the country, and the decisions were, for the most part, made by independent commissioners, not by politicians—who could and did gripe, however. It's another successful example of the use of delegated power—power delegated willingly by Congress. Congress has never appeared anxious to take that power back—which, as in the case of monetary policy, it may do anytime it chooses.

These three examples of government (mostly) by technocrats all "work"—not perfectly, but pretty well. There is always congressional oversight, as there should be. But with some exceptions, political interference has been kept mostly at bay.

That said, I hasten to add that relying on technocrats is no guarantee of success. I'm not an expert on military matters, but I wouldn't want to defend every BRAC decision. All trade agreements involve tradeoffs and judgment calls that can be, and are, questioned. The Federal Reserve has certainly made monetary policy errors. Yes, even well-intentioned, well-trained, intelligent technocrats make mistakes. They may carry ideological or bureaucratic baggage that can lead to systematic biases. They often have trouble thinking outside the box.

But in all such cases, we should ask: Would politicians have done the job better? If you're wondering where to draw the line between politics and technocracy, that's the right question. And the answer is usually no.

An Essential Amendment

Wait. I have left out something important. It is true that many economic policy decisions have major technical aspects—things at which economists excel and politicians don't. But some decisions hinge even more sensitively on value judgments, about which economists possess no comparative advantage over politicians—quite the opposite, actually. And technocrats certainly have far less political legitimacy than elected politicians. When an issue is laden with value judgments, it would be a capital mistake to transfer decision-making authority to a bunch of unelected technocrats.

Examples abound. Consider decisions about the generosity (or lack thereof) of the social safety net. Technical expertise—*illumination*, if you will—has its place. How much do food stamps and welfare payments dull the incentive to work? By how much does unemployment insurance prolong episodes of unemployment? Does Social Security induce many people to retire earlier? These and other such questions are highly relevant; policymakers should want to know the answers as best economists can provide them.

But at bedrock, questions about whether to make Paul Ryan's "hammock" more or less comfortable for the poor come down to value judgments. How generous toward the needy do we want to be? How much inefficiency are we willing to tolerate in the quest for more equity? Soft-hearted Democrats are typically more generous and more devoted to equity. Hard-headed Republicans are typically less generous and more concerned with efficiency. Their sharp partisan differences on these matters probably stem more from different value judgments than from different technical judgments. Neither economic textbooks nor economic technocrats can tell anyone who is right and who is wrong. It's political, in the good sense of that word.

A second prominent example is setting the top marginal rate in the personal income tax. Conservatives claim, with some justification, that high income tax rates create distortions and cause economic inefficiencies. But they also believe it is fundamentally unfair to "punish" successful people with high tax rates. Liberals downplay the costs of tax distortions—sometimes even denying they exist. Even more important, however, they argue that it is only fair that the rich pay higher taxes.

Economists can contribute something to the debate over efficiency costs—a topic dealt with earlier in this book. But fairness is in the eye of the beholder or, more germane to policymaking, in the eye of the politician. No one will ever convince libertarian Senator Rand Paul (R-KY) that it's fair to soak the rich. No one will ever convince socialist Senator Bernie Sanders (I-VT) that it's fair not to. Technocrats shouldn't try. These two gentlemen have starkly different value judgments, each of them thinks he is right, and each was duly elected by his constituents.

So we need to amend our list of characteristics that make an economic policy issue ripe for transfer into the realm of technocracy. An issue is a good candidate for technocratic decision making if it is technically complex, if it requires a long time horizon, and if it involves the apportionment of pain. It is a bad candidate if value judgments are central to the decision.

Can We Extend the Realm of Technocracy?

So where might that lead us? Where should we look for other areas in which politicians might be willing to delegate authority to economic experts—and where such delegation makes sense? To provoke thought, I have two suggestions. You may be able to think of others.

Infrastructure Banks

Everyone seems to agree that, for such a rich country, the United States of America has an embarrassingly poor stock of public infrastructure. Our roads, bridges, tunnels, airports, water treatment facilities, and the like are simply not up to snuff. Our passenger railroads are laughable. Perhaps the only area of agreement between Donald Trump and Hillary Clinton in the 2016 campaign was that both pledged to rebuild America's crumbling infrastructure. In fact, they both focused on the same number: $1 trillion over ten years. Once Trump became president, however, infrastructure faded into the background as other priorities (like health care and taxes) and exigencies (like the Russian investigation) consumed the administration's bandwidth.

One of the chief impediments to building more and better infrastructure is finding the money; these things tend to be expensive. Another is keeping politicians' hands (mostly) out of project selection. If we don't, we are liable to get a lot of pork-barrel spending—bridges to nowhere and the like. Years ago, when the late Senator Robert Byrd (D-WV) ran the Senate Appropriations Committee, people used to wonder whether his objective was to pave his entire home state. It seemed to be. On such matters, technocrats can do much better.

One common suggestion that dates back a long time is to establish a national infrastructure bank—or maybe fifty state banks. Such an institution, presumably run by experts on nonpolitical principles, would select projects on the economic merits. What do we need more, a new bridge, a new sewage treatment plant, or just filling more potholes so our cars don't get swallowed up? Where are the benefit-cost ratios highest? Armed with answers to such questions, the bank would select projects and raise the necessary funds in the capital markets. Finally, a bunch of technocrats would hire the contractors—who, presumably, would not be the in-laws of local politicians.

Sounds better than what we have now, right? Then why don't we have more infrastructure banks controlling more money? Well, the political attractiveness of ribbon-cutting ceremonies is one big reason. It's also why governments invest far too little in maintenance and repairs, which don't generate photo ops for publicity-hungry politicians, while new bridges do—even if they go to nowhere. Another reason is that technocratic management of infrastructure contracting would severely curtail—gracious, maybe even eliminate!—politicians' ability to dispense favors and to receive favors in return.

Think about that tradeoff from a politician's standpoint. You are asked to give up quality time on television and to relinquish your ability to dispense patronage. In return, you get more, better-selected, and better-managed infrastructure for your constituents, but receive next to no credit for doing so. Maybe not such a great tradeoff for the politicians. But for the rest of us, infrastructure banks, while hardly a panacea, could mark a meaningful improvement over today's modus operandi.

Much infrastructure building therefore seems ripe for transfer from political to technocratic hands. But it won't happen without a strong push from the electorate. In many ways, infrastructure banks offer politicians precisely the opposite deal from base closings. The base-closing commission dispenses lots of pain but little gain. So politicians were willing—maybe even eager—to hand the job over to technocrats. But when it comes to new infrastructure projects, it's mostly about dispensing gain, not pain. Asking politicians to give that up is like asking children to give up candy.

That said, a majority of states do have infrastructure banks, mainly for road building. Most state infrastructure banks began under a Clinton administration pilot project in 1995, most of them are small, and a number are totally inactive. Even in California, where highways are a way of life, the state infrastructure bank has supported only two road projects. Nationally, spending by all state infrastructure banks between 1995 and 2012 was under $9 billion—a comparative pittance. It appears that, if a serious amount of infrastructure is to be built by government, the federal government will have to step up to the plate.

Tax Policy

I have saved the eight-hundred-pound gorilla for last. The US tax code is incredibly technical and complex, probably even more so than monetary policy. Furthermore, tax laws should be written with very long time horizons in mind because it can take years for people and businesses to adjust to tax changes. (Hence the old adage, "An old tax is a good tax.") In fact, the natural time frame for thinking about tax policy is even longer than that for monetary policy. Finally, raising taxes, even more so than raising interest rates, is all about the apportionment of pain. (Cutting taxes is the fun part, even better than cutting interest rates.)

Thus the three main reasons why monetary policy should be independent of politics seem to apply with equal or greater force to tax policy. Yet the formulation of tax policy, from the broadest principles down to much of the minutiae, is left in political hands. No one ever talks of Congress delegating any of its control over the tax code to technocrats, though experts in the Treasury do write most of the detailed rules. Why not?

One obvious, and maybe even dispositive, reason is that tax policy decisions hinge on value judgments far more sensitively than monetary policy decisions do. Which groups or activities should be favored (or disfavored) by the tax code is something for politicians, not technocrats, to decide. That's true. But it still leaves the scoreboard 3–1 in favor of technocracy. Does anyone doubt that our tax code would be simpler, fairer, more principled, and less distortionary if its design was left to an independent board of experts acting under a congressional mandate—something like the Federal Reserve? I thought not. So let's explore the idea.

Imagine that Congress were to establish a Federal Tax Board (FTB) patterned on the Federal Reserve Board. Its members would be presidential appointees, confirmed by the Senate for long terms, and the law would specify that they all be experts on tax policy. I guess that would give you a bunch of lawyers, accountants, and economists. (Think of the thrilling board meetings!) It would certainly exclude almost all politicians. Its staff would presumably be drawn from the IRS, the Treasury Department, and elsewhere.

The legislation would set forth a legal mandate to govern the FTB's tax policy. For reference, the monetary policy mandate of the Federal Reserve is short and vague. It instructs the Fed to implement monetary policy "so as to promote effectively the goals of maximum employment, stable prices, and moderate long-term interest rates." Notice that the three goals are not defined numerically. Decades passed before the Federal Reserve itself, not Congress, defined "stable prices" to mean 2 percent inflation (according to one specific inflation gauge) and "maximum employment" to mean pushing the unemployment rate down to what economists estimate to be its "natural" or "equilibrium" rate (at this writing, that's estimated to be 4.6 percent).

Proceeding similarly, the mandate of the Federal Tax Board might read something like this:

> The Board shall design, implement, and maintain a tax system
> that promotes the long-run growth of the economy with due
> respect to the goals of fairness, simplicity, and efficiency.

As in the Federal Reserve Act, these goals would be stated only vaguely. However, Congress would likely want to go somewhat deeper into the details—and it should. For example, Congress, not apolitical experts, should decide within broad ranges how revenue should be raised. Is it mainly by taxing personal income, corporate income, payrolls, consumption, or what? Congress should also specify a rough distribution table, instructing the FTB, say, on what share of total revenue should come from the top 1 percent of taxpayers, the top

10 percent, and so on. If particular activities like mortgage interest, charitable contributions, or capital gains are to be tax favored, Congress should specify that, too. The technocrats' default option should always be to produce a clean and neutral tax code with no special preferences.

Given the legal mandate and congressional guidelines, the FTB could go to work designing tax laws that are much fairer, far simpler, and immensely less distortionary than those we have now. Technical judgments would have to be made, for sure. But it's actually an easier task than you may think—if you take the politics out. Finally, we can borrow the fast-track idea: rather than facing a diktat from the FTB, which would be undemocratic, Congress should get a straight up-or-down vote on whatever the board produces. If the vote goes negative, Congress should send the FTB a letter explaining what it disliked, and then leave it to the experts to work out the details.

What are the odds that such a mechanism would give us a dramatically better tax code than we have now? I'd say about 100 percent. What are the odds that Congress would relinquish its authority in this way? I'd say about zero, and for a simple reason: tax writing gives members of Congress numerous opportunities to dispense favors. To members of the Senate Finance Committee and the House Ways and Means Committee, in particular, the status quo is quite wonderful. Why upset it?

But let's ask a more basic question: Is technocratic tax writing a wise thing to do for the public interest? Should we want to take (most of) the politics out of tax policy? Some might argue no, that the halls of Congress are the right places for society to mediate competing claims, that conferring so much power on a group of unelected technocrats is undemocratic. They have a point. But I disagree, for many of the same reasons that underpin the independence of the Federal Reserve.

The goals of tax policy should be made by, and changeable by, Congress. Absolutely. Congress should also decide on the broad contours of the tax code, such as whether we tax mainly income or mainly consumption, and how progressive the tax code should be. Appointment by the president of the United States with confirmation by the Senate would imbue members of the Federal Tax Board with political legitimacy, just as it does now for Federal Reserve governors. The FTB would be required to report regularly to the relevant committees of Congress, as the Fed does today. And Congress would reserve the right to reject the FTB's handiwork and ask it to start over.

Such judgments are always in the eyes of the beholder, but that list creates enough political legitimacy for me. The chances that a runaway, autocratic board would create a tax code that flouts either public opinion or sound economics seem remote. Not zero, but remote. Compare that to what we have now.

Division of Labor

This discussion of a hypothetical Federal Tax Board that will never be established points toward a division of labor that we use at times but, in my view, could use much more: let Congress make the big decisions while technocrats make the small ones.

As I've noted, that doesn't happen in tax policy, where Congress gets deep into the weeds. But think about monetary policy. Congress gives the Fed a broad legal mandate, establishes its basic structure (a board in Washington and twelve Reserve Banks around the country), and authorizes it to use a limited set of policy instruments. For example, the Fed has complete control over its overnight interest rates but is prohibited from purchasing corporate bonds or stocks for its open-market operations.

BRAC and fast track are a bit like this, too. The law establishing the base-closing commission instructs it "to provide a fair process that will result in the timely closure and realignment of military installations inside the United States." Criteria and procedures are stated in the law, as is a process for Congress to disapprove of BRAC choices, if it sees fit. Similarly, a vote of Congress is needed to give the president fast-track authority, usually for a limited period of time and under guidelines about what to negotiate. For example, the 2015 statute that granted President Obama fast-track authority to negotiate the TPP listed twelve broad objectives and included several lengthy lists of more specific ones. More pointedly, if Congress didn't want a TPP at all—which is what President Trump later decided—it could have voted down fast-track authority. In fact, it almost did.

Another key aspect of the division of labor between politicians and technocrats is how deep into the executive branch you want to go before political appointees give way to the permanent bureaucracy. The United Kingdom and parliamentary systems in other countries offer examples at one extreme. When the government changes after an election in the United Kingdom, the cabinet ministers all lose their jobs, but virtually no one else in the government does. They are all, to one degree or another, technocrats or professionals, presumptively divorced from partisan politics.

The United States is at the opposite extreme. When we elect a new president, he has literally thousands of political appointments to fill. The so-called Plum Book (named for its color) that President Trump received in January 2017 listed about nine thousand such positions. In a typical cabinet department, it's not just a new secretary, but also a deputy secretary, a possibly long list of undersecretaries and assistant secretaries, a slew of deputy assistant secretaries, and numerous staff members below that rank. All those positions get filled by political appointees; there are many thousands of them across the federal government. If a new administration is slow to fill these jobs, as the Trump administration was in 2017, the government is hobbled.

Here's the question: Which country has it right, the United States or the United Kingdom? Put differently, how deep into the government should you have to go before you start encountering careerists instead of political appointees? My own view is that both countries have it wrong. The US system has too many political appointees, who can take forever to be nominated and confirmed and then leave too soon, who must often climb steep learning curves, and who may bring too much politics (and not enough expertise) to their jobs. The British system, on the other hand, lacks the "new blood" that we get routinely whenever the government changes. It can also foster a stubborn bureaucracy that recognizes its political masters only at the level of lip service.

As is often the case in life, the strength of the American system (fresh ideas and talent) is also our weakness (inexperience and politicization). The happy medium probably falls somewhere between the US and UK extremes. But that's a wide range. And where a country chooses to place itself will heavily influence the blend of politics and technocracy in its policymaking process.

It's Not an Either-Or Question

The key word in that last sentence is "blend," for no real system of governance will offer a stark choice between government by technocrats and government by politicians. Both will have roles to play. Financial regulation provides an excellent example. Its characteristics fit the template for technocratic decision making pretty well, albeit not perfectly.

First, the level of technical detail can be mind-boggling. The so-called Volcker Rule, which was part of the Dodd-Frank Act (2010), makes a wonderful case in point. The great Paul Volcker, whom everyone respects and some idolize, proposed a seemingly simple and reasonable principle in 2009: bankers should not be allowed to use FDIC-insured deposits to engage in what is called "proprietary trading," that is, making bets in financial markets in order to enhance the bank's profitability. Why not? Because the health of the bank could be imperiled if those bets go south, possibly even leading to a government bailout. Sounds right, right? Volcker thought a few well-constructed paragraphs could enshrine this commonsense principle into law. So, in all likelihood, did President Barack Obama when he pushed what he dubbed the Volcker Rule into Dodd-Frank.

Well, not quite. Without going into the excruciating details—and they *are* excruciating—it is devilishly difficult for regulators to tell which trades are proprietary and which are motivated, say, by hedging (which makes the bank safer, not riskier) or by customer service to bank clients. So in drafting Dodd-Frank, Volcker's few sentences mushroomed into thirty-nine pages. You can look it up; it's Section 619. (But I don't recommend you try.)

Section 619 of Dodd-Frank was just the beginning, however. In our system, Congress writes laws, and then the regulatory agencies, which have the technical expertise, translate those sometimes vague guidelines into detailed rules and regulations. In the case of the Volcker Rule, that process took three and a half years and wound up producing 268 dense pages of small type in the Federal Register. By the end of the process, Volcker himself was wondering what had happened to his "simple" idea.

The tale of the Volcker Rule, though a bit extreme, is by no means unusual. There can be no doubt that financial regulation passes the first test criterion—technical complexity—with flying colors.

Second, the natural time horizon for financial regulation is very long. Consider: The Volcker Rule took three and a half years just to finalize—and that's before any case law accumulates. Furthermore, some of the other rules called for by Dodd-Frank in 2010 have not even been written yet. Congress doesn't pass a major financial regulatory bill every year because it can't—it takes too much time and effort. The Dodd-Frank Act was supposed to last for decades, though candidate Donald Trump vowed to "dismantle" it, and the so-called CHOICE Act that passed the House of Representatives in May 2017 took several big steps in that direction. The Senate, however, never took it up.

Finally, regulations are generally a mixed bag of giving and taking, imposing costs on some, showering benefits on others—a characteristic that regulation shares with monetary policy and trade agreements. Making financial regulations tougher is, of course, the hard part. It tends to turn rich and powerful financial corporations into losers, and they have weapons with which to fight back, such as campaign contributions and legions of lobbyists. The winners from tighter financial regulations are often either the consumers of financial services or taxpayers in general. In a word, folks like you and me, who don't hire lobbyists and whose political voices are barely audible. This imbalance of political forces, I have emphasized, makes for lopsided fights when politicians are asked to dispense pain to people and institutions who have the power and inclination to push back. Might politicians want to delegate some such tasks to technocrats?

Maybe so, but don't forget the other side of the coin. When the politics of the day calls for easing regulations, that is, for showering benefits on people and institutions capable of paying you back, politicians will want seats in the front row with the mics turned on and the klieg lights shining. Like members of the two tax-writing committees, members of the House and Senate banking committees view their seats as gold mines for campaign contributions.

Is there a solution? Not a perfect one, but the American tradition of independent financial regulators certainly helps. Congress is loath to countermand the regulatory work of the Federal Reserve, the FDIC, and others—not because doing so is beyond their legal authority, but because it's almost sure to generate horrible publicity. Pandering to special interests, especially when it's on display for all to see, tends to look like exactly what it is. And if Congress overrules, say, the Federal Reserve, that action won't stay hidden for long.

But independence, unlike pregnancy, comes in degrees. The aspect of independence that matters most in this context is budgetary independence. The Fed does not go to Congress for an appropriation each year; rather, it generates its own funds from the inherent profitability of its monetary policy operations.* Neither does the FDIC, which finances its operations from the deposit insurance premiums that banks pay. (Both, of course, get congressional oversight.)

But other financial regulatory agencies, such as the Securities and Exchange Commission and the Commodity Futures Trading

---

*In a nutshell, and omitting many details, the Fed earns interest on the securities it owns but pays no interest on the cash ("Federal Reserve notes") you carry in your wallet.

Commission, are not so fortunate. They must come back to the White House and Congress each year with budget requests. If the political powers-that-be are displeased with their work, their budgets can be squeezed. This is not hypothetical; it happens. For example, the CFTC got about 11 percent less than it requested in President Trump's first budget proposal. This is not a good feature if you want the SEC and the CFTC to stand up to powerful financial interests. So put this on your checklist of things that should be changed.

Budgetary independence was one main reason why the fight over establishing the Consumer Financial Protection Bureau as part of Dodd-Frank drew so much political blood. Democrats wanted the new agency to have it, so that no future Congress could squeeze the life out of the CFPB. Republicans, who never liked the CFPB idea, wanted to keep the agency at the mercy of annual appropriations. Because Democrats had the votes in 2010, a weird compromise was struck whereby the CFPB was made part of the Federal Reserve de jure, though not de facto. The important thing was that the CFPB's budget comes directly from the Fed, not from Congress. I wouldn't want to defend this Rube Goldberg solution, but it does at least give the bureau budgetary independence.

A Possible Dream?

So the idea of moving the line in technocratic directions is not all pie in the sky. More such movement is possible.

Will we create a national infrastructure bank, or better yet a set of larger state infrastructure banks, run on economic rather than political principles? Well, actually there has been a lot of talk about that idea in recent years. So far, it's been all talk and no action at the federal level, but maybe that will change.

Will we ever get a tax code written mainly by economists, lawyers, and accountants, perhaps working for a nonpolitical government board? That's a bigger stretch, for sure. Bet against it. Campaign contributions are at stake. But the widespread disgust with the current

tax system, and our politicians' failure to make significant improvements in 2017, have kept the pot boiling. Maybe someday it will boil
over, and politicians will conclude that at least some aspects of tax
policy should be turned over to technical experts. Maybe.

But proponents of more technocratic decision making already
have several prominent success stories to tell, several of which have
been discussed in this chapter. It is surely not plausible that these are
the only viable candidates for elevating technocracy over politics. But
to move the line, both economic and political civilizations will have
to make some changes—changes that favor more economic illumination and less partisan support for policies predetermined by politics.
That's a tall order, but hopefully not an impossible dream.

Chapter 13

Last Word: On Bridging the Gap

You just don't understand.

—title of a best-selling book by Deborah Tannen

The last two chapters were devoted to hoped-for and potential changes in the political system—changes that might increase the *demand for illumination*, you might call them. If economic policy performance is to improve, politicians must learn that the *time horizons* that really matter in politics are measured in years (especially to the next presidential election), not in days or minutes. They must also come to appreciate that *logic, arithmetic,* and *facts* will ultimately triumph over spin, wishful thinking, and alternative facts—no matter how much they get away with in the short run. So by all means campaign in poetry, but once elected, govern in prose. Realize also that what *is right* will ultimately matter more to your constituents than what *sounds right* initially (and superficially). Finally, it wouldn't hurt if politicians threw a little more statesmanship into the mix. Let them all read the Constitution—or go see a performance of *Hamilton*.

But what about the *supply* of economic illumination? Can economists make their advice more useful in the policy process? You bet. The economists' to-do list is long, but I'll be brief with each item because we're the bit players in this drama. The politicians have the starring roles.

For openers, we economists need to speak English more and techno-speak less—at least when we're out in public. That would help us engage more effectively in policy debates. In particular, it is essential for economists, most of whom are academics, to realize that message matters in a democracy. In practice, it probably matters far more than purity of thought and ingenious design. A brilliant policy idea that just doesn't sound right to the citizenry is unlikely to appeal to their elected representatives.

As a corollary, economists should keep the KISS principle—"Keep it simple, stupid"—squarely in mind. Many economic problems are inherently complex, and so are their solutions. That's life. But economists need to learn to live with, even to search out and promote, simpler alternatives. Such policies may fall short of the best solutions economists can think of. But if you can't explain something to the populace, it's unlikely that you can persuade the politicians. Ranked on politically relevant criteria, the good may be better than the best.

We economists also need to remember that real people do not behave like the caricatures who inhabit our models. There's a reason we call the latter *Homo economicus*. It's a strange species. Human beings are not walking, talking calculating machines. They make systematic mistakes over and over again. Their emotions often overwhelm their intellect. They are probably more interested in better jobs than in cheaper consumer goods. And when they find themselves in economic difficulty, they want their government to provide a hand *up*, not a demeaning hand*out*.

We economists must learn to think and talk more about the concerns of ordinary people—as opposed to the things we deem important. In particular, we need to recognize that fairness is far more meaningful and important to most people than the economist's cherished notion of efficiency. One consequence is that policy proposals that enhance efficiency but strike people as unfair are unlikely to succeed in the political arena. That doesn't mean economists have it wrong; more often than not, we have it right. But when you are the only lobbying group for economic efficiency—and a tiny, powerless lobby at that—you are going to lose if you go it alone.

We must also learn something we already know but frequently ignore: that sequencing matters. Human life is mostly path dependent, not a matter of returning to previously visited equilibrium states, as so much economic theory posits. So, for example, the order in which Congress takes up a list of policy priorities may strongly influence which ones pass into law and which ones pass into oblivion.

Finally, something that may sound relatively unimportant but is actually hugely important: we economists must stop belittling transition costs. The more we denigrate "short-run" dislocations stemming from economic change as annoying "transition costs" that can be ignored, the more we ensure our own irrelevance in the policy arena. The hard truth is that almost everyone lives in transitions almost all the time. It should be possible to recognize that fact without sacrificing what economics does best: paying attention to the long term.

If the two civilizations—economic and political—are to come closer together, if we are to replace a world in which each side throws up its hands in despair at the other (*You just don't understand!*) with one in which the two sides communicate and interact productively, then each must learn some things from the other.

Politicians must learn to appreciate economic constraints and incentives, while economists must come to understand that political constraints and incentives often take precedence. The respective provinces of politics and technocracy may need to be reconfigured a bit. The starkly different time horizons of economic analysis and politics must come closer together. Economists must get over their fetish with equilibrium states (where we'll be after the dust settles), while politicians must come to understand that the laws of economics are not easily repealed. Economists must think a lot more about fairness, including the *perception* of fairness, while politicians think a bit more about efficiency.

None of this is impossible, just hard. And if we can manage it, we'll be in a position to achieve what John Maynard Keynes dreamt about more than eighty-five years ago: a world in which economists are "thought of as humble, competent people, on a level with dentists." More important, we'll have blown a hole in the Lamppost Theory and pointed the way toward more useful economic advice met by less political dissent.

NOTES

CHAPTER 1

1   **for support, not illumination:** Andrew Lang was a nineteenth-century Scottish writer. His actual saying used "statistics" rather than "economics." Same idea. The quote may be found in Alan S. Mackay, *Scientific Quotations: The Harvest of a Quiet Eye* (New York: Crane, Russak, 1977), 91.

4   **"a slogan":** Francis X. Clines, "White House Winces at Economist's Words," *New York Times*, October 28, 1982.

CHAPTER 2

15   **"40 seconds on camera":** As quoted in *Newsweek*, September 8, 1986, 14.

20   **"his not understanding it":** Upton Sinclair, *I, Candidate for Governor: And How I Got Licked* (Berkeley: University of California Press, 1994), 109.

22   **"scope of their horizon":** David A. Stockman, *The Triumph of Politics: Why the Reagan Revolution Failed* (New York: Harper & Row, 1986), 14.

35   **bills Congress ever passed:** Jacob Weisberg, "Overnight Statesman: Dan Rostenkowski's New Look," *New Republic*, March 24, 1986, 22.

CHAPTER 3

44   **"booby-trapped with hidden pressures":** David A. Stockman, *The Triumph of Politics: Why the Reagan Revolution Failed* (New York: Harper & Row, 1986), 80, 105, 123.

48   **the train in its tracks:** See Mike DeBonis, "How Health Care for 9/11 Responders Became Just Another Political Football," *Washington Post*, December 14, 2015.

49   **reform in 1993 enormously:** See Haynes Johnson and David S. Broder, *The System: The American Way of Politics at the Breaking*

Point (Boston: Little, Brown, 1996), 118–127. Ironically, that same budget reconciliation process helped health care reform get passed in 2010.

53   **balance within ten years:** US Government, *Budget FY 2018: A New Foundation for American Greatness*, May 23, 2017.

59   **"not enough for me":** Noam Scheiber, *The Escape Artists: How Obama's Team Fumbled the Recovery* (New York: Simon & Schuster, 2012), 147, 15–16.

60   **standard QWERTY keyboard:** The story is nicely told by Paul A. David, "Clio and the Economics of QWERTY," *American Economic Review* 75, no. 2 (May 1985): 332–337, on which this paragraph is based. Its accuracy has been vigorously disputed, but it illustrates my point.

CHAPTER 4

68   **"the effect is felt":** Executive Office of the President, Council of Economic Advisers, *The Economic Case for Health Care Reform: Update*, December 14, 2009, obamawhitehouse.archives.gov/sites/default/files /microsites/091213-economic-case-health-care-reform.pdf.

70   **"who gain by the new ones":** Niccolò Machiavelli, *The Prince*, trans. N. H. Thompson (New York: Dover, 1992).

77   **more than two million jobs:** Congressional Budget Office, Appendix C: "Labor Market Effects of the Affordable Care Act: Updated Estimates," in *The Budget and Economic Outlook: 2014 to 2024*, February 4, 2014, 117–128, cbo.gov/publication/45010.

77   **trumpeting this conclusion:** For a sampling of misleading headlines and quotations, see Glenn Kessler, "No, CBO Did Not Say Obamacare Will Kill 2 Million Jobs," *Washington Post*, February 4, 2014.

77   **different from being fired:** Jonathan Chait, "Obamacare, Jobs, and 'What Matters Politically,'" *New York Magazine*, February 5, 2014.

78   **"Republican ad-maker's dream":** David Nather and Jason Millman, "Obamacare and Jobs: CBO Fuels Fire," *Politico*, February 4, 2014.

79   **"economic theorists and practitioners":** James Carter, "Economists Have a Message: Clinton's Policies Are Wrong for America," *Hill*, September 26, 2016, thehill.com/blogs/pundits-blog/presidential -campaign/297719-economists-have-a-message-clintons-policies-are.

80   **"not really recovered at all":** The particular poll cited was conducted by Fox News: "Syria, Benghazi and the U.S. Economy," Fox News Poll, October 10–12, 2015, foxnews.com/politics/interactive/2015/10/14 /fox-news-poll-syria-benghazi-and-us-economy.

80   **formidable lobbying force:** See Haynes Johnson and David S. Broder, *The System: The American Way of Politics at the Breaking Point* (Boston: Little, Brown, 1996), especially Chapter 10.

CHAPTER 5

97   **"a journalist hears it":** S. Robert Lichter, as quoted in Tatiana S. Boncompagni, "Washington Coverage Is Steady but Public Doesn't Seem to Care," *Wall Street Journal*, August 13, 1997.

99   **"Broken Tax Code":** White House, "Unified Framework for Fixing Our Broken Tax Code," September 27, 2017, whitehouse.gov /the-press-office/2017/09/27/unified-framework-fixing-our-broken-tax -code.

99   **"what will advance him":** Thomas J. Friedman, "Clinton's Fibs, and Her Opponents' Double Whoppers," *New York Times*, June 1, 2016.

100   **"Pants on Fire":** The *Washington Post* kept a similar scale, though with many fewer observations. Their results were quite similar. "Comparing Hillary Clinton, Donald Trump on the Truth-O-Meter," PolitiFact, politifact.com/truth-o-meter/lists/people/comparing-hillary-clinton -donald-trump-truth-o-met (accessed September 20, 2017); *Washington Post* Fact Checker, "The 2016 Election Fact Checker," *Washington Post*, November 3, 2016, washingtonpost.com/graphics/politics /2016-election/fact-checker/?tid=a_inl.

101   **"good for CBS":** Among the hundreds of sources for this quotation, see Paul Bond, "Leslie Moonves on Donald Trump: 'It May Not Be Good for America, but It's Damn Good for CBS,'" *Hollywood Reporter*, February 29, 2016, hollywoodreporter.com/news /leslie-moonves-donald-trump-may-871464/.

102   **"purchased for that price":** James M. Fallows, *Breaking the News: How the Media Undermine American Democracy* (New York: Pantheon Books, 1996), 108–109.

103   **the price of its stock:** Among the dozens of studies that could be cited, see Ronald Stunda, "The Market Impact of Mergers and Acquisitions on Acquiring Firms in the U.S.," *Journal of Accounting and Taxation* 6, no. 2 (September 2014): 30–37.

109   **"reward friends and destroy enemies":** James Bennet, "The On-the-Record Flap About Off the Record," *New York Times*, March 8, 1998.

110   **fixates on the Fed:** My remarks were subsequently published. See "Overview," in *Proceedings of the Federal Reserve Bank of Kansas City Symposium on Reducing Unemployment: Current Issues and Policy Options*, Federal Reserve Bank of Kansas City, August 25–27, 1994, 329–342. Don't read them; they're banal.

111   **"inside the [Federal Reserve] system":** Paul Starobin, "Economy: Blindsided," *National Journal*, October 8, 1994.

111   **"hold down unemployment":** Keith Bradsher, "Fed Official Disapproves of Rate Policy," *New York Times*, August 28, 1994. Notice, by the way, the absurdly misleading headline. The Fed had just raised interest rates, and I had voted with the majority.

111   **"to lead the Fed":** Robert J. Samuelson, "Economic Amnesia," *Washington Post*, September 7, 1994.

CHAPTER 6

126   **fee has been imposed:** Central London has had a congestion fee since 2003, so we know it is workable in a huge city. Mayor Michael Bloomberg recommended such a fee in 2007, but the idea died in the New York State legislature. See Bruce Schaller, "New York City's Congestion Pricing Experience and Implications for Road Pricing Acceptance in the United States," *Transport Policy* 17, no. 4 (2010): 266–273.

127   **"older and younger scholars":** IGM Economic Experts Panel, "About the IGM Economic Experts Panel," Chicago Booth Initiative on Global Markets, igmchicago.org/igm-economic-experts-panel (accessed September 20, 2017).

128   **"what he wants to hear":** Paul A. Samuelson, "Economists and the History of Ideas," *American Economic Review* 52, no. 1 (March 1962): 1–18.

131   **"this is a spending bill":** Fox News, "In Stimulus Debate, Obama Drifts into Campaign Mode," *Fox News*, February 6, 2009, foxnews .com/politics/2009/02/06/stimulus-debate-obama-drifts-campaign -mode.html.

132   **2011, 2012, and 2013:** See Alan S. Blinder and Mark Zandi, *The Financial Crisis: Lessons for the Next One*, Policy Futures Report, Center on Budget and Policy Priorities, October 15, 2015.

134   **"neat, plausible, and wrong":** H. L. (Henry Louis) Mencken, *Prejudices: Second Series* (New York: Alfred A. Knopf, 1920), 158.

CHAPTER 7

140   *Capitalism and Freedom:* Milton Friedman, *Capitalism and Freedom* (Chicago: University of Chicago Press, 1962).

143   **"more than normal humans do":** Neil Irwin, "How a Quest by Elites Is Driving 'Brexit' and Trump," *New York Times*, July 1, 2016.

148   **of about 0.23 percent:** See US International Trade Commission, *Trans-Pacific Partnership Agreement: Likely Impact on the U.S. Economy and on Specific Industry Sectors*, TPA-105-001, 4607, US Government Publishing Office, May 19, 2016, 70, usitc.gov/publications/332 /pub4607.pdf.

148   **siding with the minority:** This idea is often attributed to Mancur Olson, *The Rise and Decline of Nations: Economic Growth, Stagflation, and Social Rigidities* (New Haven, CT: Yale University Press, 1982).

149   **"be so complicated":** Those stunning words were widely reported at the time. See, for example, Kevin Liptak, "Trump: 'Nobody Knew

Health Care Could Be So Complicated'" (video), CNN, February 27, 2017, cnn.com/2017/02/27/politics/trump-health-care-complicated.

152 **"most of their lives":** As quoted in Arthur Delaney and Michael McAuliff, "Paul Ryan Wants 'Welfare Reform Round 2,'" *Huffington Post*, March 20, 2012, huffingtonpost.com/2012/03/20/paul-ryan-welfare -reform_n_1368277.html.

153 **"in reverse—on steroids":** Robert Greenstein, "Statement of Robert Greenstein, President, on Chairman Ryan's Budget Plan," Center on Budget and Policy Priorities, March 21, 2012.

CHAPTER 8

161 **"bad trade deals":** Daily News Editorial Board, "Transcript: Bernie Sanders Meets with News Editorial Board," *New York Daily News*, April 4, 2016, nydailynews.com/opinion/transcript-bernie-sanders -meets-news-editorial-board-article-1.2588306.

162 **"oppose it as president":** Hillary Clinton, Warren (MI) Rally speech (video), August 11, 2016, youtube.com/watch?v=3rOUYlZV914.

166 **skilled, college-educated workers:** See, among others, David H. Autor, David Dorn, and Gordon H. Hanson, "The China Shock: Learning from Labor Market Adjustment to Large Changes in Trade," *Annual Review of Economics* 8 (October 2016): 205–240.

170 **18 percent higher:** Executive Office of the President, Council of Economic Advisers, Table 4: "Summary of Export Wage Premium Literature," in *The Economic Benefits of U.S. Trade*, 16, May 2015, obamawhitehouse.archives.gov/sites/default/files/docs/cea_trade _report_final_non-embargoed_v2.pdf.

174 **"in part by the federal government":** Howard Rosen, "Trade Adjustment Assistance: The More We Change the More It Stays the Same," in *C. Fred Bergsten and the World Economy*, ed. Michael Mussa (Washington, DC: Peterson Institute for International Economics, 2006), 81.

175 **surge of displaced autoworkers:** Office of Technology Assessment, *Trade Adjustment Assistance: New Ideas for an Old Program—Special Report*, PB87-203741, US Government Publishing Office, June 1987, 23–25, ota.fas.org/reports/8730.pdf.

176 **capped at $450 million:** US Department of Labor, Employment and Training Administration, *Side-by-Side Comparison of TAA Program Benefits Under the 2002 Program, 2009 Program, 2011 Program, and 2015 Program*, Trade Act Program: Trade Adjustment Assistance for Workers Programs, November 9, 2015, doleta.gov/tradeact/pdf/side-by -side.pdf.

176 **pretty slow adjustment:** US Department of Labor, Employment and Training Administration, *Trade Adjustment Assistance for Workers Program, FY 2015*, Annual Report to the Committee on Finance of the

Senate and Committee on Ways and Means of the House of Representatives, 10, doleta.gov/tradeact/docs/AnnualReport15.pdf.

176   **a comparative pittance:** US Department of Labor, "FY 2017 Congressional Budget Justification, Employment and Training Administration: Federal Unemployment Benefits and Allowances," 8, dol.gov/sites
/default/files/documents/general/budget/CBJ-2017-V1-07.pdf.

177   **"labeled a failure":** Robert J. Shiller, "Donald Trump and the Sense of
Power," *Project Syndicate* 79, November 21, 2016.

177   **dynamism is already happening:** See, for example, Ryan A. Decker,
John Haltiwanger, Ron S. Jarmin, and Javier Miranda, "Declining
Business Dynamism: What We Know and the Way Forward," *American Economic Review Papers and Proceedings* 106, no. 5 (May 2016):
203–207.

178   **"in time of war":** Henry George, *Protection or Free Trade: An Examination of the Tariff Question with Especial Regard to the Interests of
Labor* (New York: Doubleday, 1886), 51.

179   **"wages are too high":** Among many possible sources, see Maggie
Haberman, "Donald Trump Insists That Wages Are 'Too High,'" *New
York Times*, November 11, 2015.

181   **0.07 percent after fifteen years:** US International Trade Commission,
*Trans-Pacific Partnership Agreement: Likely Impact on the U.S. Econ-
omy and on Specific Industry Sector*, TPA-105-001, 4607, US Government Publishing Office, May 19, 2016, 21, usitc.gov/publications/332
/pub4607.pdf.

184   **bottom tenth would lose 63 percent:** Pablo D. Fajgelbaum and Amit
K. Khandelwal, "Measuring the Unequal Gains from Trade," *Quarterly Journal of Economics* 131, no. 3 (2016): 1113–1180.

184   **pay just 3 percent:** The International Trade Commission keeps tariff
lists at hts.usitc.gov.

189   **"common sense of mankind":** Adam Smith, *The Wealth of Nations*,
Modern Library Edition (New York: Random House, 1937), 461.

190   **10 percent premium to do so:** Consumer Reports, "Special Report:
Made in America," *Consumer Reports*, May 21, 2015, consumer
reports.org/cro/magazine/2015/05/made-in-america/index.htm. A more
recent Bloomberg poll posed a similar question and found 82 percent
of Americans "willing to pay a little more" for merchandise made in
the United States. Bloomberg Politics Poll, "International Trade / Global
Economy," Polling Report, March 19–22, 2016, pollingreport.com
/trade.htm.

CHAPTER 9

199   **total market income (36 percent):** Congressional Budget Office, *The
Distribution of Household Income and Federal Taxes, 2013*, June 2016,
14, cbo.gov/publication/51361.

200 **race between education and technology:** Claudia Goldin and Lawrence E. Katz, *The Race Between Education and Technology* (Cambridge, MA: Harvard University Press, 2008).

201 **Spain, Slovenia, and Russia:** Data are from the OECD database.

201 **twenty-fourth in reading literacy:** Joe Heim, "On the World Stage, U.S. Students Fall Behind," *Washington Post*, December 6, 2016.

204 **to 276 times in 2015:** Economic Policy Institute, "The Top Charts of 2016: 13 Charts That Show the Difference Between the Economy We Have Now and the Economy We Could Have." December 22, 2016, epi.org/publication/the-top-charts-of-2016-13-charts-that-show-the-difference-between-the-economy-we-have-now-and-the-economy-we-could-have.

205 **falls under Democrats:** See Larry M. Bartels, *Unequal Democracy: The Political Economy of the New Gilded Age* (Princeton, NJ: Princeton University Press, 2008), especially Chapter 2.

206 **(the final year of their study) as in 1979:** That's about 25 percent based on the Gini measure. See Congressional Budget Office, *The Distribution of Household Income and Federal Taxes, 2013*, June 2016, cbo.gov/publication/51361.

209 **evenly divided on this question:** The precise question is: "Should the government redistribute wealth by heavy taxes on the rich?" Notice the words "redistribute" and "heavy." See Kathleen Weldon, "If I Were a Rich Man: Public Attitudes About Wealth and Taxes," Roper Center for Public Opinion Research, Cornell University, February 4, 2015, ropercenter.cornell.edu/public-attitudes-wealth-taxes.

210 **Table 9.1:** The numbers in Table 9.1 are computed from data found at Organisation for Economic Co-operation and Development (OECD) Statistics, stats.oecd.org/. They pertain to 2012, 2013, or 2014, depending on the country.

213 **"control of their economic lives":** Robert J. Shiller, "Donald Trump and the Sense of Power," *Project Syndicate* 79, November 21, 2016.

213 **monies are taken away:** This is an instance of psychologists Daniel Kahneman and Amos Tversky's "loss aversion." A good nontechnical exposition can be found in Michael Lewis, *The Undoing Project: A Friendship That Changed Our Minds* (New York: Norton, 2017).

216 **modest minimum wage increases:** See, for example, David Card and Alan B. Krueger, "Minimum Wages and Employment: A Case Study of the Fast-Food Industry in New Jersey and Pennsylvania: Reply," *American Economic Review* 90, no. 5 (December 2000): 1397–1420.

216 **Many others do not, however:** Joseph R. Blasi, Richard B. Freeman, and Douglas L. Kruse, *The Citizen's Share: Reducing Inequality in the 21st Century* (New Haven, CT: Yale University Press, 2013), 112, estimate that 47 percent of full-time private-sector wage and salary workers receive some form of profit sharing.

216 **part or all of their higher labor costs:** Ibid., Chapter 5.

217 **offer incentive plans to all their workers:** For this and other ways to encourage profit sharing, see ibid., Chapter 6.

217 **3.7 percent in Australia:** Harry J. Holzer and Robert I. Lerman, "Work-Based Learning to Expand Opportunities for Youth," *Challenge 57*, no. 4 (July–August 2014): 18–31.

218 **risen to almost 29 percent:** See Morris M. Kleiner, *Reforming Occupational Licensing Policies*, Hamilton Project Policy Brief 2015-1, Brookings Institution, January 2015.

219 **higher earnings as adults:** Executive Office of the President, Council of Economic Advisers, *The Economics of Early Childhood Investments*, December 2014, obamawhitehouse.archives.gov/sites/default /files/docs/early_childhood_report_update_final_non-embargo.pdf.

222 **particular policy becomes law:** Martin Gilens, *Affluence and Influence: Economic Inequality and Political Power in America* (Princeton, NJ: Princeton University Press and the Russell Sage Foundation, 2012).

CHAPTER 10

225 **"dysfunctional mess":** James Stewart, "A Rare Moment of Unity on Capitol Hill, Thanks to Trump's Tactics," *New York Times*, November 4, 2016.

226 **"fella behind the tree":** Robert Mann, *Legacy to Power: Senator Russell Long of Louisiana* (Lincoln, NE: iUniverse, 2003), 333.

229 **"immortal souls were in danger":** Daniel P. Moynihan, "The Diary of a Senator," *Newsweek*, August 25, 1986.

229 **"sustainability over the long run":** Executive Office of the President, Executive Order 13531 of February 18, 2010: National Commission on Fiscal Responsibility and Reform, FR 75:35, US Government Publishing Office, 2010, gpo.gov/fdsys/pkg/FR-2010-02-23/pdf/2010-3725.pdf.

234 **"like-kind to other real estate":** See Internal Revenue Service, "Like-Kind Exchanges Under IRC Code Section 1031," FS-2008-18, February 2008, irs.gov/uac/like-kind-exchanges-under-irc-code-section-1031.

240 **"larger economy in the long run":** William G. Gale and Andrew A. Samwick, "Effects of Income Tax Changes on Economic Growth," in *The Economics of Tax Policy*, ed. Alan J. Auerbach and Kent Smetters (Oxford: Oxford University Press, 2017), 13–39, 11.

240 **is about 30 percent:** Congressional Budget Office, *The Distribution of Household Income and Federal Taxes, 2013*, June 2016, https://cbo.gov /publication/51361.

242 **opt out rather than in:** Brigitte C. Madrian and Dennis F. Shea, "The Power of Suggestion: Inertia in 401(k) Participation and Savings Behavior," *Quarterly Journal of Economics* 66, no. 4 (November 2001): 1149–1188.

242   **the default was "out":** James J. Choi, David Laibson, Brigitte C. Madrian, and Andrew Metrick, "For Better or for Worse: Default Effects and 401(k) Savings Behavior," in *Perspectives on the Economics of Aging*, ed. David A. Wise (Chicago: University of Chicago Press for NBER, 2004), 81–125.

244   **all the way to zero:** See, for example: David Kocieniewski, "G.E.'s Strategies Let It Avoid Taxes Altogether," *New York Times*, March 24, 2011; Danny Yadron, Kate Linebaugh, and Jessica E. Lessin, "Apple Avoided Taxes on Overseas Billions, Senate Panel Finds," *Wall Street Journal*, May 20, 2013.

247   **this hoard at around $3 trillion:** A January 2017 Treasury report contains an estimate of $2.8 trillion. See US Department of the Treasury, Office of Tax Policy, *The Case for Responsible Business Tax Reform*, January 2017, 41, treasury.gov/resource-center/tax-policy/Documents/Report-Responsible-Business-Tax-Reform-2017.pdf.

247   **($14 billion in back taxes.):** Among the many stories written about this case, see Natalia Drozdiak and Sam Schechner, "Apple Ordered by EU to Repay $14.5 Billion in Irish Tax Breaks" (video), *Wall Street Journal*, August 30, 2016, wsj.com/articles/apple-received-14-5-billion-in-illegal-tax-benefits-from-ireland-1472551598.

248   **Bermuda in 2010:** Executive Office of the President, Council of Economic Advisers, Table 5.1: "U.S. Controlled Foreign Corporation Profits Relative to GDP, 2010," in *Economic Report of the President*, PR 44.9, US Government Publishing Office, 2015, 214, gpo.gov/fdsys/pkg/ERP-2015/pdf/ERP-2015.pdf.

CHAPTER 11

251   **no *net* tax increase:** Climate Leadership Council, *The Conservative Case for Carbon Dividends*, February 2017, clcouncil.org/wp-content/uploads/2017/02/TheConservativeCaseforCarbonDividends.pdf.

254   **more than pay for themselves:** Glenn Kessler, "Trump Aides Sell Tax Plan with Pinocchio-Laden Claims," *Washington Post*, September 29, 2017.

254   **easy questions about financial matters:** Annamaria Lusardi and Olivia S. Mitchell, "The Economic Importance of Financial Literacy: Theory and Evidence," *Journal of Economic Literature* 52, no. 1 (March 2014): 5–44.

262   **"ruin our country":** Kimberly Schwandt, "Boehner: It's 'Armageddon,' Health Care Bill Will 'Ruin our Country,'" *Fox News*, March 20, 2010.

262   **"Everything else is negotiable":** Matt Bai, "Taking the Hill," *New York Times Magazine*, June 2, 2009.

263   **"Not once":** Terence Burlij, "Boehner: Obamacare Repeal and Replace 'Not What's Going to Happen'" (video), CNN, February 23, 2017, cnn.com/2017/02/23/politics/john-boehner-obamacare.

270   **But consider:** The bullet points that follow are adapted from Jonathan Rauch, "How American Politics Went Insane," *Atlantic* (July–August 2016).

270   **29 percent of eligible voters:** Drew DeSilver, "Turnout Was High in the 2016 Primary Season, but Just Short of 2008 Record," Pew Research Center Fact Tank, June 10, 2016, pewresearch.org/fact-tank/2016/06/10 /turnout-was-high-in-the-2016-primary-season-but-just-short-of -2008-record.

271   **incentives for small donations:** See E. J. Dionne Jr., Norman J. Ornstein, and Thomas E. Mann, *One Nation After Trump: A Guide for the Perplexed, the Disillusioned, the Desperate and the Not-Yet-Deported* (New York: St. Martin's, 2017), Chapter 9.

271   **"man taking a walk":** Stated on a *Tonight Show* interview with Jay Leno. Ed O'Keefe, "Boehner Appearing on Leno: GOP Is to Blame for Shutdown," *Washington Post*, January 24, 2014.

274   **"a perfect law":** Gary Klott, "How Tax Plan Differs a Year Later," *New York Times*, November 25, 1985.

275   **"their own to jump from":** Jeffrey H. Birnbaum, "Reborn Bill: Radical Tax Overhaul Now Seems Probable as Senate Panel Acts," *Wall Street Journal*, May 8, 1986.

275   **speaks only on camera:** Jeffrey H. Birnbaum and Alan S. Murray, *Showdown at Gucci Gulch: Lawmakers, Lobbyists, and the Unlikely Triumph of Tax Reform* (New York: Random House, 1987), 281.

277   **"It's so damn horrible":** Birnbaum and Murray, *Showdown at Gucci Gulch*, 278, 260.

277   **"somebody tries to change it":** Michael McQueen, "Hughes, Barnes Aim at Mikulski in Senate Candidates' Debate," *Washington Post*, June 16, 1986.

CHAPTER 12

283   **tax multinational corporations:** A recent and accessible version of the idea is Alan J. Auerbach and Douglas Holtz-Eakin, "The Role of Border Adjustments in International Taxation," American Action Forum, November 30, 2016.

285   **"Is Government Too Political?":** Alan S. Blinder, "Is Government Too Political?" *Foreign Affairs* 76, no. 6 (November–December 1997): 115–126.

288   **the agreement for thirty years:** US International Trade Commission, *Trans-Pacific Partnership Agreement: Likely Impact on the U.S. Economy and on Specific Industry Sectors*, TPA-105-001, 4607, US

Government Publishing Office, May 19, 2016, usitc.gov/publications
/332/pub4607.pdf.

295 **a comparative pittance:** Robert Puentes and Jennifer Thompson,
*Banking on Infrastructure: Enhancing State Revolving Funds for Trans-
portation*, Brookings Institution, September 2012.

CHAPTER 13

306 **mistakes over and over again:** Michael Lewis, *The Undoing Project: A
Friendship That Changed Our Minds* (New York: Norton, 2017).

308 **"a level with dentists":** John Maynard Keynes, *Essays in Persuasion*
(New York: Norton, 1963), 373. (The original edition was published in
1931.)

SOURCES

Auerbach, Alan J., and Douglas Holtz-Eakin. "The Role of Border Adjustments in International Taxation." American Action Forum. November 30, 2016.

Autor, David H., David Dorn, and Gordon H. Hanson. "The China Shock: Learning from Labor Market Adjustment to Large Changes in Trade." *Annual Review of Economics* 8 (October 2016): 205–240.

Bai, Matt. "Taking the Hill." *New York Times Magazine*, June 2, 2009.

Bartels, Larry M. *Unequal Democracy: The Political Economy of the New Gilded Age*. Princeton, NJ: Princeton University Press, 2008.

Bennet, James. "The On-the-Record Flap About Off the Record." *New York Times*, March 8, 1998.

Birnbaum, Jeffrey H. "Reborn Bill: Radical Tax Overhaul Now Seems Probable as Senate Panel Acts." *Wall Street Journal*, May 8, 1986.

Birnbaum, Jeffrey H., and Alan S. Murray. *Showdown at Gucci Gulch: Lawmakers, Lobbyists, and the Unlikely Triumph of Tax Reform*. New York: Random House, 1987.

Blasi, Joseph R., Richard B. Freeman, and Douglas L. Kruse. *The Citizen's Share: Reducing Inequality in the 21st Century*. New Haven, CT: Yale University Press, 2013.

Blinder, Alan S. *Hard Heads, Soft Hearts: Tough-Minded Economics for a Just Society*. Reading, MA: Addison-Wesley, 1987.

———. "Is Government Too Political?" *Foreign Affairs* 76, no. 6 (November–December 1997): 115–126.

———. "Overview." In *Proceedings of the Federal Reserve Bank of Kansas City Symposium on Reducing Unemployment: Current Issues and Policy Options*, 329–342. Federal Reserve Bank of Kansas City, August 25–27, 1994.

Blinder, Alan S., and Mark Zandi. *The Financial Crisis: Lessons for the Next One*. Policy Futures Report. Center on Budget and Policy Priorities. October 15, 2015.

Bloomberg Politics Poll. "International Trade / Global Economy." Polling Report, March 19–22, 2016. pollingreport.com/trade.htm.

Boncompagni, Tatiana S. "Washington Coverage Is Steady but Public Doesn't Seem to Care." *Wall Street Journal*, August 13, 1997.

Bond, Paul. "Leslie Moonves on Donald Trump: 'It May Not Be Good for America, but It's Damn Good for CBS.'" *Hollywood Reporter*, February 29, 2016. hollywoodreporter.com/news/leslie-moonves-donald-trump -may-871464/.

Bradsher, Keith. "Fed Official Disapproves of Rate Policy." *New York Times*, August 28, 1994.

Burlij, Terence. "Boehner: Obamacare Repeal and Replace 'Not What's Going to Happen'" (video). CNN, February 23, 2017. cnn.com/2017/02/23 /politics/john-boehner-obamacare.

Card, David, and Alan B. Krueger. "Minimum Wages and Employment: A Case Study of the Fast-Food Industry in New Jersey and Pennsylvania: Reply." *American Economic Review* 90, no. 5 (December 2000): 1397– 1420.

Carter, James. "Economists Have a Message: Clinton's Policies Are Wrong for America." *Hill*, September 26, 2016. thehill.com/blogs/pundits-blog /presidential-campaign/297719-economists-have-a-message-clintons -policies-are.

Chait, Jonathan. "Obamacare, Jobs, and 'What Matters Politically.'" *New York Magazine*, February 5, 2014.

Choi, James J., David Laibson, Brigitte C. Madrian, and Andrew Metrick. "For Better or for Worse: Default Effects and 401(k) Savings Behavior." In *Perspectives on the Economics of Aging*, ed. David A. Wise, 81–125. Chicago: University of Chicago Press for NBER, 2004.

Climate Leadership Council. *The Conservative Case for Carbon Dividends*. February 2017. clcouncil.org/wp-content/uploads/2017/02/TheConservative CaseforCarbonDividends.pdf.

Clines, Francis X. "White House Winces at Economist's Words." *New York Times*, October 28, 1982.

Clinton, Hillary. Warren (MI) Rally speech (video). August 11, 2016. youtube .com/watch?v=3rOUYlZV914.

"Comparing Hillary Clinton, Donald Trump on the Truth-O-Meter." Politi-Fact. politifact.com/truth-o-meter/lists/people/comparing-hillary-clinton -donald-trump-truth-o-met. Accessed September 20, 2017.

Congressional Budget Office. *The Budget and Economic Outlook: 2014 to 2024*. February 4, 2014. cbo.gov/publication/45010.

———. *The Distribution of Household Income and Federal Taxes, 2013*. June 2016. cbo.gov/publication/51361.

———. "Pay-As-You-Go Budgeting." CBO staff memorandum prepared by Roy T. Meyers, March 1990. cbo.gov/sites/default/files/101st -congress-1989-1990/reports/90-cbo-019.pdf.

Consumer Reports. "Special Report: Made in America." *Consumer Reports*, May 21, 2015. consumerreports.org/cro/magazine/2015/05/made-in -america/index.htm.

Daily News Editorial Board. "Transcript: Bernie Sanders Meets with News Editorial Board." *New York Daily News*, April 4, 2016. nydailynews

.com/opinion/transcript-bernie-sanders-meets-news-editorial-board
-article-1.2588306/.

David, Paul A. "Clio and the Economics of QWERTY." *American Economic Review* 75, no. 2 (May 1985): 332–337.

DeBonis, Mike. "How Health Care for 9/11 Responders Became Just Another Political Football." *Washington Post*, December 14, 2015.

Decker, Ryan A., John Haltiwanger, Ron S. Jarmin, and Javier Miranda. "Declining Business Dynamism: What We Know and the Way Forward." *American Economic Review Papers and Proceedings* 106, no. 5 (May 2016): 203–207.

Delaney, Arthur, and Michael McAuliff. "Paul Ryan Wants 'Welfare Reform Round 2.'" *Huffington Post*, March 20, 2012. huffingtonpost .com/2012/03/20/paul-ryan-welfare-reform_n_1368277.html.

DeSilver, Drew. "Turnout Was High in the 2016 Primary Season, but Just Short of 2008 Record." Pew Research Center Fact Tank, June 10, 2016. pewresearch.org/fact-tank/2016/06/10/turnout-was-high-in-the-2016 -primary-season-but-just-short-of-2008-record.

Dionne, E.J., Jr., Norman J. Ornstein, and Thomas E. Mann. *One Nation After Trump: A Guide for the Perplexed, the Disillusioned, the Desperate and the Not-Yet-Deported.* New York: St. Martin's, 2017.

Drozdiak, Natalia, and Sam Schechner. "Apple Ordered by EU to Repay $14.5 Billion in Irish Tax Breaks" (video). *Wall Street Journal*, August 30, 2016. wsj.com/articles/apple-received-14-5-billion-in-illegal-tax-benefits-from -ireland-1472551598.

Economic Policy Institute. "The Top Charts of 2016: 13 Charts That Show the Difference Between the Economy We Have Now and the Economy We Could Have." December 22, 2016. epi.org/publication/the-top-charts-of -2016-13-charts-that-show-the-difference-between-the-economy-we -have-now-and-the-economy-we-could-have.

Executive Office of the President. Executive Order 13531 of February 18, 2010: National Commission on Fiscal Responsibility and Reform, FR 75:35. US Government Publishing Office, 2010. gpo.gov/fdsys/pkg/FR-2010-02-23 /pdf/2010-3725.pdf.

Executive Office of the President, Council of Economic Advisers. *The Economic Benefits of U.S. Trade.* May 2015. obamawhitehouse.archives.gov /sites/default/files/docs/cea_trade_report_final_non-embargoed_v2.pdf.

———. *The Economic Case for Health Care Reform: Update.* December 14, 2009. obamawhitehouse.archives.gov/sites/default/files/microsites/091213 -economic-case-health-care-reform.pdf.

———. *Economic Report of the President*, PR 44.9. Washington, DC: US Government Publishing Office, 2015. gpo.gov/fdsys/pkg/ERP-2015/pdf /ERP-2015.pdf.

———. *The Economics of Early Childhood Investments.* December 2014. obamawhitehouse.archives.gov/sites/default/files/docs/early_childhood _report_update_final_non-embargo.pdf.

Fajgelbaum, Pablo D., and Amit K. Khandelwal. "Measuring the Unequal Gains from Trade." *Quarterly Journal of Economics* 131, no. 3 (2016): 1113–1180.

Fallows, James M. *Breaking the News: How the Media Undermine American Democracy.* New York: Pantheon Books, 1996.

Friedman, Milton. *Capitalism and Freedom.* Chicago: University of Chicago Press, 1962.

Friedman, Thomas J. "Clinton's Fibs, and Her Opponents' Double Whoppers." *New York Times,* June 1, 2016.

Gale, William G., and Andrew A. Samwick. "Effects of Income Tax Changes on Economic Growth." In *The Economics of Tax Policy,* ed. Alan J. Auerbach and Kent Smetters, 13–39. Oxford: Oxford University Press, 2017.

George, Henry. *Protection or Free Trade: An Examination of the Tariff Question with Especial Regard to the Interests of Labor.* New York: Doubleday, 1886.

Gilens, Martin. *Affluence and Influence: Economic Inequality and Political Power in America.* Princeton, NJ: Princeton University Press and the Russell Sage Foundation, 2012.

Goldin, Claudia, and Lawrence E. Katz. *The Race Between Education and Technology.* Cambridge, MA: Harvard University Press, 2008.

Greenstein, Robert. "Statement of Robert Greenstein, President, on Chairman Ryan's Budget Plan." Center on Budget and Policy Priorities, March 21, 2012.

Haberman, Maggie. "Donald Trump Insists That Wages Are 'Too High.'" *New York Times,* November 11, 2015.

Heim, Joe. "On the World Stage, U.S. Students Fall Behind." *Washington Post,* December 6, 2016.

Holzer, Harry J., and Robert I. Lerman. "Work-Based Learning to Expand Opportunities for Youth." *Challenge* 57, no. 4 (July–August 2014): 18–31.

IGM Economic Experts Panel. "About the IGM Economic Experts Panel." Chicago Booth Initiative on Global Markets. igmchicago.org /igm-economic-experts-panel. Accessed September 20, 2017.

"In Stimulus Debate, Obama Drifts into Campaign Mode." Fox News, February 6, 2009. foxnews.com/politics/2009/02/06/stimulus-debate-obama -drifts-campaign-mode.html.

Internal Revenue Service. "Like-Kind Exchanges Under IRC Code Section 1031." FS-2008-18. February 2008. irs.gov/uac/like-kind-exchanges-under -irc-code-section-1031/.

Irwin, Neil. "How a Quest by Elites Is Driving 'Brexit' and Trump." *New York Times,* July 1, 2016.

Johnson, Haynes, and David S. Broder. *The System: The American Way of Politics at the Breaking Point.* Boston: Little, Brown, 1996.

Kessler, Glenn. "No, CBO Did Not Say Obamacare Will Kill 2 Million Jobs," *Washington Post,* February 4, 2014.

————. "Trump Aides Sell Tax Plan with Pinocchio-Laden Claims." *Washington Post*, September 29, 2017.

Keynes, John Maynard. *Essays in Persuasion*. New York: Norton, 1963.

Kleiner, Morris M. *Reforming Occupational Licensing Policies*. Hamilton Project Policy Brief 2015-1. Brookings Institution. January 2015.

Klott, Gary. "How Tax Plan Differs a Year Later." *New York Times*, November 25, 1985.

Kocieniewski, David. "G.E.'s Strategies Let It Avoid Taxes Altogether." *New York Times*, March 24, 2011.

Lewis, Michael. *The Undoing Project: A Friendship That Changed Our Minds*. New York: Norton, 2017.

Liptak, Kevin. "Trump: 'Nobody Knew Health Care Could Be So Complicated'" (video). CNN, February 27, 2017. cnn.com/2017/02/27/politics/trump-health-care-complicated.

Lusardi, Annamaria, and Olivia S. Mitchell. "The Economic Importance of Financial Literacy: Theory and Evidence." *Journal of Economic Literature* 52, no. 1 (March 2014): 5–44.

Machiavelli, Niccolò. *The Prince*. Translated by N. H. Thompson. New York: Dover Publications, 1992.

Mackay, Alan S. *Scientific Quotations: The Harvest of a Quiet Eye*. New York: Crane, Russak, 1977.

Madrian, Brigitte C., and Dennis F. Shea. "The Power of Suggestion: Inertia in 401(k) Participation and Savings Behavior." *Quarterly Journal of Economics* 66, no. 4 (November 2001): 1149–1188.

Mann, Robert. *Legacy to Power: Senator Russell Long of Louisiana*. Lincoln, NE: iUniverse, 2003.

McQueen, Michael. "Hughes, Barnes Aim at Mikulski in Senate Candidates' Debate." *Washington Post*, June 16, 1986.

Mencken, H. L. (Henry Louis). *Prejudices: Second Series*. New York: Alfred A. Knopf, 1920.

Mishel, Lawrence, and Teresa Kroeger. "Strong Across-the-Board Wage Growth in 2015 for Both Bottom 90 Percent and Top 1.0 Percent." Economic Policy Institute Working Economics Blog, October 27, 2016. epi.org/blog/strong-across-the-board-wage-growth-in-2015-for-both-bottom-90-percent-and-top-1-0-percent.

Moynihan, Daniel P. "The Diary of a Senator." *Newsweek*, August 25, 1986.

Nather, David, and Jason Millman. "Obamacare and Jobs: CBO Fuels Fire." *Politico*, February 4, 2014.

Office of Technology Assessment. *Trade Adjustment Assistance: New Ideas for an Old Program—Special Report*. PB87-203741. US Government Publishing Office, June 1987. ota.fas.org/reports/8730.pdf.

O'Keefe, Ed. "Boehner Appearing on Leno: GOP Is to Blame for Shutdown." *Washington Post*, January 24, 2014.

Olson, Mancur. *The Rise and Decline of Nations: Economic Growth, Stagflation, and Social Rigidities*. New Haven, CT: Yale University Press, 1982.

Puentes, Robert, and Jennifer Thompson. *Banking on Infrastructure: Enhancing State Revolving Funds for Transportation*. Brookings Institution. September 2012.

Rauch, Jonathan. "How American Politics Went Insane." *Atlantic* (July–August 2016).

Rosen, Howard. "Trade Adjustment Assistance: The More We Change the More It Stays the Same." In *C. Fred Bergsten and the World Economy*, ed. Michael Mussa. Washington, DC: Peterson Institute for International Economics, 2006.

Samuelson, Paul A. "Economists and the History of Ideas." *American Economic Review* 52, no. 1 (March 1962): 1–18.

Samuelson, Robert J. "Economic Amnesia." *Washington Post,* September 7, 1994.

Schaller, Bruce. "New York City's Congestion Pricing Experience and Implications for Road Pricing Acceptance in the United States." *Transport Policy* 17, no. 4 (2010): 266–273.

Scheiber, Noam. *The Escape Artists: How Obama's Team Fumbled the Recovery*. New York: Simon & Schuster, 2012.

Schwandt, Kimberly. "Boehner: It's 'Armageddon,' Health Care Bill Will 'Ruin Our Country.'" Fox News, March 20, 2010.

Shiller, Robert J. "Donald Trump and the Sense of Power." *Project Syndicate* 79, November 21, 2016.

Sinclair, Upton. *I, Candidate for Governor: And How I Got Licked*. Berkeley: University of California Press, 1994.

Smith, Adam. *The Wealth of Nations*. Modern Library Edition. New York: Random House, 1937. Originally published 1776.

Starobin, Paul. "Economy: Blindsided." *National Journal*, October 8, 1994.

Stewart, James. "A Rare Moment of Unity on Capitol Hill, Thanks to Trump's Tactics." *New York Times*, November 4, 2016.

Stockman, David A. *The Triumph of Politics: Why the Reagan Revolution Failed*. New York: Harper & Row, 1986.

Stunda, Ronald. "The Market Impact of Mergers and Acquisitions on Acquiring Firms in the U.S." *Journal of Accounting and Taxation* 6, no. 2 (September 2014): 30–37.

"Syria, Benghazi and the U.S. Economy." Fox News Poll, October 10–12, 2015. foxnews.com/politics/interactive/2015/10/14/fox-news-poll-syria-benghazi-and-us-economy.

US Department of Labor. "FY 2017 Congressional Budget Justification, Employment and Training Administration: Federal Unemployment Benefits and Allowances." dol.gov/sites/default/files/documents/general/budget/CBJ-2017-V1-07.pdf.

———. "Overtime for White Collar Workers: Overview and Summary of Final Rule." May 18, 2016. dol.gov/sites/default/files/overtime-overview.pdf.

US Department of Labor, Employment and Training Administration. *Side-by-Side Comparison of TAA Program Benefits Under the 2002 Program, 2009 Program, 2011 Program, and 2015 Program.* Trade Act Program: Trade Adjustment Assistance for Workers Programs. November 9, 2015. doleta.gov/tradeact/pdf/side-by-side.pdf.

―――. *Trade Adjustment Assistance for Workers Program, FY 2015.* Annual report to the Committee on Finance of the Senate and Committee on Ways and Means of the House of Representatives. doleta.gov/tradeact/docs /AnnualReport15.pdf.

US Department of the Treasury, Office of Tax Policy. *The Case for Responsible Business Tax Reform.* January 2017. treasury.gov/resource-center/tax -policy/Documents/Report-Responsible-Business-Tax-Reform-2017.pdf.

US Government. *Budget FY 2018: A New Foundation for American Greatness.* PREX 2.8. US Government Publishing Office, May 23, 2017. gpo.gov/fdsys/pkg/BUDGET-2018-BUD/pdf/BUDGET-2018-BUD-3.pdf.

US International Trade Commission. *Trans-Pacific Partnership Agreement: Likely Impact on the U.S. Economy and on Specific Industry Sectors.* TPA-105-001, 4607. US Government Publishing Office, May 19, 2016. usitc.gov/publications/332/pub4607.pdf.

Washington Post Fact Checker. "The 2016 Election Fact Checker." *Washington Post*, November 3, 2016. washingtonpost.com/graphics/politics /2016-election/fact-checker/?tid=a_inl/.

Weisberg, Jacob. "Overnight Statesman: Dan Rostenkowski's New Look." *New Republic*, March 24, 1986.

Weldon, Kathleen. "If I Were a Rich Man: Public Attitudes About Wealth and Taxes." Roper Center for Public Opinion Research, Cornell University. February 4, 2015. ropercenter.cornell.edu/public-attitudes-wealth-taxes.

White House. "Unified Framework for Fixing Our Broken Tax Code." September 27, 2017. whitehouse.gov/the-press-office/2017/09/27/unified -framework-fixing-our-broken-tax-code.

Yadron, Danny, Kate Linebaugh, and Jessica E. Lessin. "Apple Avoided Taxes on Overseas Billions, Senate Panel Finds." *Wall Street Journal*, May 20, 2013.

INDEX

Alan S. Blinder is one of the world's most renowned economists. He is a professor of economics and public affairs at Princeton University, vice chairman of the Promontory Interfinancial Network, and a regular columnist for the *Wall Street Journal*. Dr. Blinder served as vice chairman of the Federal Reserve Board, 1994 to 1996, and before that was a member of President Clinton's original Council of Economic Advisers, 1993 to 1994. He has advised the presidential campaigns of Bill Clinton, Al Gore, John Kerry, and Hillary Clinton, and he continues to advise numerous members of Congress and officeholders. Dr. Blinder is the author or co-author of twenty books, including the best-selling *After the Music Stopped* (Penguin, 2013), which the *New York Times* named one of the five top nonfiction books of 2013. He lives in Princeton, New Jersey.

Photo courtesy of Denise Applewhite, Princeton University, Office of Communications